Camp David

Camp David

The Autobiography

DAVID WALLIAMS

MICHAEL JOSEPH
an imprint of
PENGUIN BOOKS

MICHAEL JOSEPH

Published by the Penguin Group
Penguin Books Ltd, 80 Strand, London WC2R ORL, England
Penguin Group (USA) Inc., 375 Hudson Street, New York, New York 10014, USA
Penguin Group (Canada), 90 Eglinton Avenue East, Suite 700, Toronto, Ontario, Canada M4P 2Y3
(a division of Pearson Penguin Canada Inc.)
Penguin Ireland, 25 St Stephen's Green, Dublin 2, Ireland (a division of Penguin Books Ltd)
Penguin Group (Australia), 707 Collins Street, Melbourne, Victoria 3008, Australia
(a division of Pearson Australia Group Pty Ltd)
Penguin Books India Pvt Ltd, 11 Community Centre, Panchsheel Park, New Delhi – 110 017, India
Penguin Group (NZ), 67 Apollo Drive, Rosedale, Auckland 0632, New Zealand
(a division of Pearson New Zealand Ltd)
Penguin Books (South Africa) (Pty) Ltd, Block D, Rosebank Office Park,
181 Jan Smuts Avenue, Parktown North, Gauteng 2193, South Africa

Penguin Books Ltd, Registered Offices: 80 Strand, London WC2R ORL, England

www.penguin.com

First published 2012
001

Copyright © David Walliams, 2012

The moral right of the author has been asserted

Set in 13.75/16.25pt Garamond MT Std
Typeset by Jouve (UK), Milton Keynes
Printed in Great Britain by Clays Ltd, St Ives plc

A CIP catalogue record for this book is available from the British Library

HARDBACK ISBN: 978-0-718-15861-3
TRADE PAPERBACK ISBN: 978-0-718-15862-0

www.greenpenguin.co.uk

ALWAYS LEARNING   **PEARSON**

For Lara.
How I wish I had met you sooner . . .
x

'When I used to read fairy-tales, I fancied that kind of thing never happened, and now here I am in the middle of one! There ought to be a book written about me, that there ought! And when I grow up, I'll write one.'

Alice in Lewis Carroll's
Alice's Adventures in Wonderland

Contents

vii

CONTENTS

Introduction

May I begin by offering my sincere apologies. If you have bought this book assuming it was a history of the President of the United States' country retreat, sorry.

This is the autobiography of a camp British comedian, me.

I always vowed never to write about my life unless I was completely honest, and *Camp David* is a completely honest, perhaps too honest, account of my life. The book starts with my birth in 1971 and ends in December 2003, after the first series of *Little Britain* was broadcast on BBC2 in the autumn of that year. The part of my life you will know the least about is here in this book, in all its joy and sadness. From the moment *Little Britain* aired, my life was documented in tabloid newspapers. However, little did the press know of the extraordinary life I had lived before I became famous.

So here it is. For the first time ever. My story.

David Walliams

PS I am not the bald one in *Little Britain*. I am the taller, less funny one.

I

A Religious Start

'Guess what me and your dad saw on the high street today,'
said my mum. She was breathless with excitement.

'I don't know,' my eight-year-old self replied.

'Guess!' implored my dad.

'I don't know.'

My mum took a pause to add suspense.

'A black man!' she said.

I was as surprised as they were. A black man in Banstead in Surrey?

'What was he doing?' I asked.

'Was he lost?' asked my ten-year-old sister Julie.

My mum and dad searched each other's faces for an
answer.

'He was just walking along the street, I suppose,' said
my mum.

'Maybe shopping?' added my dad, helpfully.

That was what growing up in Banstead in the 1970s
was like for me. So spectacularly uneventful that seeing a
black man in the street was a major incident.

I am told I was born in the early hours of 20 August 1971.
At a maternity hospital in Wimbledon called St Teresa's,

which was run by an order of nuns. A religious start to a very irreligious life.

So eager was I to be born, I came out quickly and my dad missed my birth.

My father had two main obsessions. Bridges and tunnels. Peter Williams (he didn't have a middle name because his parents couldn't afford one) was an engineer for London Transport for the best part of fifty years. He loved looking at railway bridges and tunnels, and if we travelled on the train anywhere he would point out a bridge and say proudly, 'I worked on the maintenance for that.'

Peter Williams was born in 1936 and so as a child lived through World War II. My father told me a story once that seemed to have little significance to him, but that had huge significance for me in trying to understand him. When he was boy, as Nazi rockets flew over his little terraced house in Balham, south London, his parents bought a rabbit. My dad, who could only have been six years old, naturally assumed it was a pet, named it and grew to love it. Peter cared for it, he fed it, he even mucked out its cage. Then one day he came home from school and saw the rabbit hanging dead outside the back door. In that lean time of rationing it had been food all along. My dad had loved, but the thing he loved was killed. In my opinion he never found it that easy to love again.

My mum Kathleen was a laboratory technician in a school, one of those shadowy and often dysfunctional figures that help the science teachers bring out and put away the equipment for experiments. At my secondary school we used to refer to the lab technician as Igor, after the hunchbacked assistant of Dr Frankenstein. Though I never saw my mother at work, I cannot believe the pupils at Sutton Grammar School, where she worked, called her Igor. If my dad could be cold, she couldn't have been warmer. She has spent her whole life doing things for others. One evening a week she was a Brown Owl to generations of Brownies until she was forced to retire at sixty-five. A Banstead artist once painted her portrait. It was of her in the local community centre bent over the sink doing the washing-up.

Kathleen Ellis met Peter Williams in 1961, when she was sixteen. She married him at eighteen. She has two younger twin sisters, Sue and Janet, whose extremely close bond excluded her. A lot of my mum and dad's courting took place at Tooting Bec Lido, so swimming must be in the blood. My dad even had a chipped front tooth from showing off as a youth, diving into a pool. Loving came much more naturally to my mum than my dad, and despite not breastfeeding me (which I would later correct with one of *Little Britain*'s most memorable sketches) she couldn't have loved me or my sister or her husband any more.

We grew up in a quiet little close in Nork, the posh end of Banstead (not that it has a ghetto), in a nice detached house with a garden and crazy paving out the front, where my mum still lives. Both my parents were working class Londoners, my dad from Balham and my mum from Mitcham. They moved out into Surrey suburbia in the hope of becoming middle class. It felt like a safe place.

We had a cat called Smokey and assorted hamsters that all have now very sadly died.

My life revolved around school, Cubs, watching situation comedies, especially *Are You Being Served?* and *Hi-de-Hi!* (Mollie Sugden and Ruth Madoc would later both feature in *Little Britain*) and eating my mum's home-cooked food. There were no surprises: on Monday it was bubble 'n' squeak, on Tuesday it was shepherd's pie, on Wednesday it was bangers 'n' mash, on Thursday it was macaroni cheese and on Friday it was fish 'n' chips. Saturday lunch was Heinz tomato soup and a toasted cheese sandwich.

My mum and dad were always a conservative couple. They voted for Thatcher again and again; Dad took the *Daily Telegraph* and Mum the *Daily Mail*. It wasn't just their politics that were conservative, their tastes were too. I would eagerly flick through their collection of vinyl records to find that topless picture of Sinnita from the original cast recording of the David Essex musical *Mutiny!* But as I did I was always amazed that they had lived through the 1960s but didn't own a single Beatles record. They really belonged to the '50s – they favoured Frank Sinatra or the Everly Brothers over '60s psychedelia – and in the 1950s they remained.

My mum and dad rarely went out, unless to another couple's house for dinner on Saturday. Dad never met his friends alone, nor mum her's. At breakfast the next morning after dinner at another house my mum would pass comment on the wife's cooking: 'Jeanette said the cheese soufflé was home-made, but I swear she bought it at Marks and Spencer's.'

Right from an early age I listened, and what I heard I often found funny, even if it wasn't intended to be. I was storing moments up for the future, though as a child I had no idea how or if I would ever use them. The funniest things I have ever witnessed happened around my family's dining table. There was the time when over Sunday lunch my mum said, 'There's something crawling along the floor,' and then leaned down to pick something small up and put it in her mouth.

'What was that?' I asked.

'Oh, I saw an earwig crawling across the floor, then I saw a pea on the floor and I ate that.'

Or the time when Mum had some sad news to impart to her elderly mother. 'Have you heard,' Mum said slowly and clearly, 'that Winnie Wright has died?'

My grandmother looked at her for a long while, before replying, 'I'll eat whatever I'm given.'

The trouble with a detached stance is that it does put you outside things. Unfortunately I think this is inevitable for most comedians. We are on the outside looking in. So many of the comic characters I have played exhibit my parents' mannerisms. I was observing all the time.

My dad was quite a remote figure during our childhood. As was typical of many men of his generation, he tended not to hug or kiss my sister or me or tell us that he loved us. On occasion anger would overwhelm my dad and I would be on the receiving end. I never felt good enough to be his son.

'All I ever wanted was to make you proud,' I wrote in the card for the wreath at his funeral in 2007.

My father and I only had a couple of days out together when it was just the two of us in the whole of my childhood. One was to watch a rugby match and the other a boat ride to see the Thames Barrier, which in his job he had some role in helping build. I remember them both clearly as they stood out so much from my everyday life. Sitting in the Vauxhall Viva eating ham sandwiches before watching the rugby match, I had no interest in which team won. Both times he was trying to reach out to me from father to son to share some interest he had. Sadly, both times I was uninterested.

Something my dad did share with me was his love of the films and Saturday morning serials he had seen as a boy, such as the Buster Crabbe *Flash Gordon* series, which would be shown occasionally on BBC 2 when I was growing up. That's what I loved, fantasy. Sitting together in the living room watching films was probably the time I felt most at ease with him. But my dad was never quite able to give me his approval. That didn't stop me trying. My mum sensed this tension and overcompensated, giving me all the love and more that he denied.

Mum had her issues when I was growing up too. She suffered from 'nervous tension', and remains obsessed with everything in the house being spotlessly clean. After you used the bathroom she would rush in to polish the spots of water off the mirror over the sink. Biscuit crumbs on the living-room carpet would be picked up one by one as they were dropped.

*

Two years before my arrival my sister Julie was born, just in time to see the moon landing live on television in 1969. If anyone from our family was going to enter show business it was destined to be Julie. She would delight, she would amuse; I would only appal. Julie would stand on the pouffe in the living room and recite Pam Ayres poems, especially 'I wish I'd looked after me teeth' (complete with accurate Bristolian accent) for my grannies and granddads. I didn't know any Pam Ayres poems, but God I wanted to be on that pouffe so bad. I had to get on the pouffe. I had to have the attention. So aged three, I would push her off, climb on and say, 'Pah, pah, pah . . .' That was my version of a poem – 'Pah, pah, pah.' I suppose that success in show business can be as much to do with the need to perform than necessarily any discernible talent to do so. Julie performs to this day, as a teacher in a primary school, to probably the toughest audience of them all.

I have three cousins, all girls around my and my sister's age. When we were all together at our grandparents' house for a family member's birthday we would put on a play. After the buffet lunch, all the grown-ups ushered into the living room and we children would announce that we were about to put on a performance. We would bound upstairs and raid our grandma's wardrobe, and before we had decided what to do, would announce that the play was about to start. The adults would wait expectantly on the sofa and armchairs arranged in a semicircle with cups of tea waiting for the performance to begin.

One was entitled *The Cat Burglar*. Being the only boy I would normally be given a plum part, and this time I was playing the lead role, the cat burglar himself. So with my Nan's tan tights on my head, we were ready. There were four scenes, in which my cousins Laura, Natalie and Sarah, and my sister Julie each pretended to be a rich lady putting on her jewels. I would creep up behind them silently and rob them. They would then notice that their jewels had gone and scream. This happened three times with little change, and the grown-ups applauded after each scene, probably in the hope it was now over. However, when I robbed the final lady of her pearl necklace, my eldest cousin Laura pulled the tights off to reveal my face and improvised the line, 'My husband!' This was a masterstroke. We children thought it was the most marvellous twist in the history of the theatre, though it didn't bear close scrutiny. Why was the husband stealing jewels from his own wife? Sadly we will never know.

Julie desperately wanted a baby sister who she could dress up and parade around like a dolly. However, my gender was not a barrier to young Julie. To make things easier we even had a dressing-up box at home. It contained no male clothing, just a few old dresses, ladies' hats and some bits of costume jewellery. Julie would dress me up in a combination of these items, most fetchingly the mauve bridesmaid dress and white fur hat ensemble, and I would be led up and down the road. Of course all this was a long, long time ago now. In fact the last time Julie dressed me up like this was way back in 2009.

Boom boom!

Yes there will be jokes in this book. The next one is in fact on page 176.

Julie and would cycle up and down our quiet little close on our bikes holding hands pretending to be the motor-cycle cops in *CHiPs* – though in hindsight I don't remember the cops holding hands on the TV series. However, like most siblings my sister and I fought. Of course over nothing, like who had the bigger half of the Mars Bar. Or who had cheated in the board game Operation. Many games would end with the board being thrown into the air. Julie would sometimes even roll around on her bed shouting, 'David, David get off me! Stop hurting me!' until either Mum or Dad came running up the stairs to whack me. One time this backfired when my dad ran upstairs to give me a slap only to find me in my room quietly doing my homework while Julie was rolling around and letting out mock screams of pain.

We didn't go out as a family much – perhaps a visit to Bovington Tank Museum in half-term, a trip to Wisley Gardens (my parents were keen gardeners) or a ramble around Corfe Castle in the rain. Once a year we could take the train up to London to see a film at the Odeon, Leicester Square, usually a James Bond one. I had my first erection during *The Spy Who Loved Me* when Barbara Bach leaned over Roger Moore in a low-cut dress. Twenty-five years later I spotted my first love sitting next to my friend Stella McCartney in the audience for the Queen's Diamond Jubilee Concert. I texted Stella, 'Please can you introduce me to Barbara Bach? I had my first erection watching her in *The Spy Who Loved Me* . . . Dx'.

Stella texted back, 'Just showed her that! Come over and I will introduce you.'

So I sat next to my first Bond girl for a few minutes as Sir Cliff Richard sang 'Congratulations'. Barbara very gamely posed for a few pictures with me, and I retreated to my seat and texted Stella, 'Thank you for the introduction. That really made my night.'

She replied, 'So sweet, you were like a teenager!'

I hope Barbara's husband Ringo Starr doesn't read this.

After seeing the latest blockbuster in Leicester Square we children would have chicken and chips at an Italian restaurant on Gerrard Street called Peter Mario's, which felt like the height of sophistication, then take the train home (my dad got cheap travel for his family as a perk of his job with London Transport). Holidays would be at Cliff House in Swanage, where the landlady Nora's basset hound Caesar bit my mum on the arse. As I grew older, Julie and I liked performing together, singing 'Ten Green Bottles' over the child intercom at the guesthouse. We thought we were on the radio, beaming out to the nation, rather than just Nora and her husband Bert downstairs.

I learned to swim the hard way. Aged four I had a little tricycle (I have graduated to stabilizers now) and was circling a swimming pool when inevitably I fell in. I had no inflatable armbands, but instead of rushing to my aid, my parents assumed I would be able to swim unaided. Fortunately for me, they were right.

If I had to name the time in my life when I was happiest, I would say it was just before I was old enough to go to school. Mum would look after me at home. Just me and her. I was a complete mummy's boy and still am. The two of us would sit and eat mince and mashed potatoes at lunchtime listening to the Jimmy Young show on Radio 2. Just hearing his voice takes me right back to those lunchtimes, just me and my mum. After my first day of school my mum asked me, 'Did you enjoy it?'

'Yes,' I replied, 'but I won't be going back.'

Unfortunately there was no choice . . .

2

The Demon and the Ogre

My first day at Collingwood Boys' School was dominated by a strong sense of foreboding. Thirty little boys in their new uniforms were led into a classroom. Most cried and tried to leave before registration was called, but our mothers abandoned us there. If you wet your pants, you were given a spare pair to change into and the soiled ones to take home in a clear plastic bag that you could present to your mother at the school gate. Did it have to be clear?

On the surface it was just another suburban private school with pretensions to being Eton; we would walk from the main building to the dining hall by crossing the road, doffing our caps to waiting motorists as we did so. The delight of the motorists taught me the value of good manners. Any frustration at being delayed would be banished by a simple old-fashioned gesture. However, the headmaster was a furious little man with a beard who reeked of cigars and dog.

We boys didn't see him much, although we could always smell where he had been. The pupils only met him when he wanted to punish some minor wrongdoing. To instil a deep sense of fear in all of us, corporal punishment was not done in the privacy of his office. No, he preferred to punish boys in the dining hall at lunchtime. The young offenders would be marched out and lined up, some already in tears. As the rest of us tried to eat our Spam fritters at the long tables, they were ordered to unfold their hands. Mr Richardson would then take a wooden ruler and whack them hard and repeatedly on their palms. His face went a furious colour as he did this. The boys' hands would inevitably waver as he punished them, so he would grab their wrists and hold them in place so he could keep whacking. Sometimes the ruler would break, half of it flying into the air. This would elicit nervous laughter in all of us sitting on the uncomfortable benches staring at our now even less appetizing fritters. However, within moments, another wooden ruler would be produced and the whacking would continue. It is strange to think I am describing England in the late 1970s; it reads more like a Charles Dickens novel.

If the headmaster at my primary school was a demon, the dinner lady Mrs Pierce was an ogre. She had the face she deserved, one contorted over the years to a permanent expression of sourness, as sour as her dreaded gooseberry crumble, and a thick moustache above her lip. She never smiled. She couldn't. Mrs Pierce despised children, so she was in the perfect job to make their lives a misery day after day. It was as if she was an evil villain who had escaped from a Roald Dahl story. One boy, Wilson, had a written note from his mother stating he did not have to eat any fruit or vegetables except chips. However, if any of the rest of us dared turn our little noses up at her boiled cabbage or fishcakes or dreaded stews she would jab her long steel serving spoon in your direction like a weapon and bark, 'I will rap your knuckles faster than you can say Jack Spratt!'

One Friday, after barely edible liver and onions, it was stewed peaches for pudding. I didn't like peaches at the best of times, but stewed? It seemed cruel even to the peaches. Unlike Wilson (who has now probably since died of scurvy) with his extraordinary excuse note, I had no choice but to try and eat them. I fished some out of the bowl with my spoon. Even the smell disagreed with me. Holding my nose I put them in my mouth. I chewed and found their hairy texture revolting, let alone the taste. I tried hard to swallow, but I couldn't. I knew I would throw up if I did. So now I had warm stewed peaches in my mouth, and uneaten cold stewed peaches in my bowl.

Mrs Pierce was patrolling the tables with her spoon ready to rap the knuckles of any child who dared not finish every last morsel of her dessert. 'Finish your peaches, boy,' she snarled, spitting over my bowl as she did so.

Quicker than I could say Jack Spratt, I spooned the remaining peaches into my mouth, but again I just couldn't bring myself to swallow. But then I hatched a brilliant plan. I would store the stewed peaches in my cheek and spit them into a bush on the walk back from the dining hall to the main school building. However, Miss Kinetter (a pretty young lady teacher we all loved who had hair like an Afghan hound – I still look at Afghan hounds with longing today) walked alongside me all the way, so I sat all afternoon through maths and history with stewed peaches in my cheek. I'm not sure how long I planned to store them in there like a hamster, but when the bell rang to signal the end of school that day I still had them. As usual my mum picked me up in the family Vauxhall Viva.

'Nice day at school, love?'

'Mmm, erm, umm, erm,' I mumbled. It was difficult to speak with my cheek stocked with stewed and now decomposing fruit.

'What's that in your cheek?'

I checked in the rear-view mirror. My left cheek was a lot rounder than my right.

'Stewed peaches,' I mumbled.

Mum laughed and found a tissue, and then invited me to spit the peaches out into it. It was a minor victory over Mrs Pierce.

My first appearance on stage was at Collingwood and it was a dismal failure. I was cast as Father Christmas in the end-of-term play. The role of Father Christmas is normally associated with an older actor – for example Lord Attenborough waited until he was seventy to play him. However, I was thrust into the red outfit aged five, with a large bag of cotton wool sellotaped to my face.

'NO, WILLIAMS, NO!' bellowed Mr Kirby, a karakul hat(loaf-shaped headgear made of sheep fleece favoured by Soviet leaders)-wearing teacher, from the back of the sports hall as we tried to navigate through the dress rehearsal.

I only had one line: 'The children are all waiting for

their presents.' However, the cotton wool had made my one and only contribution inaudible.

'You're mumbling through your beard!' proclaimed Mr Kirby.

'I can talk louder, sir,' I mumbled through my beard.

'What?' replied Mr Kirby.

'I SAID I CAN TALK LOUDER, SIR!'

'No, no, lose the beard.'

Reluctantly I took off the beard. In the car on the way home my sister Julie asked me, 'Were you meant to be an elf?'

Aside from being invited up on stage with some other children during a pantomime on the end of the pier in Bournemouth starring Radio 1 DJ Ed 'Stewpot' Stewart as Buttons in *Cinderella* – when I got an inadvertent laugh from the matinee audience when he gave me a packet of sweets and I told him, 'I don't like Spangles' – I didn't appear on stage again until the early 1980s. During those years, when my age and weight were both still in single figures I had no desire to be an actor; I wanted to be Tarzan, lord of the apes. Having seen all of the Johnny Weissmuller films on BBC2 at teatime, I thought the best way to emulate Edgar Rice Burroughs's hero was to leap around the house wearing only my pants calling,

'AAAAAYYYYYYAAAAAAAAYYYYYAAAA AAA!!!!!!!'

After being Tarzan didn't work out, I decided to be Sherlock Holmes. Having seen all of the Basil Rathbone films on BBC2 at teatime, I put a sign on my door that read, DAVID WILLIAMS, MASTER DETECTIVE. One of my uncles travelled a lot through work and had bought me a silk dressing gown on a business trip to Hong Kong, and at a Cub Scout jumble sale I had found a magnifying glass. So I sat alone in my bedroom in my dressing gown holding my magnifying glass waiting for someone to knock on my door with a case to solve. No one did.

When I was young I had the full set of grandparents. My mother's father we called Grampie. Of the generation who thought smoking was good for them, he developed throat cancer when I was very young and had a laryngectomy, which promised to prolong his life for a couple of years. One day I walked in on Grampie clearing the fluid out of the tube that sat behind a piece of gauze on his neck. It was connected to a metallic suitcase, and it was making a whirling gurgling sound. Grampie looked deeply ashamed that I had seen him like that, and I walked out of the room. He knew he didn't have long to live and heaped love upon me and my sister, his only grandchildren. He even bought me the most beautiful Hornby railway set, which he couldn't afford, but died before he could give it to me for my eighth birthday. I never really got to know him.

Fortunately I did get to know my dad's dad, Grandad. He was the person who made me laugh most as a child. Arthur Williams had left Wales on his own aged fourteen to try and find a job in London. He worked in hotels most of his life and even shot down a Nazi plane in World War II. Julie and I would squeal with delight when he took his false teeth out and talked gobbledygook, and like all children we wanted him to do it again and again and again. He let my sister and I stay up late to watch the wildly violent TV show *The Professionals* when we slept over on a Friday night.

'Yes, Grandad, we're allowed to watch *The Professionals* at home, aren't we, Julie?' I lied.

He knew I was lying but let us stay up and watch it anyway. On Saturday morning Grandad would take us swimming in Morden Baths (twenty-five years later Matt and I would by chance shoot our most famous *Little Britain* sketch there, the Lou and Andy diving board one, as well as Vicky Pollard smoking in the swimming pool). I would swim into my grandad's big fat stomach and pretend I was bouncing off. Afterwards we would have a race home. We children would run through the alleyway and he would drive his brown Princess on the road, no doubt pulling over for five minutes at a bus stop to let us win. Then he would cook us a big fried breakfast.

Being around him was pure pleasure because he was like a child too. One day he surprised us and took us to the circus, the one and only time I have ever been. Grandad took me to see *Star Wars* at the cinema again and again because he knew I loved it so much, and bought me my first *Star Wars* figures. He and my nanny had a pond in their garden, and one day I was using an old McDonald's polystyrene burger box as a boat for Han Solo, Chewbacca, Princess Leia, C-3PO and R2-D2. Now the Wookiee was a great deal bigger than the other figures, and I hadn't balanced it right. To my horror the 'boat' capsized. I burst into tears. I had lost my favourite toys. And my short life was over.

When I ran into the kitchen to tell him, Grandad

followed me out to the garden and rolled up his sleeve. He knelt down and spent all afternoon with his arm deep in the pond, searching through the sludge and frogspawn for my beloved figures.

'Now, there's R2-D2.'

'Thanks, Grandad,' I said as I wiped the green slime off the little robot figure.

'Who else is still down there?'

'Luke Skywalker,' I said.

He spent a good few hours dredging for the simple farm boy from Tatooine who turned out to be in the spare bedroom upstairs all along, but if Grandad was angry he didn't show it.

Years later Simon Pegg and I would meet some of the actors and crew at the premiere after-party of *Star Wars Episode* III*: Revenge of the Sith*, the least shit of all the prequels. Kenny Baker (R2-D2) was charming; Antony Daniels (C-3PO) was flirty; even the great George Lucas spoke to us. Then Simon approached Peter Mayhew, who played Chewbacca.

'Hi, Peter, it's Simon Pegg. I met you at Comic Con —'

Peter waved him away with his giant hand as one might swat a fly. He was so fantastically rude, it made Simon and I laugh for years afterwards.

When I was nine years old I decided I was going to leave home. I had had an argument with my parents over having my TV viewing rationed. That was the worst punishment I could imagine – not being able to watch *The Dukes of Hazzard*. My plan was to go and live in Banstead Woods, so

I packed some Kendal mint cake and my magnifying glass into the little nylon camouflage rucksack bought at the Royal Tournament. Then I wrote a short goodbye note to my family and slipped out the front door, not closing it behind me so as not to make a sound. I raced up to the woods and tried to find a bit that wasn't muddy so I could sit down. There rather embarrassingly I bumped into my Cub Scout leader, who was out walking her dog.

'Oh hello, Akela.'

'Hello, David.'

'In case you were wondering, I am just waiting for my mum and dad to pick me up. I told them that tree there.'

'Oh OK,' muttered an unconvinced Akela. 'See you on Monday for Cubs.'

'Oh yes,' I replied. I suppose I could still go to Cubs. Damn it, I forgot to bring my uniform.

After an hour or so of crouching by a damp tree I got bored and returned home, thinking that my family wouldn't have missed me. However, my mum was in tears and my dad was full of rage. They had been driving around and around looking for me. Little did I know then what fate might meet a small boy alone in the woods.

My dad sent me straight to bed even though his parents were coming over that afternoon. The curtains were drawn and I lay in bed unable to sleep. After an hour or so I heard their Princess pull up in the drive. When they came in, I listened to their conversation downstairs.

'Where's David?' asked my grandad.

'He's been sent to bed. He tried to run away from home,' replied my dad.

'Oh no. Why?'

'I don't know.'

There was a pause before my grandad said, 'I want to see him.'

'You can't,' replied Dad. 'He's being punished.'

'Please, I want to see him.'

Then I heard the stairs creak as my portly grandad made his way upstairs and opened my bedroom door. I pretended to be asleep for a moment, but then he came and sat on the bed and gave me a hug.

'Don't run away, David,' he said. 'We don't know what we'd do without you.'

'Sorry, Grandad.'

A few years later he would die a long slow painful death. The last time I saw him he was sitting in the back room of his little house in Morden. He had a red tartan blanket over his knees, his face grey with pain. Grandad had a brain tumour. When I walked into the room, he tried to smile, but the pain was too great, and his face wouldn't let him. I wanted to show him some of my new *Star Wars* figures. He nodded slowly, and then I was led away by my father. I didn't know it then, but we had been brought round to say goodbye.

Grandad always had Imperial Leather soap in his bathroom, and whenever I smell that, I think of him and how he made me laugh and laugh and laugh just by taking his teeth out and talking gobbledygook.

I hope I'm like him when I'm a grandad.

My grandmothers only came into focus for me when their husbands died. They had both been disapproving of their more mischievous partners. My mother's mum, Violet Ellis – Nanny E – never cared for me much; my sister was her favourite, something she never disguised. Arthur's widow, Ivy Williams – Nanny Williams – adored me though, and I adored her. I saved up my pocket money and bought her a brooch of a little owl sitting on a crescent moon for her birthday. I took her upstairs to my bedroom to give it to her, as I knew my immediate family would have disapproved of me spending so much money like that. It was twenty-five pounds, which then was a fortune to me, and my nanny was so touched she cried. She couldn't keep it a secret but immediately put it on and paraded around the party showing it to people.

Perhaps I wouldn't have wanted to run away to live in the woods without the guiding influence of Lord Baden-Powell, who at that time nearly forty years after his death still instilled in young boys a love of the outdoors. From the age of eight I was a Cub Scout. On Monday nights I would put on a thick green jumper and itchy grey shorts and learn to tie knots and that the most important thing to keep in your pocket was a piece of string. I managed to acquire an armful of badges. For the entertainer badge I had an idea that will not surprise you: I was going to do a hula dance. Elvis Presley had recently died on the toilet and his *Aloha From Hawaii* concert had been repeated on television. So I donned a grass skirt, a bikini top, a garland of flowers and a wig (20p in a jumble sale), and baffled the other Cubs and their parents in a night of otherwise more traditional entertainment. The music was 'Bali Hai' from the musical *South Pacific*. I performed the dance with another boy, Tom, who very reluctantly put a grass skirt over his uniform and burst into tears through sheer embarrassment during our routine. Despite me being considerably more committed to cross-dressing and performing a Hawaiian dance than Tom, Akela rewarded us both with badges.

The next week it was my turn to cry.

It was the sports badge, and I, despite all that leaping around in my pants pretending to be Tarzan, liked my mum's cakes too much and was a fat child. However hard I tried, I just couldn't jump high enough or run fast enough and was the only boy Baloo failed that day. It was nigh on impossible to fail a Cub badge – the tasks for each one were little more than a formality. If you expressed an interest in something, anything, there was a badge for it, and your mother had better get her sewing kit out. But, however hard I tried, the sports badge eluded me. As we walked back down the alleyway to the Cub hut, I felt so humiliated in front of all the other boys I cried. It was the first time I was made to confront my lack of physical ability. Perhaps I'm the only person in the history of the world to both fail my Cub Scout sports badge and be honoured at the BBC Sports Personality of the Year Awards.*

On a Cub camp our Akela took us all on a march along a river, resplendent in our completely-inappropriate-for-the-hot-summer's-day green woollen jumpers and thick

---

* In 2006 I was given a special recognition award for swimming the English Channel in record time and raising £1m for Sport Relief.

grey shorts. We stopped for a picnic, and I noticed a sprinkler watering the field that backed onto the canal. Stepping back to avoid the sprinkler, I fell backwards into the canal. Down and down I went, into the cold murky water. I couldn't hear a thing. I opened my eyes. All I could see were out-of-focus green weeds either side of me, and above me the sunlight dancing on the ceiling of water. Was my short uneventful life to end here in a watery grave?

Slowly I floated up, and as my head bobbed out of the water I was hastily hauled onto the bank. My heavy uniform was soaked with river water, so I was told to take off my clothes, and sat on the bank in my white underpants, eating a packed lunch of jam sandwiches. My clothes were laid out on the grass to dry. Thick wool doesn't dry in the time it takes to eat a jam sandwich and some Hula Hoops, so by the time we were ready to leave, my Cub uniform was still saturated. So the pack marched back to the campsite, all the other boys in their uniforms, me in a damp and dirty pair of white underpants. My shoes squelching with every step. It would not be my last experience of river swimming.

On Saturday 29 July 1981 Prince Charles and Lady Diana were married, and their wedding clashed with that year's Cub camp. Now I don't know if Akela called Buckingham Palace and asked the royals to change the date of the ceremony, but if she did they must have refused. So Akela and Baloo set up a little black and white television in a field and powered it off a car battery so we could watch this sadly unsuccessful marriage commence.

However, it was all quite long and boring if you were a ten-year-old boy. What's more us boys had become very distracted by something in one of the tents. A penis.

One of the boys had got out his willy and it had gone all hard. He was inviting other boys (even those not in his six) to come into his tent and hold it for a short while. Now I don't know if seeing me do that hula dance had given him the idea that I might like that sort of thing, but I was beckoned inside for my turn. I held his willy for the allotted time, and as I heard the crowds lining the Mall cheer as Charles and Diana kissed on the balcony of Buckingham Palace, I had my first sexual experience.

On the last night of camp we sat around the campfire, and one of the older boys who already had a wisp of armpit hair asked, 'Do you still play with toys?'

'Oh yes,' I replied. 'I love my Action Man; sometimes he even marries my sister's Barbie when Ken is away.'

'I don't.'

I was incredulous. What was there in life without play-ing with toys? 'What do you do?'

'Listen to the radio. Sit on a wall with my mates,' he replied.

How on earth could either of those things be more exciting than choosing honeymoon outfits for Action Man? I thought.

It was the first time I contemplated that my childhood would end. And soon.

Little by little I was growing up. The Falklands War in 1982 proved to be a turning point. Having been brought up on World War II films, I was thrilled that Britain was at war again. I was eleven and unthinkingly patriotic. I had grown up saluting the Union flag at Cubs and singing the national anthem at school. At church parade (the first Sunday in every month, when the Scouts and Guides were made to attend) the vicar gave a sermon about the war and asked us, 'If there was an Argentine boy here you wouldn't want to fight him, would you?'

'Yes!' we all answered.

I eagerly watched the war unfold on television, from the tin of Argentinian corned beef being thrown through their embassy window to the British fleet leaving port for their 'surprise attack' (as Sue Townsend so wittily put it in *The Secret Diary of Adrian Mole*), to the sinking of the *Belgrano* and then HMS *Sheffield*. The terrible injuries. The loss of life. My excitement faded as I began to realize that war was hell. My Action Men were boxed up and put in the loft, never to come down again. Slowly I was growing up.

It was time to leave Cubs. And join the Sea Scouts.

Sea Scouts sounds funny. Scouts sounds camp, but Sea Scouts sounds really camp. However, being a Sea Scout wasn't funny or camp.

It was disturbing . . .

3
A Dutch Nudist Camp

I didn't go to a conventional Sea Scout group. Our leader
lived with his mother, was an ex-merchant seaman and
didn't like the official Sea Scout uniforms and so kitted us
all out in Navy surplus. Most of the games we played in
the hall involved him chasing and spanking us. Our leader
would thoughtfully hire out a sauna so we could all sweat
together, and on camp holidays bathtime would go on for
hours. This would involve us all queuing up in the nude,
and then being dunked in a big barrel of water before
being spanked again. It wasn't all spanking though; sometimes we would go canoeing or sailing – we were Sea
Scouts after all. Water sports involved putting on wet-
suits. One time I saw the leader easing a young recruit
into rubber.

'The wetsuit won't go on unless you take your swimming trunks off,' he said.

The boy reluctantly took off his trunks.

'And it's best I rub baby oil into your legs to help it on.'

Which he did. It took a long while to get that wetsuit on.

One day on a Scout sailing trip I forgot my cagoule and
the leader ordered me to take down my shorts and pants

and bend over. At first I thought it was some kind of joke – he couldn't really physically punish me in front of all these people, standing outside in the marina? Although my parents sometimes whacked me at home, I had escaped the ruler or slipper or cane at school. However, for him the forgotten cagoule (on a day with not a hint of rain) was a perfect opportunity to unleash his sadistic streak. At first all I heard was the sharp *thwack* of the baton make contact with my skin; I felt nothing at all. But a fraction of a second later the burning sting that spread like wildfire across my buttocks was so terrific that all I could do was gasp. I held onto a boat for support, otherwise I might have toppled over. As I stood up unsteadily, tears ran down my cheeks.

When I returned home two days later I secretly examined my buttocks in the bathroom mirror and saw the baton-shaped raised red block of skin was still there, even then hot to the touch. The leader then hand-picked a few of his favourite boys (some current and ex-Scouts) to go on a special unofficial Scout camp with him. It was a nudist camp. In Holland. Once through the gates we took off all our clothes. We cooked, washed and dried up completely naked. We even slept in the same tent together as him. Naked, of course. Now I don't know what the rules are for Scout leaders, but I'm assuming you have to remain clothed at all times when with the boys in your care. When I returned home I told my mother where I had been.

'We went to a nudist camp, Mum.'

'No, you can't have done,' she replied.

'We did.'

'Don't lie, David.'

'I am not lying!'

It's so unthinkable it still seems like a lie. But it isn't. It's true. What happened at the Sea Scouts wasn't sexual abuse as such, it all felt more innocent than that, but it was still very strange.

However, there were good times at Sea Scouts. The leader's helper had a guitar, and we would sit around the campfire and sing songs, 'Yellow Submarine' and 'Puff the Magic Dragon', the latter of which I would pretend to be so moved by that I would make out I was crying, much to everyone's amusement. We would do impressions of the characters in *The Young Ones* or listen to the Smiths, though I was laughed at for not knowing what 'mammary glands' were, mentioned by Morrissey in the song 'Handsome Devil'.

The older boys would tell scary stories in the tents at night. One involved an old woodcutter who axed his whole family and could still be heard chopping wood in the forest at night. Another was even more gruesome. A young couple are driving in the country at night, and their car breaks down, so the man goes out to try and find a phone box. Later she hears a tapping sound on the roof of the car. The police arrive and tell her to get out of the car but not to look back. Unable to help herself, she looks back and sees a beast tapping her boyfriend's head on the roof.

And of course we would fiddle with each other in the dark. And in the light sometimes too. One boy I developed a sustained attraction for, and we would often pair off. After we were intimate he would be so full of anger at what he had done he would become violent with me. That would be enough to make anyone deeply confused about sex. What's more this boy had lost a parent, and in my childish mind I believed they were looking down on us. My whole experience of sex at this time can be summed up in one word. Shame.

It was at Scouts that I attempted to kill myself.

Looking back on my childhood now, I remember how much I felt isolated and alone. How withdrawn I was. How deeply things would upset me. How often I would cry and not quite know why. Now I realize I was suffering with depression, a disease that has blighted my adult life.

Once a year we went on a camping weekend as a pack, without the leaders. My pack was called Kestrel. Without the watchful eye of the leader, it all went very *Lord of the Flies*. Arguments turned into fights, and one boy nick-named Frazzle – we all had nicknames; mine, carried over from school, was Cuthbert – hit me with a log. (If you are familiar with William Golding's masterpiece, I was defin-itely Piggy.) It was dusk and I ran off into the darkening woods. Being hit by the log compounded my misery, and even though I was only twelve, I had long felt that my life was not worth living.

Earlier in the day we had all been playing with a rope swing over a stream, and I returned there. Having an extensive knowledge of knots from my years as a Cub and Scout, I knew how to make a noose. I walked up the muddy bank of the stream, put the noose around my neck, then launched myself off the bank. I felt the rope tighten and crush my neck. My eyes started watering and I choked, feeling as if I was going to throw up. My feet skimmed the bank and dragged in the cold stream. I was too tall. I tried other positions, but it was impossible, so I removed the rope from around my neck and hid in the woods. Now it was dark, 'real country dark' as Anthony Burgess writes in *A Clockwork Orange*, and I crept back up to the camp, lay down behind a tree and watched as the other boys sat around the fire. Frazzle was crying, I wondered why. I watched them for quite a while. Outside of it all again.

I watched and waited behind the tree, and when a Land Rover pulled up I worried that I would get into trouble and walked back into the camp. Frazzle leaped up and tried to attack me again, but was held back. Now he was attacking me for running away.

The boy nominally in charge said to the man in the Land Rover, 'It's all right – we found him!' The car drove off. 'Where the fuck have you been?' asked the boy.

'In the woods, hiding,' I replied.

'You fucking cunt. We had to call out the warden.'

'Sorry.'

'I don't want you in our group any more.'

'OK,' I said, trying not to look at anyone.

I never told them about trying to hang myself. That would have made them even angrier. I never ever told a single person. Until now.

It would not be the only time I would try to take my own life.

*

By now I had passed an exam to go to senior school a year early. My mum bought me the seven-inch single of Queen's 'Flash' by way of congratulations. I still have it. I loved the film *Flash Gordon* so much (I still have a huge crush on Ming's feline daughter Princess Aura played by Ornella Muti) I even wrote a letter to *Jim'll Fix It*.

Dear Jim'll,

Please can you fix it for me to meet Brian Blessed who plays the King Vultan in Flash Gordon. And please can you fix it for me to be a Hawkman for the day? Basically I just really want to be on TV.

Yours Sincerely,
David Williams age 10

Now I realize I should have written in with a more unusual request, like 'Please can you fix it for me to be Muslim for the day.' The more imaginative fix-its always made it onto the show. Needless to say Jim never fixed it for me. However, twenty-five years later while on the Little Britain Live tour I spotted Brian Blessed in a theatre car park. We had a performance that night and he was about to appear in pantomime there as Captain Hook. Feeling pretty famous at the time, as *Little Britain* had been running on BBC1 for a few years and the tour was on its way to playing to a million people in the UK, I approached him, assuming he would recognize me. He didn't.

'Mr Blessed?'

He turned around to face me, obviously a little annoyed that I had distracted him from rummaging around in the boot of his car, probably for Captain Hook's hook.

'Yes?' he boomed.

'Well, I er . . .' I soldiered on. 'Well, when I was young I wrote to *Jim'll Fix It* and asked to meet you.'

'Yes'.

'Well, er, now I have . . .'

Without a word he returned to rummaging around in his boot. However famous you think you are, there will be always be someone who hasn't a clue who you are and thinks you are just another nutter. I tiptoed off into the dark.

So the release of the single 'Flash' heralded the beginning of eight years at Reigate Grammar School. The change was an immediate shock to the system. Having been among the tallest at Collingwood, now I was among the shortest. Some of the older boys at my new school had facial hair; others even drove themselves in every day.

Perhaps I found this new environment disorientating, as for the first time in my school life I did something bad. I copied another boy's work in a French test, and the teacher spotted the same mistakes in our answers. I was therefore given a detention, but knowing neither of them was in a well paid job and they made huge sacrifices to send me to this school I was too afraid to tell my mum and dad. Inexorably the day of the detention came. I would have to stay after school for an hour, and since I took the school coach home and we lived seven miles away I couldn't lie about it. Every morning I sat next to an older boy called

William Conqueror (WC or Bogs as he was nicknamed) on the coach, and he told me what I should do.

'Go to the toilets at breaktime, stick your fingers down your throat until your eyes water —'

'What?' I squeaked.

'Trust me. Then come into your next lesson and tell the teacher that you've been puking up. The secretary will call your mum at work and she'll come and pick you up and you'll miss your detention.'

It sounded like a brilliant plan. So I did exactly what he said, very nearly puked up for real sticking my fingers down my throat, and was duly ushered to the sick bay, which was really just a cupboard under the stairs. My mum turned up an hour later looking very worried, and we went home. I forced down some mince and potatoes and listened to Jimmy Young before lying in bed for the rest of the day.

I was free.

However, what I hadn't envisaged was that the school would simply give me another detention the next week. This time I just didn't turn up. So they gave me another. And another. And another.

One Saturday morning a letter from the school to my mum and dad arrived.

Dear Mr and Mrs Williams,

We regret to inform you that your son David Williams was given a detention for copying another boy's work in a test. He failed to attend detention on the 2nd, 9th, 16th, 23rd, 30th of January, 6th, 13th, 20th, 27th of February, and 4rd, 11th and 18th of March.

We therefore have no option than to give him a double detention on 24th of March, from 4 p.m. to 6 p.m. Please confirm receipt of this letter.

Yours Sincerely,
Mr P. Hamlyn (Headmaster).

Aged ten I was a serial detention dodger.

'It costs us so much to send you to that school,' yelled my dad.

My mum couldn't speak for crying. I had let them both down badly. They were giving me the education their parents could never afford for them, and I was ruining it for myself. And been given a double detention. I still feel bad about it. For the first hour of the detention I had company, a boy who during a chemistry lesson had burned another boy's blazer with some tongs. The language teacher Miss Benson was invigilating, and set him 100 lines and me 200. For the second hour I was on my own, and unlike one of those criminals who is hardened by punishment, I never did anything bad like that again.

Miss Benson made a huge impression on a group of us boys in the first year while she was attempting to teach us Latin. Learning Latin involved lots of verb conjugating, in this case listing all the present indicative versions of a word. The verb in question was *facio*, which translates as to make or do. So we sat there bored out of our brains on a hot summer's afternoon as Miss Benson asked us to repeat after her . . . '*Fáciō, facīs, facit, fácimus, fácitis, fáciunt.*'

Now when you are an eleven-year-old boy, your teacher

nearly saying the word fuck is the funniest thing in the world. One particularly brave boy at the back murmured 'fuckio' instead of *'fáciō '*. Of course we all exploded with laughter but were shocked into silence when Miss Benson, a scary-looking lady with an upturned nose and long black hair who was nicknamed Booga Benson,* demanded that the boy repeat what he had just said. Of course he didn't want to say it, but she cajoled him.

'Fuckio,' he finally said.

'That's funny is it? Fuckio? A man and a woman fucking? To fuck, to be fucking, to have been fucked?'

Being a Latin teacher, Miss Benson couldn't help conjugating the verb.

Now I have a juvenile sense of humour at the best of times, but aged eleven this was the funniest thing I had ever heard and I burst out laughing.

'Do you think that's funny, Williams?'

'Yes,' I replied.

'Get out!' she screamed.

For the rest of the class I stood outside in the afternoon sunshine, trying to laugh as quietly as possible so Miss Benson wouldn't hear. I still think it's funny now. However, soon it would be my turn to make everyone else laugh . . .

---

* The name of a pupil in the long-running BBC school drama *Grange Hill.*

4

The First Laugh

Reigate Grammar School put on plays twice a year. When I was in the first year they staged an operetta called *All The King's Men*, set during the English Civil War. The school only had girls in the sixth form, and this was to be performed by the younger boys only. The operetta featured the King's wife, Queen Henrietta Maria. The boy who was originally cast pulled out; he probably couldn't face putting on a dress. For me that was a plus.

My English teacher Mr Shipton always wore shoes with steel toecaps. This led to wild theories that he had no toes or special mechanical toes or robot toes, depending on what you chose to believe. One day he asked me to stay behind when the lesson had finished.

'Williams? Would you like to play the Queen in this term's operetta?' he enquired.

'Yes!' I shrieked excitedly.

Why had he chosen me? I wondered. Perhaps Mr Shipton had seen me playing Wonder Woman in the school playground, spinning around singing the programme's theme tune pretending to transform from mild-mannered Diana Prince into the superheroine herself.

I was inescapably effeminate. I never contrived it. I couldn't help it.

The way I ran, the way I threw a ball, the way I talked, the way I flicked my hair . . . was just like a girl. In my case, a big fat ugly girl. In early life this tends to go unchecked, though as soon as secondary school starts and boys start asserting their masculinity, being effeminate gets you noticed. Not in a good way. 'Gay!' was shouted at me in the playground most days. It was the worst thing you could be called at school.

A few years ago I was walking through Covent Garden in London, and some youths recognized me and yelled, 'Oi oi, Little Britain! Fucking queer!' Even though I was clearly on a date with a woman, they still shouted it. So I am fully aware of how effeminate I am. Of course I play up to it on TV to elicit laughs, pretending to have a crush on Simon Cowell on *Britain's Got Talent* and calling him 'my Simon'. It's naturally within me, and always will be. And of course my Simon is pretty hot.

So at eleven years old I was effeminate enough to be given the role of the Queen in a school play without even having to audition. There was also the fact that no one else wanted to do it. Queen Henrietta Maria was a non-speaking role. All I had to do was sit and fan myself while my ladies-in-waiting sang me a song. My mum found me a very nice wedding dress that looked suitably queenly, and I found a curly black acrylic wig in a jumble sale for 25p. When I put on my costume at the dress rehearsal I noticed I was the only boy who wore a wig and had the best dress by far. I sat there with my nose in the air, fanning myself in rehearsals. It never occurred to me that it might be funny.

Finally the night of the performance came. My dad, mum and sister were all in the audience. There were titters when I first trolled on. Then I sat down and started fanning myself in the most regal way I could imagine, and the titters turned into guffaws. I'm sorry to say I completely upstaged Trimbee's beautiful falsetto and the pretend lute playing from Lambourne.

Stepping off the stage that night, I was a hundred times happier than I could ever say. I had generated laughter. Loud, explosive, wonderful laughter. It was as beautiful as moondust. Just by fluttering my fan or sticking my nose up higher I had created this sound that would be my drug until this day. I sat beaming in the back seat of the Maxi on the way home. 'I was telling people, my son's the Queen,' said my delighted mum.

After letting my parents down so terribly with the detention drama, I had made my mum proud. What's more I knew what I wanted to do with my life.

I wanted to make people laugh.

And more importantly I wanted to wear a dress.

Twice a year at school there was no rugby or cricket during games; instead there was a compulsory cross-country run. Three miles around Reigate park. For the first 100 yards everyone would sprint wildly, then the pack would spread out and I would find myself at the back with the other fat boy, Halliday. We would then walk the remainder of the course chatting. Despite the mud, and the rain, and the cold, and the stinging nettles, and the bracken, it was actually quite an enjoyable way to spend an afternoon. However, when we came in sight of the changing block we would see the hundred or so other boys, who had all by this time showered and changed, waiting for us. It was a tradition that the stragglers were jeered as they crossed the finish line, so we would speed up, our fat little thighs chafing together as we ran. Neither of us wanted to be last. I always prided myself on not being quite as fat as Halliday, or Fattygay as he was inevitably called by the other boys. And Halliday prided himself on not being as effeminate as me. Coming last was the ultimate shame, so both fatties would throw ourselves over the finish line as the other boys laughed in that cruel mocking way that boys do.

Even if I wasn't the fattest boy in the year, I was still overweight. I would raid the flapjack tin when I got home from school. I was sixteen stone by the time I was sixteen. Comfort eating or pure greed? Most likely a mixture of both. Pieces of cake or biscuits or chocolate could instantly sweeten the sourness of my life. If you have been called gay all day in the playgroud, a cake when you returned home from school offered some consolation. A fairy cake of course.

However, home wasn't the sanctuary it might have been. As I grew up, feelings of alienation from my family immersed me. When my parents punished me, I would fall silent. I wouldn't speak. More punishment would follow – no television, no pudding – and the hours of silence would become days. Finally my mum would plead with me. Seeing how upset she was, I would always break my vow of silence.

'I'm sorry, Mum,' I would say, meaning it.

'Right, let's try and have a bit of a better attitude in future.'

'Yes, Mum,' I said, never really sure what she meant by this.

'Now go and apologize to your father,' she would order.

So I would creep into the living room, where he would be drinking tea and watching the news.

'I'm sorry, Dad,' I would say. In my head I was saying, *I'm not sorry.*

Every time this happened, and it happened often, my defiance grew.

Like at most schools, it was survival of the fittest at Reigate Grammar. A boy in the year above me had an upturned nose so was greeted by his fellow pupils with a burst of the song 'Pigs in Space!' (from *The Muppet Show*). One day he just wasn't at school; he had left, presumably unable to take it any more. Another boy, Broach, had a twisted mouth from birth and couldn't pronounce his 'r's properly, so he became 'Bwoach'. I was friends with Broach: I was always drawn to outsiders. They tend to be the most interesting characters. Broach and I even looked at pictures of naked ladies in *Fiesta* magazine together. One day he too was gone, and never came back, most probably hoping that in another school no one would make fun of his speech impediment. Lendon was unusually hairy for his age, and was accompanied by a chant: 'Chewbacca! Chewbacca! Chewbacca Lendon!'

The teachers had nicknames too. As well as Booga Benson, there was Monkey-man Stather, a lovely slightly deaf teacher called Mr Gardener, who was known completely unfairly as Sterile John, Ratty Burnett and Mr Worthen, who was known simply as Bastard.

Ratty taught French and unsurprisingly vaguely resembled a rat. He was a very sensitive soul. Once he overheard me ask the boy in the booth next to me in the language laboratory, 'How much longer have we got of this crap?'

'Crap? CRAP?' he said, stammering with emotion. 'Williams, get out!' I left the classroom for the vague embarrassment of standing in the corridor. Through the door I could hear him weeping. 'Crap? I work so hard on these lessons . . .'

The other boys had to console him; one even offered him his hanky. Normally we would have welcomed seeing a teacher have a nervous breakdown, but Mr Burnett was a sweet man. Unfortunately Mr Burnett's complete and utter humiliation was only a term away. At Christmas the whole school gathered in the local church for a special service. The vicar took the sermon and thought that instead of starting with the Bible, he would tell us a story that ended up relating to it. It's a common trick: one time I even witnessed a vicar segue from Laurel and Hardy to the Crucifixion.

'When I was a boy I asked for a mouse for Christmas, but my parents bought me a rat . . .'

Eight hundred boys tittered.

The vicar didn't think his story was that funny, but he continued: 'And so I named him Ratty.'

There were huge waves of laughter now. This was the best Christmas service ever.

Of course the vicar had no idea about Mr Burnett's nickname or his appearance, and, emboldened by the response, went on: 'That's right. Ratty the rat!'

Collective hilarity was now rocking the church. 'Ratty! Ratty! Ratty! Ratty!' Boys were now craning for a glimpse of poor Mr Burnett, who had his head in his hands.

'So Ratty the rat became —'

The headmaster approached the lectern and whispered in the vicar's ear. Abruptly the confused clergyman announced the next hymn. We boys never knew how he would have got from Ratty the rat to the baby Jesus.

Writing was increasingly something I enjoyed. All that time spent on my own in my bedroom had given me an active imagination. A few of us boys decided to do an alternative school magazine. The official one, *The Pilgrim* (named after our school hymn), came out once a year, and was a dry list of rugby results and the like. Ours was going to be 'by the kids for the kids' and we called it *Wall Scrawl* (forgive us, we had just turned fourteen). There were video reviews (some of X-rated films that we hadn't seen) and humorous drawings of teachers. I wrote this review of a day out I had had with my friend Bowling at Alton Towers:

STUNG AT ALTON TOWERS

I was there for six hours and managed to go on only four rides. The queueing time ranged from one to two hours and the rides last one to two minutes, working out at about £1 each.

Adding to the discomfort of the day, I was stung by a wasp which crawled down my shirt, and when I enquired if there was a First Aid post at hand I was annoyed to hear the nearest one was two miles away!

I was so pleased with the pun on 'stung'.

Other pieces I wrote display the beginnings of an anti-authoritarian streak. I wrote a piece TEN FACTS YOU DIDN'T KNOW ABOUT MR NICHOLSON. Mr Nicholson was a handsome PE teacher with a resemblance to cricketer Ian Botham, and was never seen out of his shell suit.

- He is studying nuclear physics with the Open University.
- He is really 4'11" tall but his trainers add 2" to his height.
- He once met Jimmy Savile's brother-in-law at a tennis club in Wandsworth.
- His real name is Ian Botham.
- He hates poseurs.
- His moustache is 100% cashmere.
- His secret ambition is to be a Franciscan monk.
- He writes poetry for the *Financial Times*.
- He doesn't like wearing designer sportswear.

- He is the only person in the world, apart from Barry Norman, who bought the *Film '86* signature tune.

It wasn't P. G. Wodehouse, but it wasn't a bad start.

We sold copies of *Wall Scrawl* at break and lunch, and felt like we were living a plotline from *Grange Hill*. However, with declining sales (the boys realized it was not worth 25p after all and they would rather buy a Lion Bar from the tuck shop) we all lost interest, and *Wall Scrawl* closed after only three issues.

You were cool at Reigate Grammar School if you excelled at sport. Rugby and cricket were the two sports that we were poured into whether we liked it or not. However, the school did have an open-air swimming pool, and despite being overweight, I was selected to be in the school team. Martin Russell was head of PE. He was one of the nice teachers, if not the nicest, and the coach of the swimming team. A small group of us would travel to other reasonably posh schools and swim races with them. I never ever won one – someone was always faster than me – but I loved being in the water, and Mr Russell could see that and allowed me to swim in the pool unsupervised at lunchtimes. My parents also enrolled me in a swimming club, Sutton & Cheam, and I practised for an hour in Cheam Baths every Wednesday night. The highlight was stopping at the Happy Fish chip shop on the way home. At the club I never won a race either.

However, my body, so heavy and ungainly on land,

loved being in the water. The feeling of solitude under-water, and being alone with my thoughts, if only for as long as I could hold my breath, was something I also treasured. As races were all 50, 100, 200 or 400 metres, I could never beat the sporty kids. However, put me in over a distance of 22 or even 140 miles, and maybe I could win. Perhaps if Mr Russell had never let me practise on my own in the school pool at lunchtimes, I would never have one day swum the Channel or the Thames.

In the early 1980s we lived under the reign of Thatcher. Growing up in Surrey, we were expected to be right wing. There was only one black boy in the entire school, and one day our form teacher played a brilliant trick on us. We were about to have a new headmaster, and a black man was seen being shown around the school. One particularly prejudiced pupil demanded to know who the man was.

'It's the new headmaster,' he told us. We were outraged. Chaos and confusion reigned.

'He's black, sir. He can't be the headmaster,' piped up one little boy.

'Why not?' asked the teacher.

And of course we couldn't find an answer. For the first time we had been confronted with our own unthinking racism. Some teachers really are magnificent.

There were girls only in the sixth form and you had to fancy them. Our collective crush was on Sarah Prescott-Smith – or SPS as we had to call her as we mentioned her name so much, just like little girls now have to call One

Direction 1D. If you talk about one subject so much you have to abbreviate it. SPS was the prettiest girl in the school, perhaps even in the entire Borough of Reigate and Redhill.

'I just saw SPS in the canteen,' one of us would say.

'She smiled at me!' said another.

'No she didn't,' piped up another eleven-year-old. 'She loves only me!'

We even wrote 'I Love SPS' on our books. There were plenty of other girls in the sixth form, but Sarah Prescott-Smith was by far the prettiest, and besides we didn't know the names of any of the others.

In the years that followed, boys would come into school on a Monday morning full of tales of exploits with girls they had met at parties at the weekend. I wasn't cool enough to be invited to those parties. I imagined if I ever did, I would tell a girl that I was dying of a terminal disease so she might take pity on me and show me at least one of her breasts. One Monday morning Sharman came into registration with a big smile on his face and waved his middle finger under all our noses, boasting that he had put it inside some girl. It certainly smelt like he had. Sharman and others would tell stories that had me enthralled . . .

'Within minutes all the rugby team had a girl and were rolling around the floor with them.'

Images of Caligulan excess played in glorious Technicolor in my mind. The truth was probably less exciting. I wondered when I would be allowed entry to this kingdom of sex. As a teenager I was both prurient and prudish. I was so full of self-loathing that in my mind it was unthinkable that any girl would ever want me. I hated everything about myself.

The way I looked.

How I spoke.

Even how I thought.

It was a symptom of my (yet to be identified) depression.

In my head I believed myself to be completely and utterly unworthy of love. The homosexual encounters I had experienced at Sea Scouts filled me with a gigantic sense of wrongness.

Guilt.

Shame.

Self-loathing.

My life had only just begun but I felt that I had already ruined it.

My parents were generous enough to send me on a school skiing trip to Courcheval in France. One night there was a disco in the youth hostel we were staying in for all the youngsters, and the fifty or so boys from Reigate Grammar School all went. I had recently been given a Walkman by my Auntie Janet for my birthday, and had one tape to play on it, Paul Young's *No Parlez*. As I had never been to a disco before I took my Walkman.

'There'll be music at the disco, Williams,' pronounced one of the boys sharing my dormitory.

'I know,' I said, although I wasn't sure. 'But I might want to dance to my own music.'

'Prick.'

He was right. But I thought having headphones on made me look cool. So after tiring of *No Parlez*, I attempted to dance to the records that the DJ was playing, Phil Collins's 'Sussudio', Jan Hammer's 'Miami Vice Theme' and a-ha's 'Take on Me'. I was wearing moon boots, and my Walkman repeatedly slipped off my belt and fell on the dance floor. Two French teenagers spent the entire five hours we were at the disco snogging. I was utterly spellbound. It was the most erotic thing I had ever seen in my life. Just like staring at the sun, you want to look but also know you have to keep looking away or you will go blind. You glimpse. I glimpsed for most of the five hours. I had never seen kissing like that, and it would be another seven years until I would experience it for myself.

If Bogs's advice about how to evade a detention didn't turn out to be useful in the long term, the nickname he gave me was.

'I do like your digital watch' was the first thing I said to him. He laughed at my voice because he thought I sounded posh and called me Cuthbert. Cuthbert Cringeworthy was the name of the teacher's pet in 'The Bash Street Kids' in *The Beano*. The name stuck and I would use it as the name of my first comedy character (who was utterly unfunny), Cuthbert Hogsbottom III. I was only twelve so I hope you can forgive me.

In addition to the twice-yearly plays, once a term each class had to host an assembly. It could be anything really – a short reading from a book, a talk about coin collecting – and was normally boring. It was a drudge to organize, and everyone in my class hated doing it. Not me. I had big plans. I wanted to use the assemblies to stage my own comedy sketches. So I started writing spoofs of TV programmes for me to star in, with other boys from my class in supporting roles. It was reassuring finding something I could enjoy after the ritual humiliations of the cross-country runs.

The first of these spoofs was based on *Game for a Laugh*, a long-running TV prank series of the time. I dragged up and also blacked up to play Rusty Lee, who was then one of the presenters. Years later I would do both of these again to play Bubbles' nemesis Desiree in the third series of *Little Britain*. The spoof culminated in me putting a custard pie in the PE teacher Mr Nicholson's face, which made me the most popular boy in the school. Until break time. When everyone went back to calling me gay.

Then I moved on to *Secrets Out*, a short-lived Mike Smith-presented TV game show for children. I recorded the theme music by putting a tape recorder next to the television. As this was played to the 200 boys in the second and third years, I entered as Cuthbert Hogsbottom III. In my dad's old flares and adorned with a little blonde toupee I had found in another jumble sale for 15p (there must have been a lot of wig wearers in the Banstead area at the time), I entered waving to everyone, pretending to be some big TV star. The music stopped and I ran towards the stage, not quite making it in time, and falling back onto the floor as I did so, my jumble-sale toupee ending up on the floor. It wasn't sophisticated humour, but it got laughs from thirteen-year-old boys and some of the PE teachers.

My finest hour however was *Blankety Blank*. One of my favourite programmes as a child, first hosted by Terry Wogan and then the great Les Dawson (I fulfilled a lifelong ambition by appearing in a special Comic Relief episode with Paul O'Grady hosting in 2011), it was a gift for double entendres. So I wrote questions involving teachers such as, 'Miss Benson was shocked when she ran into the staffroom to see Mr Chesterton had got his *blank* out,' or, 'Mr Russell and Mr Nicholson were showering after the rugby match when Mr Russell turned to Mr Nicholson. 'My word, you have an enormous *blank*.'

As you may have gathered, just as in the TV series, the answer to every question was 'penis'. The contestant, a pupil plucked from the assembly, had to try and think of a suitable non-rude alternative. Aged thirteen, I was writing and performing my own material.

In some tiny way my career as a comedian had begun . . .

5
'Don't do it!'

Unfortunately, not everyone enjoyed my sense of humour. The metalwork master at Reigate Grammar School, Mr Rooth, was a permanently grubby man with a beard. Mr Rooth smelt of rust. He was so irritated by my constant chatter as we made things out as of metal (I only managed a letter opener though it started out as a tray), he would actually pay me 50p per lesson not to talk at all during the class. However, I was soon to see a comedy performance that would convince me that making people laugh was all I wanted to do . . .

In the mid-1980s Rowan Atkinson was much like he is now, one of the most popular comedians in the country, though his career had yet to break internationally. Rowan had made his name in the punk sketch show *Not the Nine O'Clock News*. My sister Julie and I were sometimes allowed to stay up to watch but were sent to bed if the sketches got too rude. Richard Curtis wrote a comic song entitled 'Kinda Lingers' which when sung by the quartet of Rowan, Pamela Stephenson, Mel Smith and Griff Rhys-Jones became 'Cunnilingus'. This was the cue for our parents to immediately send us upstairs.

'But we don't even know what cunnilingus is!' I protested tearfully.

Julie and I bought tickets to see Rowan Atkinson live on stage at Croydon Fairfield Halls. Our parents didn't come with us; instead we took a friend each. I counted the months and days and weeks until finally the night of the performance came.

Needless to say, with Rowan centre stage and all the sketches written by Richard Curtis and Ben Elton (one even premiered the character Mr Bean with his getting-changed-in-front-of-a blind-man-on-the-beach routine), it was an evening of laugh upon laugh upon laugh. As much as I was laughing I was observing. *How did he time that joke? What was so funny about that particular facial expression?*

Rowan is unlike most comedians as he has mastered both verbal and physical comedy. So I studied him carefully that night. Most of what I saw is burned into my memory. I thought, *This is exactly what I want to do.*

Although I wanted to make people laugh I could never quite imagine myself as a stand-up comedian; I still can't. Rowan wasn't doing stand-up; he was acting in sketches, the most economically written sketches without a single misplaced word. Rowan is an extremely precise performer; as a result the performance was like a masterclass in comedy. Even though in real life Rowan is painfully shy and has a stammer, the verbal sketches where he was a teacher or a vicar or the devil were delivered perfectly. To compensate for his stammer Rowan tends to overemphasize words, which makes them sound funnier. In *Blackadder*

II he elicits laugh after laugh simply for his pronunciation of the shortest name, Bob.

If the verbal sketches were magnificent that night, the physical comedy was even better. Even now I can remember exactly where I was sitting in the theatre, at the back of the stalls, marvelling at his huge talent, looking down the rows of seats as the entire audience doubled up with laughter. Rowan was a conductor and the audience was his orchestra. One day I wanted to conduct a symphony of laughs too.

This was in the days just before videos of comedians' live tours were common, and not long after the show finished its run an audio recording was released on vinyl. Alone in my bedroom I listened to that record over and over again. More than any piece of music before or since. I studied it. I yearned for it to yield its secrets to me. I had borne witness to its power; now I longed to harness it.

Listening to the record, I learned how to time a joke. I wrote down the lines to all the sketches. Then I would go into the bathroom and practise them in front of the mirror, copying his facial expressions from memory. I didn't perform them for anyone; I just wanted to act all the sketches to myself and work out where all the laughs were.

His influence on my acting was obvious, as this review of a school play in *The Pilgrim* demonstrates: 'The play provided a good vehicle for parading the ample talents of Messrs Dashwood and Williams. The latter's facial contortions à la Rowan Atkinson seldom fail to amuse . . .'

The very first Comic Relief Red Nose Day was in 1988.

I asked the deputy headmaster Mr Mason if I could take the assembly that day even though it wasn't my class's turn. My wish was granted, and I memorized the sketches perfectly. I put on my red nose and walked to the bus stop, taking that instead of the school coach so I could get there early to rehearse on the stage. Mr Mason, with his comb-over and half-moon spectacles, introduced me: 'As it's Comic Nose Day it seems only fitting that this morning's assembly is taken over by the school comedian.'

I stood behind the curtain, fiddling with the dog collar I had cut from a piece of white cardboard, so thrilled that anyone other than me thought I was a comedian.

First I performed the 'Tom, Dick and Harry' vicar's speech wearing a cassock I had borrowed from a boy who was in a choir. Set at a funeral service this concerns three friends, one deaf, one dumb, one blind, who get run over by a combine harvester. 'Dick saw the combine harvester. Harry heard the combine harvester. But neither could cry out. Tom, who could have cried out, never had the faintest idea what hit him . . .' Then I put on a gown and moved on to the sketch 'No one called Jones', in which the teacher takes registration, and all the pupils have rude names like Ontop, Doodoo and Genital.

It still surprises me that Mr Mason allowed me to finish that second sketch. I left out the most obscene names but it was still very rude for a fee-paying school in Surrey. Perhaps that it was for 'Comic Nose Day' made the difference. At the end I collected money from my fellow pupils at the door with a bucket as they filed out. At break

I counted the money: £53.20. I had raised my first money for people living in poverty around the world. I was monumentally proud and eager to do more.

Also in 1988 Rowan Atkinson was appearing in an evening of nineteenth-century Russian playwright Anton Chekhov's comic sketches in the West End, the collective title being *The Sneeze*. I bought tickets with money saved up from my Saturday job as a lifeguard at Banstead Swimming Pool, and my best friend from school Robin Dashwood and I took the train up to London. This time I was determined to meet my idol, so I bought a programme and we ran around to the stage door afterwards so I could ask him to sign it.

After a short while the nervous comic genius appeared.

'Please can you sign my programme?' I asked.

Without a word Rowan took out a pen and scribbled his name. While he did this I realized I had the chance to ask him a question.

'What advice can you give an aspiring comedian?'

'Don't do it!' he stammered, smiling as he moved on to the next fan.

Over a decade later I met him at an audition for the role of Bough in *Johnny English*. I wrote in my diary:

Monday 18/2/2002
Met the great Rowan Atkinson today, for the first time in 14 years. In 1988 I asked him to autograph my *Sneeze* programme. This time I was auditioning for *Johnny English* in the offices of Working Title. I recognized a couple of names on the call-back list

for the sidekick role Bough – Ben Miller (who will probably get it) and Eddie Marsan. I had been informed that Rowan is shy and has a stammer. I was saddened at how bad it was. He even struggled to read his lines confidently. I really felt for him. Rowan is also quite a scientist when it comes to comedy. No wonder his work verges on being perfect. I performed the scenes a couple of times but what I did never felt inspired and I left knowing I hadn't quite made the grade. Perhaps I just wasn't good enough, but the over-riding feeling I had was complete awe to be in the presence of my childhood hero. Just reading the scenes with him was intimidating.

Three years after that, Matt and I were stars, and we were asked to shoot a series of *Radio Times* covers for Comic Relief with various famous faces. Lou and Andy from *Little Britain* were put with Rowan Atkinson as Plantman, a superhero spoof he was doing for Red Nose Day that year. Once again he was painfully shy, but as we posed for the photograph I now had the courage to tell him the story of how I had met him as a schoolboy.

'And you said, "Don't do it!"'

'D-d-did I really?'

'Yes.'

'W-w-well I must have been joking.'

'I know, but I am so pleased I didn't take your advice!'

He had told me not to be a comedian, but Rowan Atkinson was so brilliantly funny, all I wanted to do was be like him . . .

6
Theatrical Types

I was not a model pupil. My school reports again and again pick me up on my immaturity, poor concentration and relentless exhibitionism.

January 1984
Scripture: An ebullient student who makes sensible, perceptive comments when he manages to exercise self-discipline.
Physics: Recent good work has not hidden the fact that his concentration in lessons often wanders.

December 1985
Headmaster: There are still signs of immaturity in his attitude which contrast strongly with his more serious and sensitive nature. This report presents some challenges to David that I hope he will respond positively to.

July 1986
House Tutor: He contributes where he can. The sporting activities are not for him.
Year Head: Still signs of immaturity but David has shown a more responsible attitude of late.

Summer 1988

History: In class he remains an enigmatic mixture of immaturity and perception.

General Studies: David finds it very difficult not to treat all the exercises with flippancy. I find this annoying as he could contribute much with a positive nature.

Form Tutor: David is certainly not a conformist – though he needs to learn to curb his non-conformity on occasions.

Year Head: I agree: especially, that knowing where to draw the line is important.

Deputy Headmaster: Talented and flamboyant, David had better heed a few warning shots here.

Spring 1989

Form Tutor: On an individual basis he is often charming and cooperative, in a group he can be frivolous and irritating.

The truth is I didn't want to grow up. I still wanted to play. That's why I chose a job where adults can play like children.

There were four distinct social groups in my year at Reigate Grammar School:

- the cool kids
- the rugby types
- the nerds
- me and Robin Dashwood

We were our own group – I suppose of theatrical types, or 'poofs' as the rugby types referred to us.

There were reading competitions once a year, in which you recited a poem and then a piece of prose, and mostly either Robin or I won them. The only poem I wanted to read was Philip Larkin's 'This Be the Verse' which of course has the word fuck in the opening line: 'They fuck you up, your mum and dad . . .' If only I had known about his poem 'Love Again', which contains the word cunt.

Of course we weren't allowed to read a poem with swear words, so we generally chose a First World War poem as they were familiar through class. Finally my turn came to take to the stage to read Wilfred Owen's World War I poem 'Dulce Et Decorum Est'.

> Gas! Gas! Quick, boys! – An ecstasy of fumbling,
> Fitting the clumsy helmets just in time . . .

An incredibly powerful piece; I still had some pretensions to being serious then. However, as I bounded confidently onto the platform I tripped and fell spectacularly flat on my face, my anthology of World War I poetry flying one way and my left shoe the other. Unsurprisingly the audience of 200 boys exploded with laughter. A kindly teacher picked up my book and a pupil returned my shoe. In some pain I hobbled to the centre. I knew somehow I had to be in on the joke and said, 'I don't find it very funny.'

This led to even more deafening laughter, and it was now impossible to read the poem without the whole piece feeling utterly absurd. Some boys were still laughing twenty minutes later and had to be thrown out.

My foray into public speaking was more successful. I thought my speech 'Argos catalogues are the work of the Antichrist' was funny and original, and it really wasn't bad for a sixteen-year-old. The catalogues were relatively new then, and it felt satirical at the time. What's more we had just studied Marlowe's *Doctor Faustus* and so I was newly familiar with the seven deadly sins. So the pictures of ladies in their underwear made you 'lustful', the fact that you didn't have to walk around a shop meant you were 'slothful', the toy guns encouraged you to feel full of 'wrath', etc.

Success in the school competition led to another, to decide who was best junior public speaker in the whole of Reigate and Redhill! What made this different was that you now needed a proposer and a seconder (I asked two pretty girls in the sixth form, Sarah Smith and Helen Squire) and the judges could ask you questions at the end. The night came, and in our school uniforms we met at the town hall and sat through speeches from the other insufferably precocious pupils from nearby schools. The speech got some laughs, and then it was time for the dreaded Q & A, when each judge could ask you a question. Now you had to think on your feet. One severe bald-headed gentleman judge with glasses looked determined not to give me an easy time.

'Mr Williams, you say that Argos catalogues are the work of the Antichrist, and yet those who are elderly or perhaps disabled rely on these catalogues to do their shopping.'

My mouth went dry; this was a stern response to a humorous speech.

'Wouldn't you say,' he continued, 'that these catalogues actually provide a very useful service in our community?'

'Well, sir,' I said, my brain searching for an answer, any answer. 'That's why these catalogues are so evil – they prey on the weakest in society!'

The audience laughed and burst into applause. The judge was irked but had one more question he could ask me. He wanted revenge.

'It seems to me that these catalogues are not the work of the Antichrist at all, but in fact merely an expression of a consumerist society. Do you view consumerist society as immoral?'

Now my mouth was like a desert, and I had to take a sip of water so my tongue wouldn't stick to the roof of my mouth.

'What a wonderful question,' I said, my mind still racing for something, anything to say. 'I have to say our judges tonight have been exceptional . . .'

The audience was laughing at how I had avoided his Exocet missile of a question.

I continued '. . . and I would like to ask the audience to join me now in giving our wonderful judges a well-deserved round of applause.'

Everyone applauded and laughed, I had brought the house down. Even the judge smiled at how artfully I had avoided his question.

First place was mine. Next I won the Surrey heat, and I had my picture in the local newspaper holding the trophy. A school play prevented me from taking part in the

United Kingdom finals. Winning a trophy was nice, but knowing I could improvise a funny answer and make a room full of strangers laugh was even better. You can learn in quite a technical way how to generate laughter, as I had by memorizing Rowan Atkinson's sketches and replicating what he did. Most people could read those sketches and get a laugh or two; Richard Curtis and Ben Elton's writing is so strong. However, the ability to be spontaneously funny under pressure (a skill you will need if you are one day going to go into gladiatorial combat with Jonathan Ross on his chat show) was something more precious. Slowly but surely I was gaining the confidence to take myself further and further.

When I reached the fourth form at school we were all given the choice of taking part in the Duke of Edinburgh's Award Scheme (boring) or joining the Combined Cadet Force (marginally less boring, and of course you were given a uniform). Having watched the older boys march up and down the playground, I decided that the Navy Cadets had by far the best uniform, so I joined them.

The uniform was much the best bit. You were allowed to wear it all day, even though the activities – mainly marching and standing still – did not start until in the afternoon. So I would use the opportunity to camp it up, much to the distaste of the teacher who acted as our commanding officer.

'You are making a mockery of the navy,' he barked.

'I can't help the way I march, sir.'

The marching, the saluting, the falling in line was all a game to me – to see how effeminately I could carry out the commands.

Only a few of us chose the navy, probably because of the camp reputation sailors have. We were sent off to an army camp to do a weekend of training. It was like doing forty-eight hours of national service: we cleaned boots, struggled round assault courses and consumed the greasiest food I have ever had the displeasure of eating. There were chips with every meal except breakfast.

I was singled out for ridicule. Daphne was what the older boys christened me. Apparently it was a word people in the armed forces used for homosexuals. Of course I had brought most of this on myself, as I was now in the habit of playing up to my effeminacy, and delighted in the attention.

My friend the comedian Ben Miller (of Armstrong & Miller fame) once told me a theory about comedians that helps explain this cycle of outrageous behaviour and bullying.

'A comedian's worst fear is being laughed at,' he told me when were filming the Channel 4 comedy drama *Coming Soon* in Glasgow in1998.

'Laughed at?' I asked.

'Yes, we all love being laughed *with*, but no one wants to be laughed *at*, and certainly not the comedian. He or she creates comedy to control the laughter at them, and turns it into being laughed with.'

His words resonated with me that day in Glasgow as they do now. Sometimes I read comments about myself complaining that my effeminacy is an act. It isn't. I'm really camp, and I always have been. Hence the title of this book. Effeminacy is one of the characteristics of camp. The writer Susan Sontag sought to define it in her 1964 essay 'Notes on Camp'. According to her, other characteristics of camp include theatricality and humour. 'Camp proposes a comic vision of the world. But not a bitter or polemical comedy. If tragedy is an experience of hyperinvolvement, comedy is an experience of under-involvement, of detachment,' she wrote.

As a child, when you first enter the environment of a school or Scout group, there is pressure to conform to the behaviour of the other boys – what is considered 'normal'. In an all-male environment especially, being effeminate marks you out for ridicule. When I played Wonder Woman in the playground it wasn't for effect; I really loved the TV series and wanted to be her. When I realized that the other boys were laughing at me for this, instead of shying away from it I embraced it so I could be in on the joke.

That's what I did at the army camp (!) that day in 1985, and that's what I do on television programmes today.

If the other boys were going to call me Daphne, I was going to be the campest cadet of all time. I started wear-ing my beret at a jaunty angle, swinging my arm wildly as we marched, saluting with an extravagant wobble of my arm. It was a necessary technique for survival. However, on the Sunday afternoon the attempted humiliation reached its apotheosis as a few hundred cadets were gath-ered in a semicircle on a hill.

'Right, Daphne,' said one of the older boys who was playing at being an officer, 'you have to get up now and tell us all about your sexual experiences!'

The boys all laughed in anticipation of seeing Daphne demeaned a little further. I rose to my feet and faced the toy soldiers.

'My first sexual experience may surprise you actually. It wasn't with a woman. Or a man . . .'

There were jeers of disbelief from the audience, but I didn't feel this was the time to tell them about me holding another boy's willy at Cub camp. 'No, my first sexual experience was actually with a peanut!'

It wasn't that funny, but they laughed nonetheless and I was told I could sit down. I had survived.

When reading a play out loud in our all-boy English class in the fifth form, I didn't mind taking the female role. As my teacher Mr Bruce noted in my school report for February 1987, 'His class portrayal of Lady Macbeth will never be forgotten!'

That same year there was a general election in the UK which gave Margaret Thatcher her third inexorable victory. The headmaster had the bright idea that Reigate Grammar School should have an election too, and debate the political issues of the day. Anyone could enter and represent any political party, just like in a real general election. Most participants wanted to represent the Conservatives; in our school Labour would not have stood a chance. I decided I would stand as a candidate for the 'Navy Party'. My time in the CCF must have made me realize there was a rich vein of comedy there. So I registered myself as a candidate, and began campaigning. My policies were as follows:

- The wearing of flares to be compulsory at all times.
- The school hymn 'To Be a Pilgrim' to be replaced by the Village People's hit song 'In The Navy'.
- All teachers to salute when passing each other in the corridor and say, 'Hello, sailor.'

The list went on. All the candidates would have a few minutes to speak in assembly. The boy representing the Conservatives (think of that clip of William Hague addressing the Tory Party Conference as a teenager) took a deep and quite reasonable dislike to me.

'And for Williams to denigrate this election with his so-called Navy Party . . .'

I took this as a cue to stand on my chair and wave to the boys behind me. The anarchy elicited a huge cheer.

'It's pathetic, the Navy Party . . .'

I was back on my chair. Another huge cheer.

'That you might waste your vote on the Navy Party . . .'

Chair. Cheer. However, this was the last time as a teacher ejected me for being disruptive. I was taken outside, but having been in plays I knew the secret door that led to the stage.

'He is making a mockery of this election . . .' continued the young Tory.

At that point I burst through the curtain to wild applause.

I was banned from campaigning for a week.

A poll put me in the lead but my campery peaked too soon. An older boy with long hair who campaigned for the Psychedelic Lentil Alliance (presumably inspired by Neil the hippy in the wildly popular sitcom *The Young Ones*) ultimately came first, and I was a close second. The Conservatives came last. The winner unrolled a poster with the slogan TAKE THE LENTIL PSYCHEDELIC DECISION, highlighting the TAKE, the L, the S and the D.

That was surely not what the headmaster had envisaged when he let us boys have our own election . . .

7

The White Rabbit

Mr Louis was the flamboyant classics master of Reigate Grammar School. He was also the self-appointed director of all the school plays. He rushed around the school like the white rabbit in *Alice in Wonderland*.

'Oh dear! Oh dear! I shall be too late!'

He had long grey hair and wore light-coloured suits with paisley shirts and matching ties. If he saw a piece of litter in the playground he would order the nearest boy to pick it up. He had an interesting repertoire of plays, from Russian playwright Ivan Turgenev (Mr Louis's production of *A Month in the Country* was popularly renamed a *A Month in the Concert Hall* due to its phenomenal length) to Roman 'comedy' by Plautus.

He cast me first as an illiterate servant in *Romeo and Juliet*. I only had a few lines, which were spoken to the audience:

I am sent to find those persons whose names are here
writ, and can never find what names the writing
person hath here writ. I must to the learned. In good time.

It wasn't much, but pretending to be thick always guarantees a titter or two. My parents had recently taken me to see Frankie Howerd in a revival of *A Funny Thing Happened on the Way to the Forum* at the Chichester Festival Theatre in 1986. They took me to the theatre lots, which I remain thankful for, and my mum and I still go and see everything in London together. Frankie had yet to make his appearances on *The Last Resort with Jonathan Ross* or *The Word* and was not fashionable again, so was revisiting the role that he had such success with during the 1960s. I had seen him in his two Carry On films and some old episodes of *Up Pompeii!*, but live I was utterly enthralled. Frankie Howerd had funny bones. There was something absurd about him, as if he had no choice but to be a comedian – people would have laughed anyway. As soon as he came on stage in his Roman outfit and the most unconvincing toupee the world had ever seen, he had us all in the palm of his hand.

As a nation we have always preferred our comedians – Tommy Cooper, Eric Morecambe, Dawn French, Alan Carr – to invite laughter at their own absurdity rather than to say funny lines and provoke laughter at others. I was laughing as much as anyone else in the audience, but I was studying Frankie too. That night in Chichester he effortlessly shifted from being in a scene to talking to the audience. That was something I needed to do in my pivotal role as First Servant in *Romeo and Juliet*, so I turned my performance into a little impression of him. I shamelessly stole his withering looks to the audience and his 'oohs' and 'ahs' too. Every time I stand in front of an audience now I feel like I am channelling a little bit of Frankie.

A few years later I would wait outside the stage door at the Secombe Centre in Sutton to get his autograph, which he graciously gave me though I was too in awe to speak to him. A younger man with glasses led Frankie away, and they drove off in an old Jaguar. In 2008 I would play Frankie Howerd in a BBC drama about his tormented private life entitled *Rather You Than Me*. I travelled to his house in Waverly Down in Somerset, to speak to his life-long partner Dennis (who drove the Jag that night), now almost totally blind, to understand Frankie better.

'He cried when he came,' Dennis told me, which made me sad that someone could have that much self-loathing. Impressed by my knowledge and enthusiasm for his for-mer lover (I even quoted some of Frankie's lines from the relatively obscure film *The House in Nightmare Park*), Dennis gave me his blessing. By the end of the day at Waverly Down I was even cajoled into trying on the great com-edian's toupee. It was as if a circle that had taken twenty years to draw had been completed.

First Servant in *Romeo and Juliet* wasn't the greatest part, but it was better than Second Servant and felt like another breakthrough for me.

Mr Louis was an incredibly prescriptive director. The process was not important; all that mattered was that the play would not be a disaster at the end of it. RGS was an achingly lower middle class school with aspirations of being upper middle class, so appearances were everything. Mr Louis would make you write down all your moves on your script before you had even stood up and rehearsed anything.

'Williams, you move from stage right to centre stage to say your line and then exit back stage right.'

Mr Louis was a big player in his local amateur dramatics group and was not averse to getting up on the stage and performing the line exactly how he wanted it done. He also had very old-fashioned ideas about stage make-up. He would draw thick black lines on your forehead if you were playing anyone older than your actual age, which meant most characters in a school of eleven- to eighteen-year-olds performing Shakespeare, Molière and Turgenev.

I met my best friend Robin Dashwood through performing plays together, as we never shared a classroom. I had a few friends before Robin, but he was my first real kindred spirit. The previous friendships felt like affairs, this was marriage. Short, blond and well spoken, Robin is also fiercely intelligent. We have been friends for nearly thirty years, and although we have disagreed with each other, Robin and I have never ever had an argument.

Robin had sophisticated tastes. While all our contemporaries were getting drunk on snakebite down the local pubs, we would take walks in the park and then go for dinner. Instead of watching Swedish Erotica, a series of pornographic films that made the rounds of our school, we would watch the entire series of *Brideshead Revisited* on video.

One Sunday afternoon Robin and I went to Hampton Court Palace. In the blazing sunshine we saw a woman in the distance dressed in the style of a character from a 1940s film noir. In a wide-brimmed black hat complete with veil, floor-length black dress and high heels, she had the appearance of a woman whose husband had just been found dead, and in her widow's dress was knocking on the door of private detective Sam Spade. Naturally Robin and I were intrigued.

'Let's walk over and get a closer look,' I suggested excitedly. So as subtly as we could, we moved closer and closer to this mysterious lone figure. When we were near enough we both realized that the hands were large, there was an Adam's apple and more than a hint of stubble. The figure fixed us with a withering look and flounced off behind a hedge. It was distinctly un-PC of us, but as soon as 'she' was far enough away, we burst out laughing. This vision stayed with me and ultimately gave birth to the *Little Britain* character Emily Howard. It was that 'she' was dressed in a style of women's clothing not seen for forty years that stayed with me the most – the gloves, the hat, the veil even! For Emily I made the clothing from a hundred years before. The vision at Hampton Court had definitely gone out wanting to be looked at by strangers – perhaps that was part of the pleasure – and again Emily Howard was an exhibitionist at heart.

Ten years after we left school we often reminisced about our misspent youth.

Monday 19/1/1998
I invited Robin over for dinner and we had a very relaxing low-key time, eating, talking and watching *Dr Who: State of Decay*. We talked of our life as teenagers, how we were in watching *Bergerac* when everyone else was out drinking, smoking and groping.

'Being an outsider is very useful,' I said. 'If I had been doing all of those things everyone else had been doing I don't think I would have been bothered to become a comedian . . .'

Robin was a much better actor than I was as a teenager, certainly a lot subtler. However, he never had that need to push his sibling off the pouffe to recite nonsense, like I did, and is now a very successful documentary director for the BBC. Together we did a number of Mr Louis's old-fashioned productions, most strangely *An Evening of Chinese Drama*, in which Robin narrated a story of a fisherwoman (me) who lost all her fish.

I have a strong sense of the gifts of others, and instead of pushing them away as some competitive performers do, I am drawn to talented people. As we sat together on the school coach one morning I announced, 'You are funny, I am funny; we should form a comedy double act together.'

'A comedy act?'

'Yes, we don't have to have a funny man and a straight man. We could both be funny, like Les Dennis and Dustin Gee.'

Of all the double acts I could have mentioned who are both funny, Cook and Moore, the Two Ronnies, French and Saunders, Smith and Jones, I chose Les Dennis and Dustin Gee!

Our friendship has survived the test of time. He is still my best friend and, with Matt, Robin was the best man at my wedding.

*

For all his eccentricities, I am grateful to Mr Louis for something. He was one of the first grown-ups to spot some potential in me. Perhaps I wasn't just an irritating show-off. Before I left for the summer holidays after my O levels he gave me a play to read before starting the sixth form. It was Molière's *Le Bourgeois Gentilhomme*.

'Williams, I want you to familiarize yourself with the lead role.'

'Thank you, sir.'

'And pick up that Wotsit packet.'

'I didn't drop it, sir.'

'I don't care. Pick it up!'

'Yes, sir.'

So I picked up the Wotsit packet, and in between clearing tables at Chessington World of Adventures I spent the summer reading and rereading the play.

I was about to play my first lead role . . .

8

Kenny Everett on a Monorail

Monsieur Jourdain in *Le Bourgeois Gentilhomme* is one of those roles where a good comic actor can utilize all the skills he has to make the audience laugh. The play tells the story of a middle class man who tries to be aristocratic, with hilarious consequences. Well, I assume the consequences were hilarious when the play was written in 1670, but in 1987 they were still mildly amusing. We actually performed a translation by the comic actor Miles Malleson entitled *The Prodigious Snob*.

My duties at Chessington World of Adventures (where Matt and I would later film an episode of our ill-fated first television series *Sir Bernard's Stately Homes*) involved clearing tables at the Courtyard Café while wearing a stripy red shirt and a straw boater. I was paid £2.50 an hour, but at least I could arrive early and go on the log flume.

One day Kenny Everett came to the park to review it for Gloria Hunniford's talk show *Sunday Sunday*. Kenny was one of the most popular comedians of the 1980s and sadly died in 1995. The best way I can describe him is that he was somehow mainstream but also utterly alternative.

All any of us staff could talk about that day was the fact that Kenny Everett, although by 1987 just past his peak in popularity, was coming to Chessington World of Adventures. It was beyond exciting. What's more, he was going to eat in the Courtyard Café! I might even be allowed to clear his table! Imagine wiping away a splurge of ketchup Kenny Everett had left! As it happened, an area of the Courtyard Café was sectioned off for Kenny and only the permanent staff were allowed to serve him or wipe his table. Still I spied him from afar eating some chicken nuggets.

My shift ended and I was dejected. I had missed my big chance to meet one of my favourite comedians. With a heavy heart I returned to the staff block to take off my stripy shirt and straw boater and change into my slightly less embarrassing normal clothes. Suddenly one of the litter collectors rushed into the changing room with some amazing news . . .

'Kenny Everett is on the monorail and he's heading this way!'

We all ran out onto the balcony of the staff block, which was adjacent to the monorail. In the distance I could see a very bored-looking Kenny Everett and a few other people approaching in one of the monorail carriages. He was too far away to shout anything out yet. *What would endear me to him most?* I wondered. Shouting one of his catchphrases surely? 'Sid Snot here!' 'All done in the best possible taste!' or perhaps 'Round 'em up! Put 'em in a field! And bomb the bastards!' This last one felt too long, as the monorail would pass quickly.

There was a general mood among all us summer job teenagers that we should play it cool. This is Kenny Everett after all. He's bound to say something wacky and zany to us and have us all in stitches for the rest of our lives.

The monorail carriage was getting closer and closer . . . Kenny Everett was passing right by the balcony . . . We all watched expectantly . . . He merely looked the other way.

We watched the back of his head disappear into the distance as Johnny Morris of *Animal Magic* fame wittered along wistfully on the audio commentary.

'Hi Kenny!' I shouted quietly as the monorail carriage turned a corner. He was now too far away to hear. We were crushed.

These days when people approach me for an autograph or photograph I always oblige them, but as with my experience with Kenny Everett, I think meeting any famous person will always be a huge disappointment.

Back at school rehearsals for the play began. However, it wasn't until the first night of *Le Bourgeois Gentilhomme* that I realized how funny it could be.

Despite Sarah Smith, who was playing my wife, forgetting her lines and saying 'Oh shit!' very loudly on stage, it was a huge success. I remember coming off at the end exhausted and lying on the table of the classroom that was also our dressing room as the audience filed past. A few of the parents tapped on the window and said 'Well done' as their offspring gave me the thumbs up. I was thrilled.

As the four-night run continued, I gained in confidence, and by the third night I had shamefully added in some business we never rehearsed, such as falling asleep during the scene when a girl came on to sing a song to me. However, on the final night, the night when my parents were coming, I disastrously lost my way in the first half. The pressure of wanting to impress them, and in particular my father, made me screw things up.

I forgot to come on in the first scene wearing my coat.

It doesn't sound important, but in this play to enter not wearing my coat was a disaster. A whole section of comic business followed in which Monsieur Jourdain kept on asking for his manservants to take off his coat and put it back on him again. So with no coat this was not going to work. At all.

Realizing my mistake I improvised a few lines of Molière . . . 'Manservant, fetch my coat! At once!' . . . but I was really thrown. My mouth was dry, my timing was off, and the first half of the performance was a shambles. I left the stage utterly dejected. I was sure I didn't have the strength to be an actor, if my nerves were going to get the better of me like that. And of course my mum and dad were watching. After all those hours I had spent practising my funny faces and voices in the bathroom mirror, I was desperate for them to see me make everyone laugh.

I wandered off in my tights and wig and found a long, dark empty corridor. Then I gave myself a good talking-to, like a manager might at half-time to a footballer. 'David, you have got to go out there in the second half and turn it around. You have to be the funniest you have ever been to turn this night into a triumph.'

So I stepped back onto the stage, and attacked my role with renewed vigour. Now instead of just falling asleep during the song, I was snoring loudly. What's more,

79

I rested my head on my hand, and improvised some business where with each snore I leaned further and further over until I fell off my chair. Utterly shameless upstaging, but the audience loved it. At the end of the night the audience were all cheering and applauding; it was only a school play but they had had their £2's worth, in fact I had probably given them a £2.50 show.

I was delighted with my review at the end of the school year in *The Pilgrim*:

THE PRODIGIOUS SNOB

The production was carried firmly on the ample shoulders of David Williams, whose Jourdain was a comic delight. From an initial entry which immediately injected the piece with energy and pace, he proceeded to give us a splendidly uncouth, social-climbing buffoon, and had a flexibility of facial expression that reminded me of Charles Laughton. The scene with the batty and pretentious philosopher (exuberantly portrayed by Robert Shearman) and the dinner at which he drooled sycophantically over the Marchioness (Lara Lass-Burch/Helen Squire) and then fell asleep during the song, were joyful moments, and exhibited a level of visual humour and snappy timing that made them the comic high-points of the piece. The singing of Belinda Teale and Vicky Shearman was impressive, especially since they were ruthlessly (and hilariously) upstaged by the antics of David Williams.

Now there was just one thing that could distract me from my pursuit of being a comedian.

A girl.

9
'Age cannot wither her'

According to the ancient Greeks, to be truly perfect you have to have an imperfection.

Zoe Shorey had a scar on her forehead.

Other than that she was perfect. Flawless. Complete. Nothing needed to be added or taken away from her.

In the late 1980s girls could only join Reigate Grammar School in the sixth form, so after years of having no female contact at school, aged sixteen you were pushed into a classroom with a gaggle of teenage girls. I remember my first English literature class as a sixth former and becoming absolutely tongue-tied.

Mr Paxton announced, 'This year we are studying Shakespeare's *Antony and Cleopatra*. Have any of you seen the play?'

I put my hand up.

'Where did you see it, Williams?'

'Erm, um, the er . . . National Theatre.'

I could sense all these girls looking at me as I spoke, and I became increasingly panicked.

'And who was in it, Williams?'

'Erm, um, Judi Dench and erm . . .'

How could I forget Anthony Hopkins at a time like this!

'Erm, oh a man, really famous actor, oh erm . . .'

He even had the same first name as the character he was playing! But I couldn't remember. I could hear a few giggles and stared at my mock-wood desk in embarrassment.

'Thank you, Williams. Antony is normally played by a man.'

Mr Paxton put us all at ease with that joke. He was the most entertaining teacher I ever had. He looked a little like Eric Morecambe, with a bald head and glasses but big Dickensian sideburns. We used to watch *Antony and Cleopatra* on video. He found the BBC adaptation so boring that he would take off his glasses, put his handkerchief over his face and put the glasses back on. Then he would sit there and pretend to snore, blowing the handkerchief into the air as he did so.

Then we moved on to ITV's RSC version, which starred Janet Suzman as Cleopatra. Anyone who has read *Antony and Cleopatra* or seen the far superior *Carry on Cleo* will know that Cleopatra is so sexy she brings down the Roman Empire. Janet Suzman purred through her mesmerizing performance, as well as appearing in a number of revealing outfits. Every time she appeared on screen Mr Paxman would moan with desire . . .

'Phowoar! Janet Suzman.'

It was utterly hilarious. It's a miracle any of us passed our A level as he was making us laugh most of the time.

The term started with Zoe Shorey being a distant figure, although I had noticed her in the playground and assemblies. Everyone had noticed her. She was so beautiful I could barely look at her. Zoe and I didn't share lessons until a couple of months into the first term when one day as if by magic she arrived in Mr Paxton's class.

'This is Zoe, everyone,' he announced. For some reason the girls were all referred to by their first names, whereas the boys by their surnames. 'She has just changed from business studies. Now I need someone to help Zoe go through all the coursework we have done up to now . . .'

His eyes scoured the room as my heart beat faster and faster.

'Williams! Will you help Zoe?' asked Mr Paxton. He had selected me because I was the class swot, not because he knew I was already deliriously in love, even though I had never even spoken to her.

'Erm, yes, um, OK . . .' I said, acting as nonchalantly as I could.

Zoe smiled over at me, and I could have happily drowned in that smile.

When the bell rang to signal the end of the class, Zoe walked over to me. Even though she was stunningly beautiful with her long blonde hair and perfect features, she underplayed her looks, wearing no make-up, a big baggy school jumper, and covering her long legs in an even longer skirt.

'Thanks, William,' she said. Even her voice was lovely. She purred.

'It's David.'

'I thought he called you William?'

'Yes, but it's David Williams.'

She laughed. I wasn't making a joke but I didn't mind. Her laugh was even lovelier than her smile.

'What are you doing on Sunday afternoon?' she asked.

'Nothing,' I replied a little too quickly. 'Absolutely nothing. Completely free.'

'Well, if you want I can come over to your house and we can go through the coursework?'

Oh. My. God. We were going to be alone in a room together, but I didn't want it to be at my house. I knew my mother would be crouched spying through the keyhole, or worse coming in and asking me for my pants and socks to put in the wash, as she did most days.

'How about I come to you?'

'Great,' she said. 'It's the big house on Garratt's Lane. See you at three.'

That Saturday night I couldn't sleep and on Sunday got up early and looked through my wardrobe options. I had recently been shopping at Next and bought a pair of grey trousers and a stripy red shirt. I hadn't worn them yet and was waiting to be invited to a party, though I never was. I sprayed every inch of my body with Sure deodorant, dabbed some of my dad's Old Spice on my face and put on my Next clothes, which made me look like a child stockbroker. Then I waited and waited until it was late enough to avoid arriving any more than an hour early, and stepped out into the autumn afternoon.

Marching up the close I saw my neighbour Mrs Shilito, who had been out walking her red setter. I patted the dog, which leaped up as dogs do and put its muddy paws all over my best new shirt and trousers.

'Oh sorry,' said Mrs Shilito. 'Not going anywhere special, are you?'

'Oh no, not at all.'

In the alleyway I frantically tried to rub the mud off my clothes. Then I walked the short distance to Zoe's house just the other side of the Reigate Road, arriving a mere twenty minutes early.

Her father answered the door. 'Hello?'

'Oh hello, I'm Williams, David Williams, and I'm here to help Zoe with her coursework,' I said. *And marry your daughter*, I added, but not out loud.

'Come in, come in . . .' he said beckoning me inside with a smile.

'Zo? There's a young man here come to help you with your coursework.'

'He's early,' she said from upstairs.

I smiled awkwardly at her father.

Then Zoe sailed down the stairs in a baggy T-shirt and shorts, looking unutterably gorgeous.

'Hello, David. Thanks for coming. Would you like a drink of something?'

Dom Perignon. Slightly chilled. Two glasses is what James Bond might have answered. 'Some orange squash, please' is what I actually said – I was still too immature to drink tea.

Zoe led me into the dining room; we sat down and went through some of the main themes of Shakespeare's play, love being the principal one.

Our legs and elbows nearly touching, which alone made my heart sing, I looked into Zoe's eyes and read Enobarbus's description of Cleopatra:

> Age cannot wither her, nor custom stale
> Her infinite variety . . .

'What on earth does that mean?' asked Zoe.

'That Cleopatra is the most beautiful woman in the world, and she will never ever be boring,' I replied as I looked into her deep blue eyes.

'Oh right. It's beautiful.'

'Yes, you a— I mean, it is.'

'More squash?'

For the next two years I pursued Zoe, not physically but romantically. I had this very old-fashioned sense of chivalry, which I still have. So I sent her a dozen red roses on her birthday; I wrote her little love notes with quotes from romantic poems; I took her to the cinema to see *Angel Heart*, even up to London to the theatre. I never tried to kiss her, though my heart ached to do so. The truth is, I didn't know how to get our lips to meet, let alone actually kiss. And I couldn't stand being rejected and losing everything we had. At sixteen she was very mature and I was painfully immature. However, spending

1. A star is born. My mum had strange hair then.

2. The funniest person in the world ever. My grandad.

3. Still a baby, I am already admiring my sister Julie's dress.

4. Why did I not persist with the knee-high white socks look?

5. Moments before I attempted my Channel crossing in 2006.

6. An early fashion shoot with my sister Julie.

7. Me at my most angelic at my Auntie Janet's wedding.

8. Of course I wouldn't wear fur now. The mauve dress is fine though.

9. (*right*) In my CCF outfit. Hello sailor!

10. (*below*) In my first starring role as Queen Henrietta Maria in *All The King's Men*.

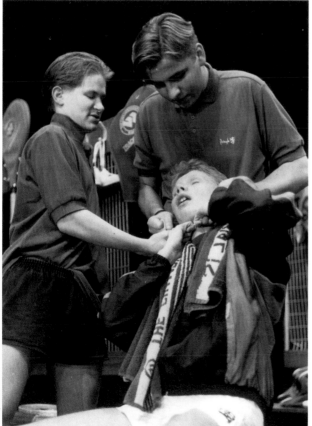

11. (*above*) Me and my many chins in *Romeo and Juliet* at Reigate Grammar School.

12. (*left*) My best friend Robin Dashwood and me strangling Edward Luck in *Ball Boys*.

13. (*right*) On the way to the Sixth-Form Ball, with my Ford Fiesta, thinking I am James Bond.

14. (*below*) Channelling Frankie Howerd at my eighteenth birthday party.

15. Sharing my Bottom in *A Midsummer Night's Dream* at Bristol University.

16. Gratuitously pulling a stupid face at my graduation as my mother pretends to be amused.

17. An average night out for my first girlfriend Katy Carmichael and me.

time with her made me at last grow into being a man. I was in love.

First I fell in love with Zoe's beauty – I couldn't imagine there being a more beautiful girl anywhere in the world ever – then as we spent more and more time together I loved Zoe for her kindness and intelligence and humour. She never made me feel like a fool for loving her. Zoe certainly never encouraged it – in fact she had boyfriends for most of the two years we were at school together. However, there was an unspoken agreement between us that however much I loved her we would never be more than friends. She loved being my friend. My love for Zoe will always be perfect, as it was never requited.

From that first time I saw her at school, for the next twenty years I thought about her every single day. My heart still longed for her. When *Little Britain* took off on television, I registered myself on the website Friends Reunited. With fame and success came a new-found confidence. I posted a message asking if anyone was still in touch with Zoe. Little did I know what consternation it would cause her family, with journalists from tabloid newspapers knocking on their door and photographers waiting outside their house for days, desperate to run a story about my great unrequited love. Eventually a friend of hers put me in touch, and I finally saw Zoe again.

I went round to her parents' house on Christmas night in 2005 and my eyes fell upon her for the first time in nearly fifteen years. She hadn't changed. Still incandescently beautiful. Age could not wither her. Next I met her

Austrian husband and her three lovely daughters. Zoe now lived in Vienna. We went off into the kitchen to catch up alone.

'You know, Zoe, I have to tell you. When we were at school, I loved you so much.'

'You should have told me how you felt,' she said as her daughters screamed with delight as they opened another present in the next room.

'I didn't really know how to then . . .' I said.

Now I did. But it was a thousand years too late.

10
'A couple of queers'

My other great love was my best friend Robin. Despite him wanting to take *Querelle* (a Jean Genet story about a sailor, turned into a film in 1982) out of the video shop on a Saturday evening, I never thought to ask him if he was gay. It didn't matter, and I suppose he didn't tell me because being gay didn't seem like a possibility in Surrey in the 1980s. There were camp men on the television when we were growing up, from John Inman's Mr Humphries in *Are You Being Served?* to Larry Grayson presenting *The Generation Game* with his catchphrase, 'He seems like a nice boy,' which never failed to create explosions of laughter. It seems strange now, but you didn't really think they were homosexual, just camp.

One night my dad decided to give me a warning about 'queers'. His word.

'Now if you go to the toilet and stand at the urinal,' began my dad, 'and you see a man moving towards you and trying to look at your thing . . .'

'Yes, Dad?' I was intrigued.

'. . . shout at the top of your voice, "GET LOST, YOU QUEER!"'

'Get lost, you queer?'

'Yes, they're in all the toilets these days.' Well he did work for London Underground, with its abundance of public conveniences.

'A friend at work said they found a group of queers in a circle,' he continued. He shuddered as the image he was painting filled the canvas in his mind. 'They all had an arse each.'

'Thanks for the advice, Dad.'

'Any time, son.'

That was the only piece of sex education either of my parents gave me.

The early 1980s was when the hysteria around the Aids epidemic reached its apotheosis. An advert featuring a giant black tombstone falling to the ground with 'AIDS' chiselled on it as discordant music played was shown repeatedly on TV, with John Hurt's voice warning, 'There is now a danger that has become a threat to us all. It's a deadly disease and there is no known cure. The virus can be passed during sexual intercourse with an infected person. Anyone can get it.'

Sex = Death. That was what we thought. Our religious education teacher Mr Manfield cranked up the terror even further, telling us in class, 'Aids can get through condoms. When you grow up none of you will be able to have sex.' The disease destroyed the monolithically handsome Rock Hudson's looks, and he died in 1985. I remember there being serious speculation at the time that his *Dynasty* co-star Linda Evans might have contracted Aids by sharing the briefest on-screen kiss.

So despite Robin and I being interested in sex (though

not with each other), we both felt too scared to act upon our impulses. Instead we spent the late 1980s tottering around like an old married couple. When I finally passed my driving test and my mum and dad helped me buy a sky-blue Ford Fiesta, we played the *Cabaret* soundtrack on the stereo. When the stereo broke, we sang the songs instead.

Zoe received some tickets to be in the audience for *Top of the Pops*, but it was half-term and she was going on holiday with her family. So she gave me the tickets, and Robin and I took a number of trains up to BBC TV Centre. *Top of the Pops* counted down the top forty best-selling songs of the week, interspersed with performances and by this time videos. If you were a teenager, being in the audience was about the coolest thing you could imagine. You were filmed dancing as the acts sang, and you might even end up on TV! Even more exciting was the fact that this week our favourite band in the world, the Pet Shop Boys, were still in their imperial phase, and thus number one in the charts with 'Heart'. We were going to be in the same room as our idols.

As we queued outside the studio with other much cooler teenagers with spiky hair and leather trousers (I was sticking to my stripy red shirt and grey trouser en-semble) a joke of mine went embarrassingly wrong. The first of many.

I turned to my diminutive friend and said, 'Well, here's to show business!'

Robin looked a little ashamed as the cool kids who overheard me groaned at what an absolute tosspot I was.

Inside there was a DJ spinning records to get everyone warmed up for the show. This involved a dancing competition. Whoever was the coolest dancer won all the top forty singles on seven-inch discs. Having no one else to dance with, Robin and I danced together, me moving my heavy frame around the studio with no concession to rhythm or beat whatsoever. Unsurprisingly we didn't impress the DJ and found ourselves placed behind the scaffolding that made up the set when the programme was recorded.

One artist who performed that night was Patsy Kensit, who as part of Eighth Wonder had a hit with the Pet Shop Boys-written song 'I'm Not Scared'. She was the absolute girl of the moment, an actress turned singer who was mind-blowingly beautiful, sexy and cool. Kensit didn't know it then, but the big ungainly teenager in the red stripy shirt peering out at her from behind the set as she sang would one day share her bed.

Next it was the short-lived duo Climie Fisher, a kind of less good Lighthouse Family, if that's possible. Then we watched Mike Smith count down the top ten. Robin and I looked hungrily around the studio. *Where were the Pet Shop Boys going to sing their latest chart-topper?* We had to elbow our way to the front. 'And for the second week at number one it's Pet Shop Boys and "Heart"!' announced Mike Smith as the video started playing on the screen. Robin and I were so disappointed. Behind us were a couple of rough-looking teenage girls from Essex in luminous tracksuits.

'Shame the Pet Shop Boys aren't here,' said the blonde one.

To which the brunette replied, 'Don't worry, they're just a couple of queers.'

The Dame Edna Experience was at the time one of the biggest entertainment programmes on television. It was a chat show which has since been imitated countless times in which real-life celebrities were humiliated by the host. Such was the esteem in which Barry Humphries, the creator of Dame Edna, was held that the biggest stars of the day would queue up to be destroyed by her (Cliff Richard and Sean Connery were guests on the first episode). Dame Edna is one of the greatest comedy characters of all time, if not the greatest. Despite 'her' actually being a man, the character is so utterly believable it would be demeaning to call Dame Edna a drag act. *The Dame Edna Experience* dominated Saturday night television, and when a season in the West End was announced, Robin and I booked tickets. We sat in the cheapest seats, at the very top and back of the theatre, and Dame Edna referred to us as the 'paupers'.

'Once in a while I will glance up at you, in strict accordance to the amount you have paid. [Pause.] Goodbye.'

Just like the experience of seeing Rowan Atkinson live, it was like being struck by lightning, but this show had a lot more spontaneity. If Rowan Atkinson was a scientist, Barry Humphries was an artist.

For the West End run, instead of celebrities, members of the audience were humiliated. When a large lady was brought up on the stage Dame Edna touched her newest victim's dress.

'Lovely material, darling.'

'Thank you,' said the large lady, basking in her moment in the spotlight.

'I'm surprised you could get so much of it.'

The whole evening (which began with Humphries' second most famous character, Sir Les Patterson) was explosively funny. A couple of thousand of us shook the Strand Theatre with laughter. The entire performance remains imprinted in my memory. It's no coincidence that many of the characters Matt and I created for *Little Britain* such as Carol 'Computer Says No' excelled in cruelty, though they never managed to humiliate their victims with as much wit as Dame Edna.

My hero-worship of Barry Humphries dates from that night.

Friday 7/11/1997

On tour with Matt I brought a video of Barry Humphries' *South Bank Show* to watch in the van during the journey home. I said, 'He's the man I want to be in forty years' time: elegant, intellectual, impossibly funny.'

Monday 16/2/98

A read-through at the American church just off the Tottenham Court Road for the Channel 4 sketch series *Barking* I am doing. I read through scripts with Rhys Thomas, who is playing opposite me in a couple of scenes. We sneaked a peak in the rehearsal room next door. Barry Humphries rehearsing his new *Edna* show. I felt completely awestruck even though I didn't even catch a glimpse of him.

In 2005 such was the huge success of *Little Britain* that Matt and I would be honoured with our very own *South Bank Show* special to be broadcast that Christmas. I told the producer how inspired I had been by seeing Dame Edna perform that night, and Barry Humphries very kindly agreed to appear on the programme with us. A breakfast at the Connaught Hotel in London was arranged, which would be filmed for the documentary. Matt and I sat like eager schoolboys waiting for our favourite teacher, and he didn't disappoint. He arrived in a beautiful Savile Row suit, topped off perfectly with a fedora. Although this was meant to be a conversation all I wanted to do was listen. When the waiter asked Barry, 'Would you like some freshly squeezed orange juice, sir?' he replied, 'Have you by any chance got any that was squeezed a week ago, that's now going very slightly off?'

The waiter looked bemused.

'I will ask kitchen, sir.'

Filming hadn't even started but already Matt and I were in hysterics.

Two years later we returned the favour when Barry asked us to be guests on his new Saturday night chat show *The Dame Edna Treatment*. The only downside was that at one point we had to share the sofa with the most annoying man in Britain, Piers Morgan. He turned to Matt and me and in a typically Morganesque charmless attempt to break up a double act asked, 'Who do you think is funnier out of you two? Because I know who I think is funnier.'

'Well luckily we are both funnier than you,' I said.

The audience applauded, and Barry Humphries stepped outside his Dame Edna persona for half a second and gave me a wink as if to say, *That showed him!*

Seeing Barry Humphries that night at the Strand Theatre gave me the confidence to accept my first paid gig as a comedian. I was seventeen . . .

11

A Swimmer Who Dabbles in Comedy

Soon everyone in my year at Reigate Grammar School was turning eighteen. That meant we could all drink alcohol, so birthday parties were held at local nightclubs with names like Bachelor's, Vortex or Cinderella's. They were universally awful. My cool friend Richard Gadd planned to have his at Reigate Rugby Club.

'Williams, will you do some stand-up comedy at my party?'

'Stand-up comedy?'

'Yes.'

'I don't really do stand-up comedy.'

'You're funny. Of course you can do stand-up comedy.'

I thought for a moment.

'Yes, Gadd, I'd love to.'

'I'll pay you five pounds.'

'I'll do it for free.'

'No, I want to pay you. Is five pounds OK?'

'Wow! Thank you.'

Of course I didn't have an act, just the belief that I might be funny. I went through lots of ideas. I would sing. I would appear in drag.

Quickly I remembered I couldn't sing, and I thought drag was risky for a rugby club. So I wrote some material and stole a great deal more, mostly from a video, *Steve Martin Live*, which captured one of the greatest comedy performances of all time. I wrote down my script on cards and arrived at the club three hours early to sound-check. I was so early that Richard Gadd had yet to arrive, and there were lots of tough-looking men who had been playing rugby all afternoon drinking in the bar.

I approached the barman. 'I'm here for Richard Gadd's party.'

'The party's not for two hours, son. What do you want to drink?'

'Just some tap water, please.'

He rolled his eyes and got me some water. I took my glass and faced the room. There was nowhere to sit and I felt distinctly uncomfortable standing at the bar while all these rugby types were jostling to buy a drink. I spotted the end of a banquette that was unoccupied.

'Do you mind if I sit here?' I asked.

'No,' said the rugby type, having changed out of his rugby shirt into another more casual one in case anyone doubted his love of the sport. His ear was severely mis-shapen; perhaps it had been chewed in a scrum.

'What the fuck are you doing here?' he asked.

'I'm here for Richard Gadd's party. I'm the stand-up comedian.'

'Ha ha ha!'

I wasn't sure why the idea that I might be a stand-up comedian was funny in itself. As a comedian you defin-

98

itely want people to laugh, but when you decide and not before. The late Bob Monkhouse had the best self-deprecating one-liner on this theme: 'People laughed when I said I'd become a comedian, well they're not laughing now.'

'Tell us a fucking joke then,' goaded the rugby type.

'I don't really do jokes.'

'You're a stand-up comedian who doesn't do jokes. Good fucking luck! Ha ha! You're going to need a drink. We are all having whiskies. Do you want a whisky?'

'Just another tap water, please.'

'A tap water for the fucking comedian over here!'

Finally Richard Gadd arrived. I was so relieved. I couldn't think of a single thing to say to the man with the misshapen ear.

As I was the kind of person who would arrive at 7.55 for a party at 8.00, I was confounded that I had to wait for a few hours until everyone had arrived and I could take to the stage, which was little more than a wooden box.

The music stopped and I could hear boos.

'Here to do some stand-up comedy for my birthday is Williams,' announced Richard Gadd. There was a smattering of reasonably enthusiastic applause from my contemporaries in the upper sixth.

'Good evening, everybody,' I said too loudly into the microphone. The clicking sound was actually my mouth dry with fear.

'Boy, those French. They have a different word for everything! I like a woman with a head on her shoulders. I hate necks! I gave my cat a bath the other day – they

99

love it. He sat there, he enjoyed it. It was fun for me. The fur would stick to my tongue, but other than that . . .'

Of course they weren't my jokes; they were Steve Martin's. Jokes that propelled him to playing stadiums in America in the late 1970s. To become the biggest stand-up comedian in the world. Even though I was reading them from cards because I was scared I would forget them, I got laughs. The jokes are so good they would still get laughs if Professor Stephen Hawking was delivering them. I was seventeen so I hope I can be forgiven. I have never really understood that Oscar Wilde quote, 'Talent borrows. Genius steals.' In comedy originality is every-thing. A joke is a surprise. And there's no surprise when you've heard the joke before.

A few days after I swam the Channel in 2006 I was introduced to the great Steve Martin, whose jokes I had stolen, by Alan Yentob at Wimbledon, where I had been invited to watch the tennis by the BBC.

'Steve, do you know David?' said Alan.

'Ah! Are you the gentleman who swam the Channel? I read about that in the newspaper.'

'Yes, Steve, that's me,' I beamed. Steve Martin, one of the greatest comedians of all time, knows who I am. 'But I also do comedy. Have you ever heard of a TV series called *Little Britain*?' I asked excitedly.

'No,' he said.

Steve Martin obviously assumed I was a swimmer who dabbled in comedy. (Maybe he was correct!) It served me right for stealing his jokes twenty years before.

*

After Richard Gadd's eighteenth, which went so well that in my elation I refused to take his five pounds, I was asked to perform at a ball that some boys in the upper sixth were organizing. They thought this would make them rich, as at the time all most people in the year wanted was an opportunity to cop off with someone of the opposite sex. This would be a much bigger event, with hundreds of teenagers not just from Reigate Grammar School but also from all over Surrey.

Emboldened by my success I said yes, and agreed a fee of twenty pounds, which was then reduced to a free ticket, which seemed odd as I was going anyway. I was never any good at the business side of things, and still take little interest in what I get paid. Just like today, all I cared about was being up on that stage again.

So I went about writing a new set, by which I mean re-renting *Steve Martin Live* from the video shop. The problem was I had already taken all the jokes that could be transmuted for a British audience, so I was left with the more bizarre routines such as 'Cat Juggling'. I borrowed my dad's dinner suit, as this was a black-tie event, and my mum drove me to the hall in Redhill.

I stood by the DJ holding the microphone waiting for my moment. Finally Jive Bunny and the Mastermixers faded down and the DJ (who I was told had great connections in the show business world in London) announced me.

'Now for some comedy with a very funny man . . . David Williams!'

There were boos when the music stopped. But this

time the boos never stopped. These teenagers wanted to drink and dance and snog. What's more I was probably the worst stand-up comedian of all time. Seventeen and reading someone else's jokes off cards. A few of my friends from Reigate Grammar School gathered around the stage, but soon even they were wandering off to buy drinks, such was my unfunniness. I could see the hall emptying, so I looked down at my cards and read from them as quickly as I could, trying to get the ordeal over as quickly as possible. The boos grew louder, and soon a slow handclap echoed around the room.

'Get off!' A drunk girl in a purple ball gown that made her look like a Quality Street chocolate shouted from the back of the room.

'Thank you; you've been a great audience. Goodnight,' I finally said.

The worst thing was that the DJ pretended to find me funny as he faded in Yazz's 'The Only Way Is Up'. 'Ha ha!' he said. 'Cat juggling, very funny.'

Even I looked at him with contempt. I knew I had been epically unfunny.

I just wanted to walk off the stage and disappear for ever. The thought of hanging around in a room full of people who had all been booing me moments before was humiliating. However, I had told my mum not to pick me up until midnight, as I had thought I would be the guy all the girls would want to talk to or even kiss after I had made the whole room laugh. Instead I waited for my mum on a wall outside, as teenager after teenager came out into the cold night air to snog or throw up or both.

'So, how did it go?' enquired my mum.

She already knew it had gone badly as my face was white and I was still shaking when I got into the seat beside her in the Vauxhall Cavalier.

'Not well.'

'Oh dear. What happened?'

'I don't want to talk about it.'

'Were you nervous?'

'Of course I was nervous.'

'Well maybe your nerves got the better of you.'

'Maybe.' I couldn't begin to paint the scene in all its horrifying detail. This was the Guernica of gigs.

'Maybe the comedy thing isn't for you,' she said kindly.

I thought for a moment.

'No. I still want to do it.'

If you are aspiring to be a comedian and you get booed off and you still want to be a comedian, one day you will be.

Life at Reigate Grammar School became easier the older we became. I was even made a prefect, most likely as a reward for my acting and public speaking. There was a special prefect's tie, though no one wore one as it was deeply uncool. My mother had different ideas. She took me to the school outfitters in Reigate.

'David, I want to buy you the prefect's tie.'

'It's OK thanks, Mum. No one wears them.'

'Please. For me. Please . . .' she implored.

Reluctantly I let her buy me the tie, though I changed it when I arrived at school. Her pride in my achievements has always outweighed my own.

One of the perks of being a prefect was that you were allowed to leave the school grounds if you didn't have a lesson. Robin was also made a prefect and we would walk into downtown Reigate at lunchtime. We would buy chips from the cafe and then go to Our Price and sort through the latest releases from the Pet Shop Boys, saving up to buy the twelve-inch remixes of 'Suburbia' or 'It's a Sin', songs that spoke to us more than any other. We loved Neil and Chris and we still do. Robin and I have never met up and not discussed them. I chose 'Later Tonight' from the album *Please* as one of my Desert Island Discs. A story of waiting and waiting just to catch a glimpse of the one you love, without them even knowing you exist.

> That boy never cast a look in your direction,
> Never tried to hook for your affection . . .

It was typical of their songs, as most were full of longing, as I was at the time. Moreover, they dominated the charts in the late 1980s. Everything the Pet Shop Boys touched turned to gold.

And we wanted to touch them.

During the summer holiday Robin secured a part-time job answering the telephone at a theatre booking office. This allowed him access to a computer database of everyone who had booked tickets for West End shows. So one day he just happened to insert the words 'Neil' and

'Tennant' into the database and found out that the Pet Shop Boy was going to see the Oscar Wilde play *An Ideal Husband* on Saturday night.

'Neil's going to be at the theatre at 7.30 p.m. He's booked two tickets,' said Robin breathlessly.

'Shall we wait outside?' I asked. I was no less a potential stalker than my friend.

'Let's book tickets for the play, then we can go up to him in the interval.'

'Brilliant!' I exclaimed. 'I'm sure he'll be delighted to meet two of his biggest fans.'

'His two biggest!' proclaimed Robin.

So Saturday came, and we went up to London on the train in the afternoon. When you have grown up in Surrey and you are seventeen, London is beyond thrilling, and just walking around is entertainment in itself. So we enjoyed an all-you-can-eat buffet at Pizzaland, then went for a walk in Covent Garden. On Long Acre the most extraordinary thing happened. We saw Neil Tennant!

So we followed him. For around an hour.

We followed Neil Tennant into a stationery shop and watched him buy pens. Then we followed Neil Tennant into a bookshop and watched him browse through some books and magazines. Then we followed Neil Tennant to a clothes shop, where he looked in the window at a shirt for a short but thrilling while.

Then Neil Tennant walked to Shaftsbury Avenue and tried to hail a cab. We had to approach him. And fast. So we crept up behind Neil Tennant.

'You say something,' I whispered.

'No you . . .' said Robin.

'Mr Tennant?' I said, my voice trembling.

The Pet Shop Boy turned to face his stalkers.

'Yes?' he replied in his lovely north-eastern lilt.

'I just want to say you are a living god,' I spluttered.

Neil smiled uncertainly, and then fortunately for all of us a cab stopped, and he got in. He smiled weakly out of the window at us as it sped off. We stood on Shaftesbury Avenue and watched the cab disappear out of sight.

'A living god?' said Robin. 'Why did you say that?'

'Well he is!' I protested.

'I know he is, but he must have thought we were a pair of weirdos.'

After a pause I said, 'We are a pair of weirdos.'

'I know,' agreed Robin.

'It's fine,' I said brightly. 'I can apologize to him later when we see him at the play.'

Robin's face darkened with worry. 'Oh yes, the play. Well we can't go now.'

'Why?'

'He'll know we're stalking him.'

'We are stalking him,' I said.

'I know, but we just can't go. He might put two and two together and I could lose my job.'

'No more stalking today then?'

'No, let's just go to the cinema.'

So we went to see the Pet Shop Boys film *It Couldn't Happen Here* at the Odeon, Tottenham Court Road instead.

*

A very important person stepped into our lives at this point, a new English teacher at Reigate Grammar School called Mr Grant. He had the appearance of Billy Bunter* and even dressed in pre-World War II style complete with neatly combed hair and round wire spectacles. However, his ideas were modern, and what's more he desperately wanted to direct school plays.

Spotting the potential in Robin and me, he asked us if we wanted to appear in a production of *Ball Boys* by David Edgar. This was a short contemporary political play about two ball boys at Wimbledon who strangle a tennis champion with string from a racket. This was a production way outside Mr Louis's conservative ideas about drama – dark, homoerotic and sadistic, much like the 1929 play *Rope* by Patrick Hamilton. As it was too short to put on in the evenings on its own, we performed the play at two lunchtimes. We recruited the tall blond and handsome Edward Luck (who had never lived down taking out his penis in the language laboratory) to play the tennis champion.

Mr Grant had a completely different approach to Mr Louis. Instead of giving us all preset moves, he allowed us to find our own way around the play and the stage. We had to find the characterizations, rather than copy what the teacher did. Needless to say we loved every moment of it. We were finally learning how to be actors, rather than copying the teacher.

* The corpulent schoolboy character from the stories by Charles Hamilton.

There was a moment when Robin, playing One-Eye, had to snap a tennis racket over his knee. So a racket was sawn in half before the performance and reassembled so that it would break at the appropriate time. However, before that point in the play there was another sequence in which we mimed a game of tennis. When Robin pretended to serve, the head of the racket flew across the room, nearly decapitating some poor fourth former in the process. We looked out at the audience even more stunned than they were, and in a state of shock got through the rest of the play.

A thwarted Mr Louis turned up the second lunchtime, not to watch the performance but to berate Robin and me. 'You are meant to be in the school canteen now supervising the dinner queue!' he bawled.

'I'm sorry, sir. I forgot,' I said. In the excitement of the play we had forgotten our prefect duties.

'Unbelievable!' he screamed. 'Unbelievable!' With that he turned on his high heel and slammed the concert hall door behind him. Robin and I waited a moment and laughed. We had outgrown him.

Even more audacious was Mr Grant's production of *The Collection* by Harold Pinter. This short play was written in 1961, and Laurence Olivier took the role I was cast in for a television adaptation in 1976 – so no pressure then. The play concerns a young man named Bill (Robin) leaving his ageing gay lover Harry (me!) to have an affair with Stella (Helen Punt, sister of Hugh from the comedy double act Punt and Dennis), to the anger of her husband James (Robert Shearman, who now is a playwright that Whovians will know wrote a brilliant episode of *Dr Who* entitled 'The Dalek').

I had a terrific speech as Harry that made me aware of how great dialogue should sound.

'Bill's a slumboy, you see, he's got a slum sense of humour. That's why I never take him along with me to parties. Because he's got a slum mind. I have nothing against slum minds per se, you understand, nothing at all. There's a certain kind of slum mind that's perfectly all right in a slum, but when this kind of slum mind gets out of the slum it sometimes persists, do you see, it rots everything. That's what Bill is. There's something faintly putrid about him, don't you find? Like a slug . . .'

I loved that speech so much, I immediately fell in love with Pinter's work and saw every play of his I could. For me, as a writer of dialogue Pinter is without equal, someone whose work makes you aspire much more with your own writing. Just a sighting of the great man was enough to make my heart beat faster.

Wednesday 4/4/2001

I had a strange premonition I was going to see someone really famous at the National Theatre. And indeed I did, along my aisle at Pinter's adaptation of Proust's *Remembrance of Things Past* was Pinter himself. In a black suit with a black shirt. Poking out of my pocket was Michael Billington's biography of him! My dream is to be introduced to him, so I resisted the temptation to launch myself upon him.

In 2008 I would sit next to Harold Pinter in his book-lined study. For an actor this was the modern equivalent of being invited to meet Shakespeare. Pinter is one of the most celebrated playwrights of all time, and like Shakespeare I have no doubt that his work will be performed for ever. I was in the great man's study with Sir Michael Gambon, David Bradley, Nick Dunning and the pointlessly handsome director Rupert Gould to read his play *No Man's Land* to him. Soon we would open the play at the Gate Theatre in Dublin before taking it to the West End. Everyone else was too intimidated to sit next to Pinter himself, including the great Gambon (I had waited twenty years since seeing the television masterpiece *The Singing Detective* as a youth to work with him), so I was forced to take the chair.

'I was in a production of *The Collection* at school,' I told the legendary playwright.

'Was it any good?' he asked.

'Some say it was the definitive production,' I answered cheekily, and Harold laughed.

I made the greatest playwright in the world laugh.

A few months later on Christmas Eve Harold's long battle with cancer would end, and Michael, David, Nick and I would return to the stage on Boxing Day trying our best to honour his memory by giving the greatest performance of *No Man's Land* we could.

Back in 1989 Robin, Helen, Robert and I were called to Mr Grant's house to discuss *The Collection*.

'What do you think is the nature of the relationship between Harry and Bill?' asked Mr Grant, like most teachers asking a question he already knew the answer to.

'They could be friends,' I said.

Mr Grant said nothing. It was an extremely bold choice for a school play: *The Collection* explores infidelity, homosexuality and how people can be imprisoned in relationships. The four of us all felt incredibly grown-up being part of it. I even smoked a cigar on stage; there were references to stroking a pussy, and Mr Grant played Joy Division's 'Love Will Tear Us Apart' before the play started.

However, the choice of play was too daring for a deeply conservative school like Reigate Grammar, and it was given a bad review in *The Pilgrim*, a magazine that never ever gave any school play a bad review . . .

Here were the heavyweights, the local RSC, Dashwood, Punt, Shearman, Williams. I placed them unisexually in alphabetical order, so as to not indicate favouritism.

Harry (David Williams) and Bill (Robin Dashwood) have some conversational passages together which require very nice timing and more than a little menace. Harry's words at times should convey a cold menace to Bill, but it seemed to me that throughout, Robin was exhibiting complete self-possession and lack of concern. There should be tension between all the characters. It is quite awfully difficult to achieve this, and I have to give my opinion that this production failed to achieve it.

I saw Jim Grant at a fundraising evening at Reigate Grammar School in 2012, and he called the review 'a stinker'. He still seemed quite hurt by it.

So as my days at Reigate Grammar School drew to a close, it was time for the exams that would help determine all our fates. I sat in the sports hall for hours and hours on long hot summer days. I wrote and wrote until my left hand ached as I took A levels in English literature, history and business studies. I still have no idea why I chose that last one.

The final event in the school calendar was the end-of-term ball. This was when we could say our goodbyes. Some for good. I wore a dinner suit and a horrid little red bow tie, and posed for my mum next to my Ford Fiesta, hoping that I looked like James Bond. I didn't get to kiss Zoe that night, but as we stepped out into the summer night to take some air, I looked up at the stars and the moon looking down at us and wanted the night to last for ever. Never again would I be able to see her every day, a thought which drained the world of colour.

It was a school legend that the most anti-authoritarian boys swam in the school pool at midnight after the leaving ball. The caretaker was wise to this and waited by the pool to intercept everyone who wanted to leave the school with this badge of dishonour. That year nobody managed it – except Robin and I, the boys least likely to. We were clever enough to wait an hour or so until the caretaker had gone to bed.

We scaled the fence, stripped down to our boxer shorts

and dived in. The water was warm and silky. The moon reflected on the water. It was the most magical swim of my life. Moreover, it was the perfect way to say goodbye to the school that we had loved and loathed for the last eight years. I drove Robin home in my little pale blue Fiesta, singing 'Maybe This Time' from *Cabaret* as we sped down the Reigate Road in the early hours.

12
Enter Daffyd

A group of thirty young people who wanted to be actors more than anything in the world sat on some grass outside St Aloysius School in north London. It was August 1989 and I had been waiting for this day for years. After two unsuccessful auditions, my third trip up to London to the National Youth Theatre's rehearsal rooms on the Holloway Road had proved successful. One summer day the letter arrived. By chance I opened it sitting out in the garden eating a choc ice with Zoe, who had given me a lift home from RGS in her poo-brown Ford Fiesta, and for a moment everything seemed right in the world. A beautiful girl, an ice cream and a letter that meant I was a step nearer being an actor.

Sporting a pair of ghastly purple shorts that clearly showed the outline of my genitals (it did say wear 'loose comfortable clothing' in the letter), I made my way to the school. For the next three weeks these thirty strangers and I would devise a play. It was a disparate group – from Clive Manyou, black and from a council estate, whose place on the course was being paid for by the Prince's Trust, to Joe Talbot, head boy at the most expensive public school in the country, Millfield. We were all waiting on the grass for the director to turn up. It seemed unrealistic to expect a film star to arrive, but a film star was who walked up to greet us that day.

In his baseball cap and jeans, it wasn't easy to recognize him at first.

'I'm Ralph,' he said in rough tones. 'Ralph Brown. I'm an actor and I'll be taking the course this year.'

Still the name didn't give him away, but there was something very familiar about him.

'Are you the bloke who makes the Camberwell Carrot in *Withnail and I*?' asked Joe.

'Yes,' replied Ralph modestly. 'I played Danny the drug dealer in that film.'

We all looked around at each other. We couldn't believe it! He might not have been Harrison Ford, but he was in one of the funniest scenes in one of the most celebrated films of the time, the brilliance of which the passing decades have still not dimmed.

In that famous scene Danny rolls a joint with twelve skins so long it resembles a carrot. The film follows the story of two out-of-work actors, which is what most of us were destined to be. Even after one viewing, Ralph's lines (written by the occasional genius Bruce Robinson) about hairdressers being in the employment of the government and hairs picking up signals from the cosmos were burned in my memory.

After memorably playing a racist copper in the first series of *The Bill*, Ralph had become a much-sought-after film actor, having appeared in major roles in *Buster* and *Scandal*. (Since then he has acted in *Alien³*, *The Crying*

Game, Wayne's World 2 and *Star Wars Episode I: The Phantom Menace.*) All we wanted to do was ask him questions about *Withnail and I*, but Ralph wanted to move from acting into writing and directing, so devising a play was as important to him as it was to us.

The theme was the environment, with global warming a relatively new crisis in the late 1980s. Although it may seem corny now, in 1989 it was a new topic, and infinitely more original than Aids or nuclear war, the staple themes for youth theatres creating 'issue' plays around this time. One such NYT-devised piece I saw at the time had two girls holding hands and berating the audience 'Who says our love is wrong?' in much the same way Daffyd from *Little Britain* would many years later.

In fact I met the person who provided the inspiration for Daffyd that year. Although there were many gay people in the NYT, not many were out about it. They were still teenagers, and Aids had provoked a huge upsurge in homophobia. Shadwell was different. Shadwell was not in fact his real name. It was Paul. However, being from Wales he had picked up the nickname (the comedian John Sparks had a morose Welsh poet called Shadwell on the Channel 4 sketch series *Absolutely* at the time). Shadwell was gay, and it was the first thing he told anyone about himself.

'Hello, I'm Shadwell and I'm homosexual,' he would say to new NYT members on the Tube. 'I am the only out gay in the whole of the youth theatre.' Because Shadwell was out everyone in the NYT knew him, and his Welsh accent made him instantly imitable. It was if his whole identity was based around his sexuality, not that there was any evidence of a boyfriend or sexual encounters. There was something comical about the way he said 'homosexual' in that musical Welsh accent of his. Mimicking him at the time, I played out the scenario for my friends of someone else in the NYT who was gay too. 'No, *I'm* the only gay in the youth theatre!' I would say. Unbeknown to me, my brain stored up the idea, and many years later when Matt and I were trying to think of ideas for a character-based sketch series, Shadwell still shone bright in my memory.

Ralph Brown was a cool character and set a very cool tone. One day he announced he wanted us all to dance to the rap song 'Do the Right Thing' by Redhead Kingpin and the FBI. Ralph enlisted two friends who danced with the Cookie Crew to choreograph it. Of course I was utterly hopeless at any form of dancing let alone hip-hop, but I threw myself into it anyway. My lack of dancing skills hardly mattered – as long as you excelled at something you were noticed – and I excelled at making the others laugh, and it wasn't just the purple shorts.

I really made Ralph laugh one day when, as part of a stage fighting workshop, I started my demonstration with my hands around another boy's throat and uttered the bizarre line, 'You'll never work in the circus again, Charlie Chan!'

Those who didn't live in London stayed at the Tufnell Park student residences. Most of us sat at the bar all evening, pausing briefly to go out and buy some chips for our dinner. I didn't drink – I was too inhibited to get drunk – but I loved that everyone else did. We played spin the bottle, and these attractive young people talked about sex, and I listened with great interest. Some of them even had sex up in the small hot bedrooms, though this activity once more eluded me. However, it was as if we had all finally found our soulmates, the formerly isolated acting types from secondary schools around the country were finally all together and revelling in each other's company.

On 20 August 1989 I turned eighteen. After rehearsals a group of the guys took me out to a local pub and kept on buying me drinks. The only alcoholic drink I could bear was vodka and orange, as you couldn't taste the alcohol. When we returned to the halls of residence I was led stumbling into the bar.

'SURPRISE!' they all shouted. There were balloons and a 'Happy Birthday' sign and a cake. Not since I was small had I been given a birthday party, and that these people who had known me for only a couple of weeks had organized a party for me made me feel really special. We all danced to 'Do the Right Thing'. Finally I had left behind the sometimes brutal atmosphere of school, and was now with people who mostly had the same playful side to them that I had.

One morning I called my mum from a phone box that reeked of urine next to Tufnell Park Tube station to find out my A level results.

'Well . . . ?'

'You've got into Bristol, love! Three Bs.'

Bristol University was the most prestigious place to take a drama degree, and my grades meant that I had a place. I was thrilled but didn't want to look too pleased with myself as some others on the NYT course were in tears at hearing their grades.

In the finished production, called *Zone*, I was given an amusing piece to do. The premise of the play was that at some time in the future humanity had so raped the earth only a selected few got to live in a special area called the Zone. My role involved selecting those who gained entry, so I could be amusing and dark at the same time – much as I am now.

'I am so sorry, madam, you can't come in. You are rather large and will take up too much room. The Zone is quite small, you see.'

We performed at the newly built Business Design Centre in Islington. The mums and dads sat baffled in the audience, but other NYT course members cheered and stamped their feet as if *Zone* had changed theatre for ever. Being young and naive, we all thought *Zone* would tour the world and halt the earth's impending environmental catastrophe, but of course it was never heard of again.

Someone who was heard of again was Daniel Craig, who that year was in an NYT production of *Marat/Sade* in the West End. Arguably the best Bond ever played Marat and so was topless in the bath for the entire performance. His presence, voice and torso marked him out for future greatness, and needless to say all the girls and some of the boys in the NYT fell instantly in love with him. The actor who played opposite him in the role of Sade was equally mesmerizing, Dickon Tyrell. However, Dickon never went on to be on the cover of *Vanity Fair* or marry Rachel Weisz. Indeed, I can recall many other brilliant actors in the NYT who we all thought would be international stars whose careers never took off. Further down the cast list of *Marat/Sade*, playing one of the inmates of the asylum, was a young Jamie Theakston. Now I wish I could see the play again – watching the ex-children's TV presenter in the background pretending to be a mental patient might just be the funniest thing in the world ever.

To fill in the month before university started, I took a job as a kitchen porter at the Thorndike Theatre in Leatherhead. Being a kitchen porter, you do the washing-up, peel the potatoes, mop the floor – all the worst jobs. Of course this wasn't any old job as a kitchen porter; it was at a theatre, and I thought somehow I was closer to being an actor by peeling potatoes within spitting distance of a stage. A show celebrating the music hall which starred Ruth Madoc played at the Thorndike for a week. Ruth had just had a huge success playing Gladys Pugh, the love-struck chief yellowcoat in the 1950s holiday camp sitcom *Hi-de-Hi!* I loved the series and knew Ruth Madoc was eating in the restaurant with the rest of the cast between the matinee and evening performance. We all did – the chef had been preparing for her arrival all day. He cooked appalling roast beef with even more appalling Yorkshire pudding, and I carried the potatoes out.

There, in Victorian dress was TV's Ruth Madoc, spooning some peas onto her plate. The chef could see me loitering and barked, 'Get back in the kitchen now and mop the floor!' However, for a few brief wondrous moments I saw Ruth Madoc spoon some overcooked vegetables onto her plate.

In 2004 Matt and I asked her to play Daffyd's mother in a couple of *Little Britain* sketches. The first of these, for which I had the idea that Daffyd should come out to his spectacularly unsurprised parents, remains one of the best sketches we ever recorded, and Ruth's performance stole the show. The studio audience was so pleased to see her the night of the recording and clapped and cheered her, but no one was more pleased than me. Her performance in *Hi-de-Hi!* was beyond brilliant, and I was delighted that she was back on BBC1 making people laugh. Ruth had some outrageously rude lines in the sketch.

'Auntie Sioned stays in on a Sunday and eats minge.'

'I know who's mad for cock . . . Gay Aled!'

Like a naughty schoolboy, I would say in interviews while promoting series two of *Little Britain* that Matt and I had 'put cock in Ruth Madoc's mouth'.

13
The Bongos

In September 1989 the family Vauxhall Cavalier was loaded up with my books, my clothes and some old pots and pans for the long drive to Bristol. A letter informed me I was not going to live in a hall of residence but a student house, and had to share a room with a total stranger. When we arrived, my mum tried to hide her shock at how squalid the house was. The kitchen walls were thick with grease; the bath looked like someone had died in it, and the bedroom was more like a prison cell.

When my belongings had been unpacked, and it was time to say goodbye, my mum began to sob.

'I don't want to leave you here,' she said.

'He'll be all right,' said my dad, attempting to lead her out of the room. 'He's just got to get on with it.'

'I'll be all right, Mum. I promise.'

'Will you call me tonight?' she asked.

'Yes.'

There was a payphone at the bottom of the stairs after all. I sat on the hard bed and watched as my dad took her out. The sprung door slammed shut and I listened as her sobs echoed through the corridor.

After a few hours my room-mate arrived and took an

instant dislike to me. He would rearrange the furniture to his advantage when I was out, played hip-hop music really loud when I was writing an essay and refused to put any money in the heater.

At 9 a.m. the next day the new students had to report to the Drama Department. Even though I have an exhibitionist streak, I can be painfully shy – the exhibitionism masks the shyness – so I listened as others made jokes, in particular Jason Bradbury, who immediately made his presence felt (he would later find fame as a presenter on Channel 5's *The Gadget Show*).

I'm not the funny one any more, I noted to myself. Jason was not just funny, but confident and cool. He even played the bongos. I had lived such a conservative life I don't think I had ever even seen bongos, and certainly couldn't imagine striking them. Jason passed around a photograph of his pretty girlfriend, who had a quirky name, Twoo, and everyone felt compelled to comment on how attractive she was.

Finally someone in charge appeared, his name was Martin White. (He is the Martin that Linda the un-PC university secretary in series two and three of *Little Britain* calls when she is confronted by a dwarf she describes as an oompah loompa.) Martin was tall and thin and dressed quite unlike a teacher, sporting jeans and a corduroy jacket. Of course we didn't have teachers any more; we had lecturers. He led us into the department's studio theatre, and he led us into some embarrassing bonding exercises, such as rolling around on top of each other. My biggest fear was an unwanted erection. There was after all an extremely pretty girl from Liverpool in our group, Katy Carmichael. Fortunately I did not have to roll on her.

Thankfully the rolling-on-top-of-each-other business would never feature again in our three years of studies. The degree was mostly an academic course in theatre, film and television. We would study such diverse work as:

- cubist cartoons
- *'Crocodile' Dundee*
- performance art
- medieval theatre
- Bertolt Brecht
- futurist* cabaret
- Michel Foucault
- Jacobean tragedies
- Anton Chekhov
- the avant-garde
- Friedrich Nietzsche
- vagina dentata (this is as crazy as it sounds)

It was for the most part a pretentious course, even *'Crocodile' Dundee* was deemed somehow not a straightforward fish-out-of-water comedy but actually a postmodern take on cultural identity. *Alien* was concerned with the 'monstrous feminine'. One night I watched the film with my fellow student and friend Myfanwy Moore or Myf

---

* Futurism was an artistic movement in early-twentieth-century Italy that celebrated technology, speed, youth and violence.

(pronounced 'Miff' though Jason liked to call her 'Muff')*
so we could make notes for our essays.

Myf and I sat on the sofa together and loaded a VHS
of Ridley Scott's masterpiece into the video player. The
film started, and we watched as the camera tracked along
the corridors of a spaceship. A door opened automat-
ically. Even though the film had been playing for less than
a minute, out of the corner of my eye I saw that Myf had
already written something on her pad. *What has she seen
that I've missed?* I thought. I peered over and she had written one word.

Hymen.

Hymen? That's how brainwashed we had become. A
door didn't represent a door any more, it represented part
of a woman's vulva. Years later I had dinner with Sir Ridley Scott when we both happened to be on holiday in the
Turks and Caicos Islands and I told him the story. He
laughed uproariously. Everything on the course would be
intellectualized into oblivion.

One lecturer, Alison Butler, even asserted that *Star
Wars* reflected the confusion of President Carter's America after the Vietnam War as to who was good and who
was bad. 'Look at the storm troopers – they're wearing
white – and the rebels are wearing grey. George Lucas
has swapped the colours to point up this confusion.'

---

* Myfanwy Moore provided the name for Daffyd's barmaid friend in *Little
Britain* and would produce the first series before she left television to live
in the country and have babies.

But Darth Vader is dressed all in black with a cape, wearing a mask that looks like a bloody terrifying skull so I think we know who the baddies are! I wished I had said.

What's worse, even though I am left wing and always have been, the department was so far to the left it was on the verge of being a totalitarian state. Any comment that in any way could be construed as sexist, racist or homophobic meant instant social banishment. This is where the idea for the Linda sketches from *Little Britain* came from.

'Hello, Martin, it's Linda . . .'

Once a student was trying to identify a girl in her year who happened to have one arm. So scared to mention her most obvious distinguishing feature, she described everything else about her . . . 'Shoulder-length brown hair, medium height, brown eyes.' The other person was bemused as to who this girl might be, not thinking it could possibly be the girl with one arm or the student would have mentioned that! Similarly the only black male on the course was described as having 'curly black hair'.

Of course in *Little Britain* Linda finishes by insulting those students she is describing: 'the big fat lesbian', 'the ching-chong Chinaman', 'fatty boom-boom'.

I knew Jason and I would become friends when we were sitting together in the cinema watching a series of cubist cartoons. These consisted of black and white squares moving around the screen getting smaller and larger.

'This is so sexist,' I said, and he laughed.

A few moments passed.

'Who do you think you are kidding, Mr Hitler?' sang Jason – the cartoons made you think of that giant arrow on the *Dad's Army* title sequence. And I laughed.

Soon we would form a comedy double act.

Jason was a divisive figure in the department. He would upset people with his jokes. For example he said to a fat girl called Fatima on the course, 'Wow! You're fat and your name's Fatima!'

We had all thought it, but Jason said it.

Another outsider of a different sort was Sarah Kane. She went on to write a series of brilliant but bleak plays and become one of the most celebrated playwrights in the world. Back then she asked us all to call her Wildhorse.

'That's my Sioux name,' she would say.

Myf, Sarah and I did our performance studies course together. Sarah, being a hugely sensitive soul, was very kind and gentle with me. And I latched on to her. One night I turned up at Goldney Hall, where she lived, to see her. Both of us carried sadness. I couldn't express mine. Sarah was just starting to express hers with the stunning short plays she would write and perform at lunchtimes. That night I held her and didn't want to leave, and she let me stay the night. During the following morning's class she smiled at me, and I felt slightly better as I was worried I had done something wrong. We never mentioned my visit again. Nothing happened. We just stared at each other a lot into the early hours, silently trying to communicate something. I found out later that

I had freaked Sarah out a bit, and the story had gone round he department. Getting worse every time, I imagine.

In 1995 I was delighted to see the world premiere of Sarah's play *Blasted* at the Royal Court Theatre in London. However, four years later I read on the front page of the *Guardian* that she had checked into London King's College Hospital suffering from depression, and hanged herself with her shoelaces.

In my first year at Bristol I auditioned for and was cast in the plum comic role of Bottom in the Drama Department's production of *A Midsummer Night's Dream*. This gave me confidence that the success I had had at school was not a fluke. In this much more competitive environment I was deemed talented enough to play the funniest role in Shakespeare's least unfunny play. Dominik Diamond, who would later go on to present *GamesMaster* on Channel 4, played one of the lovers, Lysander. In the dressing room after the performance he would say loud enough so I could hear, 'What I would do with a part like Bottom . . .'

I realized I had very strong competition when I went to the first studiospace party at the end of term. This was an evening held in the studio space (wanky term for theatre) when all the students were allowed to get up and perform something if they wanted to without any interference from the lecturers. Simon Pegg took to the stage. He was in the year above and already had a comedy act that was original, charming and most of all funny. Simon would read poems to a carrot in a fishbowl he would claim was his pet goldfish, called Rover, and talk about his love for Woody Allen's muse Diane Keaton, and all the girls would swoon.

Most comedy has a victim, which is why it often courts controversy. Simon showed that the best joke is one played on oneself. I could tell instantly that Simon was going to have a huge career. From the first time I ever saw him perform to this day I remain a fan. Twenty years later he is of course a major film star, appearing in *Star Trek*, *Tintin* and the Mission Impossible films. Simon was so hilarious the first night I saw him on stage I am surprised it took so long for the rest of the world to recognize his genius.

Less likeable but more ambitious was Dominik, also in the year above me. He was a conflicted character, a public schoolboy from a very poor Scottish working class family. He wanted to be an angry comedian like Bill Hicks. So Dominik's stand-up act consisted of him pacing the stage smoking attempting to be polemical. Still for a student and not a real comedian his confidence was impressive, and I knew I would have to work hard to earn my place on stage alongside him and Simon.

So for my first performance I borrowed my friend Graham Eatough's acoustic guitar and performed a song. Despite not being able to sing or indeed play the guitar. I wrote the shortest song ever written called 'Don't Patronize me, Mrs Thatch', Mrs Thatch being of course the then prime minister Margaret Thatcher. I walked earnestly onto the stage and unsmilingly announced that

I was here tonight to sing a protest song. Then I proceeded to strum the strings and sing (in a northern accent),

> You can make me pay the poll tax,
> You can put me in prison,
> But don't patronize me, Mrs Thatch,
> Everybody! Don't patronize me, Mrs Thatch.

And that was it. The students at the party that night liked it – well at least it was short. It was original too, and a little subversive to send up those who despised the deeply right wing prime minister in Bristol's deeply left wing Drama Department.

If this minor success brought me happiness, it was momentary. That Christmas I returned home to Banstead, and the depression that I have struggled with all my life swelled within me like a storm. Living without love or affection was becoming more and more unbearable. Every day the self-loathing would grow. Death seemed like the answer. I was eighteen and didn't understand what depression was. All I knew was that there were times in my life when light became dark, colour faded, and all that was beautiful became ugly. What's so pernicious about depression is that you lose all perspective, and all past happiness seems false.

I decided that what I really wanted was to die.

In early January 1990 I waited until my parents had left for work and then looked through the family home for ways to kill myself. First I experimented with putting my head in the oven, but didn't want the house to explode when my mum came home from work and turned on the light. Then I thought about hanging myself – there were plenty of belts and ties and shoelaces in the house – but being unusually tall there was nowhere high enough. So I decided that I would take an overdose, and found some bottles of painkillers that my mum kept in the kitchen cupboard. In the dining room I discovered some Basildon Bond light blue writing paper that my sister and I had been forced to write thank you letters on to distant relatives. Retreating to my bedroom, I decided to write three notes: one to my mum and dad, one to Zoe and one to Robin. All apologizing for what I was about to do.

I then took out my CD of the Beatles' *White Album* and selected the penultimate track on disc two, 'Goodnight'. It sounded like a song that you could say goodbye to. I put the track on repeat then sat on the end of my bed and looked at myself in the cupboard mirror. *That's the last time you'll see yourself*, I thought. With tears rolling down my cheeks I watched as I swallowed pill after pill. I looked at my watch: 10.15 a.m. I then lay on my bed and waited and waited as the song played and played.

'What have you done? David? What have you done?!'

My mum was crying so much she could hardly speak. It was 4 p.m. and she had returned from work.

As a Brown Owl she was trained in first aid and knew exactly what to do. She hurtled down the stairs to fetch a glass of warm salty water. This was to make me throw up. In my semi-conscious state I couldn't take much down, so my mum led me down the stairs into the car and drove me to the local hospital. There doctors and nurses took over, and, lying on a trolley, I was forced to drink something much more potent. And then the sickness started. I retched and retched into a yellow plastic bowl, seeing the remains of the partially digested pills splatter into it.

I was taken up on a trolley to a private room.

'Why?' my mum implored. 'Why?'

I didn't have an answer.

Finally my dad arrived – he finished work later – and they sat and looked at me as the nurses came in and out every half an hour or so to check my pulse and blood pressure. It was decided I would stay in overnight for observation. My dad led my weeping mother out of the room, and I lay there looking at the ceiling trying to understand both why I had tried and why I had failed.

In the morning I ate some Rice Krispies and a kindly-looking young doctor with shoulder-length hair came in and asked with a smile, 'Now you're never going to do that again, are you?'

'No,' I said after a pause. It would be thirteen years until I would try again.

My mum assumed it was because Zoe had rejected me, though really it was because I had rejected life. However, it was easier to go along with what my mum thought, and my parents drove me back to Bristol a couple of weeks later.

I didn't tell anyone in Bristol what had taken place, but my mum called the university and I received a letter asking me to make an appointment with a psychiatrist. Thinking that my talent and my sadness were intertwined, I never called. No follow-up letter was sent.

My poor mum would ask me on the phone, 'And how do you feel in yourself?'

'Fine', I would answer. Lying. In truth I couldn't put into words what was wrong.

Soon it was easier for everyone to pretend it had never happened. Although the thoughts of killing myself became quieter, they would never fall silent.

14

A Giant Egg

At the first studiospace party Jason Bradbury and I had performed separately, but now we decided to put on a sketch together. One of the things we enjoyed doing was making stupid noises and creating words, so I had this idea for a piece in which we would be two very serious intellectuals who made stupid noises. We wrote it in his room in Manor Hall. It was heavily influenced by my idols at the time, Stephen Fry and Hugh Laurie, whose masterful series *A Bit of Fry & Laurie* was then playing on BBC2. I was in the Stephen Fry role as an eccentric host interviewing an academic writer (Jason in the Hugh Laurie role) about his new book. All the quotes from the book were surreal sounds, so by the end of the sketch there were no words but just the two of us on stage looking serious but making loud discordant noises at each other. It was a decent if studenty sketch with a beginning, middle and an end, and when we performed it the laughter grew and grew and loud applause and cheers broke out at the end.

'That was really funny, guys,' said Simon Pegg. There is nothing like the approval of those you admire.

'Oh thanks, Simon,' I replied like a bashful schoolgirl.

'You could put that straight onto television,' added Domink's friend David Young, who ended up being one of the most successful producers in British television.

Suddenly we found ourselves accepted into the comedy clique, and Dominik had a plan. He suggested we should all set up a comedy night together separate from the department or the university. We would be forced to work hard to create a new set each week, and might even take home some money at the end of it. Unlike many students at Bristol, none of us had rich mummies and daddies. My parents gave me a small allowance and I ate jacket potatoes with beans every night. An extra ten pounds or so meant I would be able to transform my meals with a sprinkling of grated Cheddar.

Dominik would run the club and compère the night. Two other performers would also appear, Barney Power, a short bald energetic man who somehow never managed to be all that funny, and Myfanwy Moore. Myf had a very likeable onstage persona, and was gently amusing as a stand-up with material like a humorous column you might read in the *Guardian*.

Jason and I had a continuous identity crisis as a double act. For some reason now lost in the mists of time we decided upon an utterly misguided name, the Dr Johnsons of this World. We were both called Dr Johnson and wore lab coats and had toy stethoscopes around our necks. Worse than our name was the one Dominik had chosen for the whole group, David Icke and the Orphans of Jesus. The popular sports presenter David Icke had recently become a national laughing stock by claiming on the TV chat show *Wogan* that he was 'the son of a god-head' but even worse he wore a turquoise shell suit.

A venue was selected, the Dome Café in Clifton, and the plan was to perform there once a week for six weeks, and we would split the profits, with Dominik taking a double share as he was administrating. I couldn't believe I was going to get paid to perform. Before we were allowed to step onto a professional stage Dominik called us all to his flat for a 'heckler workshop'. Having done a few professional gigs around Bristol, Dominik was the expert on all things stand-up comedy. He instructed us to do our acts as he shouted out interruptions.

Eventually it was me and Jason's turn to perform in his living room.

'Tell us a joke!' shouted Dominik.

I immediately broke out of the act: 'Two lesbians walk into a bar . . .'

Everyone laughed except Dominik.

Actually no one heckled on our first night, or on any other night. Simon always went down the best, and Jason and I received generous laughs from an audience made up principally of our university friends. We would perform out-front sketches: that is to say we spoke to the audience rather than just each other. One concerned me mistaking a milk bottle left on a doorstep for a baby. Another time we dressed in Victorian bathing suits and performed a bizarre circus strongman act.

For me what I was performing didn't matter; it was

enough that we were performing at all. And of course taking home ten pounds a week was a boon.

At the end of the first year I went back to the National Youth Theatre to perform a play. That summer I would meet the one person who would change my life for ever.

Matt Lucas.

'You have to meet Matt – he's so funny,' said a mutual friend at the NYT. I had noticed Matt. Everyone had noticed Matt. He was fat and bald and pale. Like a giant egg. 'Wait here,' I was instructed.

I was standing in the bar of the Tufnell Park hall of residence where all the National Youth Theatre members gathered at night. I was cast in a play called *Surrender Dorothy*, which was heading to the Edinburgh Festival Fringe. Matt was on a course as it was his first year in the company.

The bald sixteen-year-old walked over, his appearance even more startling up close. His skin was so pale it was almost translucent, and he had no eyebrows. He looked like a cross between a baby and a very elderly man.

'Matt,' said Matt.

'David,' I said. I was nearing nineteen.

'Matt does the most amazing impression of Jimmy Savile!' said our friend.

Inwardly I groaned. *Everyone does an impression of Jimmy Savile.*

'And David does this impression of Frankie Howerd.'

'I'd love to hear it,' said Matt with a tense smile.

'You go first,' I said.

'OK,' he said a little too quickly. 'Now then, now then . . .'

I had to admit it did sound very much like the *Jim'll Fix It* presenter.

'I have a letter, I have a letter . . .'

'Very good!' I said, no doubt cutting him off before he got to the punchline.

'Now you do Frankie Howerd.'

'Oh no, oh missus, oh yes, get your titters out!'

Matt smiled. There was an awkward silence when we realized we had nothing whatsoever to say to each other.

'Well I better be getting back to my friends,' he said.

'Me too.'

We nodded and smiled at each other. Then we retreated to opposite sides of the bar. We would not speak again for a year.

Meanwhile, a girl had caught my attention. She was pretty and funny, and as I had floppy long hair at the time she called me the Eskimo Princess. (I do have small eyes like an Inuit.) Her name was Jessica Stevenson (now Hynes), and she went on to appear in *Spaced*, *The Royle Family* and *Twenty Twelve*. Despite the National Youth Theatre being a company, it had its stars and Jessica was definitely one. She had been given the lead role of Mrs Bitzstein in a revival of Lionel Bart's musical *Blitz!* Katy Carmichael and Jessica were best friends, and Katy organized a date. So I took Jessica out for a pizza at a greasy restaurant on the Holloway Road in London. As if to deliberately sabotage the evening, Katy came too and sat at a nearby table, waving and laughing at us throughout.

Unsurprisingly the date was a disaster, and so was *Surrender Dorothy*. It was a play about students who go mad and take on the identities of characters from the books they are studying. 'Surrender Dorothy' is of course what the Wicked Witch of the West writes in the sky in *The Wizard of Oz*. I played Doctor Chaney, who turns into a werewolf. We played in the big theatre at the Pleasance in Edinburgh, which seats around 400. Comedy rarely works with only a handful of people in the audience, and unfortunately nobody wanted to part with money to see a play they had never heard of performed by a group of teenagers they had never heard of.

However, *Surrender Dorothy* was only an hour long, and as I was in a show at the Pleasance I could see anything there for free as long as I didn't mind standing at the back if it was sold out. So that summer I gorged on comedy. Steve Coogan and Frank Skinner were doing an hour together; Jim Tavare was performing, as was Norman Lovett. I saw them all time after time. The one I loved the most was *The Bob Downe Show*. Mark Trevorrow's outrageously camp safari-suited lounge singer had me laughing time after time. Mark Trevorrow has a great gift for physical comedy, and all of Bob's songs were accompanied by absurd and frenetic dance moves.

When you're a comedian or someone who wants to be a comedian, sometimes it's hard to laugh at a gig. You are so intent on studying how the performer is eliciting laughter, you end up watching like a scientist observing an experiment. I had watched many stand-up comedians, and I found them very hard to relate to. Their observations were not the same as mine. Buying Rizlas from all-night garages to roll joints, or girlfriends complaining about how quickly lovemaking was over were comic staples at the time. Of course I had neither smoked a joint nor had sex with a woman. So that summer as I died on stage night after night in *Surrender Dorothy*, howling through my change into a werewolf to an otherwise silent theatre – something that had seemed so funny to the rest of the cast in the rehearsal room – I made an important break-through. Like with the Dame Edna show I had seen a couple of years before if confirmed that you don't have to be a stand-up comedian to make people laugh; you can play a character. What's more, it's probably best if that character is an extension of you. I decided I had to go back to the Edinburgh Fringe one day and perform professionally.

I approached Mark Trevorrow after a performance. 'Hi. It's the third time I've seen your show and I abso-lutely love it.'

'Why thank you,' said Mark, only slightly less camp than his alter ego.

'It's such a funny character . . .'

'Thank you.' He was really smiling and staring at me now.

'The dance moves are hilarious.'

'Oh yes.' He was looking me up and down.

'Well, nice to meet you.'

'Do you fancy a drink?'

'I have to get back to the place we're staying. I'm with the National Youth Theatre.'

'Oh, right. I see. How old are you?'

'Nineteen.'

'You look older.'

Walking to the bus stop I realized why he was looking me up and down like that. He was coming on to me.

In 2007, when Matt and I were touring Australia with Little Britain Live, Mark came and saw us perform in Melbourne and invited us to his apartment the next day for lunch. I was glad to have the opportunity to tell him how seeing his act seventeen years before had inspired me. I didn't mention that we had met before.

Back at university for my second year I noticed most of the girls had become lesbians over the summer holidays. Indulging in a bit of 'licky licky' was the best option politically in the Drama Department. It meant you were right all the time about absolutely everything.

Jason's ambition was growing daily. He said to me, 'I have this dream that I'm driving around in a brand-new open-topped sports car and I stop at the lights. Then all these kids start recognizing me and shouting, "Jason! Jase!" and I smile and wave and then the lights change and I drive off.'

'Really?' I asked.

'Surely you have dreams like that?'

'No, never,' I answered. And I was telling the truth. I never once thought what it would be like to become famous.

Deep down Jason really saw our comedy act as a stepping stone to what he is today, a TV presenter.

Trevor (Neal) and Simon (Hickson) were an amusing double act on Saturday morning children's TV, famous for their catchphrase 'Swing your pants.' They spanned two hugely popular series, *Going Live!* and its successor *Live & Kicking*. In 1991 they temporarily left *Going Live*, and despite still being in the middle of our university course Jason decided we were the perfect people to take over from them.

For some reason we had changed our name to Bunce 'n' Burner.

'I'm David Bunce.'

'And I'm Rally Burner.'*

Somehow Jason managed to secure us an audition at the BBC. We had done a few local things such as a series for BBC Radio Bristol entitled *Bunce & Burner Visit Interesting Places* and an appearance on the local TV news performing a sketch in a local café. Jason was very pushy and somehow managed to convince people to give us a chance. I remember making the grumpy stand-up comedian Stewart Lee laugh out loud when we rehearsed a guest spot on a long-forgotten Radio 4 comedy series which he and Richard Herring wrote. The programme travelled around the universities, showcasing a little local talent along the way. Jason and I had written a piece that ended with me saying, 'At Christmas I love nothing more than settling down in front of the fire with my family and having a jolly good wank.'

Stewart Lee exploded with laughter perhaps because

---

* The Raleigh Burner was a popular BMX bicycle at the time.

nothing Jason or I had said previously was all that funny and his expectations were low.

The stressed-looking producer came up to have a word. 'Yes, yes, it's all very funny but you can't say "wank" on Radio 4.'

'Jerk off?' I suggested hopefully.

'No.'

'Whack off?'

'No.'

'Masturbate?'

'No.'

'Play with myself?'

'Absolutely not.'

Jason and I looked at each other. This was the biggest laugh we would get and it was going to be cut.

'I've got it!' said the producer.

'Yes!' I said, my voice soaring with hope.

'Wink,' he said.

'What?' I replied.

'You can say ". . . settle down in front of the fire and have a jolly good wink".'

'Wink isn't funny,' said Jason.

'Can I pronounce it "wank"?' I asked innocently.

'No!' said the producer angrily. 'Now take it or leave it. I have a show to produce.'

Our contribution in the final programme was edited down to less than ten seconds.

We were pretty sure you couldn't say 'wank' on children's television, so we wrote a number of new sketches for our *Going Live!* audition. We took the train to London and made our way to the BBC rehearsal rooms in Acton for our audition. Somehow having an audience of three people was worse than having 300. We repeated our milk bottle baby routine from the Dome Café. I was so nervous my hands were shaking and the bottle dropped out of my hands and landed with a *thud* on the floor of the huge rehearsal room.

Of course we didn't pass the audition. Two Cambridge Footlights performers called Nick and Jamie took over, died week after week live on TV, and Trevor and Simon heroically returned the next year. Nick and Jamie were never heard of again. In retrospect it was a lucky escape for us, because Jason and I were not ready for television. In fact together we never would be.

That summer I was cast in the National Youth Theatre's production of Shakespeare's *The Tempest* in the supposedly comic role of Trinculo. Given the task of moving the scenery around was the bald boy from the bar who did a Jimmy Savile impression, Matt Lucas. Fate had thrown us together again.

15
One Person Laughing

University terms are only ten weeks long, so I had a couple of months before rehearsals for the National Youth Theatre production of *The Tempest* were to start. My dad knew a man who knew a man who ran the Fortune Theatre on Russell Street in Covent Garden, where *The Woman in Black* was (and still is) on. I was an usher. I earned fifteen pounds a night, thirty pounds on matinee days. My duties were selling programmes and ice creams, and then clearing up when the play was finished, which wasn't too bad, as you often found coins that had dropped out of people's pockets. One night a man asked me to show him to his seat and gave me a 50p tip. I was ecstatic.

Often coaches full of tourists would park outside the theatre. One night I was standing on the first floor looking out the window at a large group of European teenagers in their coach. It was the second half of *The Woman in Black*, and I all I had to do was collect the discarded ice-cream tubs at the end of the play. I could see that a few of the teenagers were looking at me, so I thought to amuse myself I would amuse them.

At first it was a little wave, then I would disappear behind a curtain and wave again. Soon I saw that a few of them were laughing and telling their friends to watch me too, so I started running up and down the stairs and waving each time I did so. Then I pretended to be really out of breath, got some tap water from the bar, and drank it like a toddler might with two hands, pouring most of it down my red Fortune Theatre usher's waistcoat in the process. Next I ran downstairs again and into the street. I took off my waistcoat and acted as I if I was a matador, the waistcoat was the cape, and the coach was the bull. Unbelievably the coach driver played along, and the coach lurched forward towards me as I pranced around. I have no idea if the teenagers were Spanish, but this delighted them no end. They all crowded towards the front of the coach and peered out of the grimy windscreen to get a better look.

Finally I felt a swarm of people brushing past me and realized the audience were exiting the theatre. Knowing that both the play and my little performance were now over, I took a bow. The teenagers all applauded, and a girl got off the bus and gave me a bunch of flowers. This only added to the performance, as now I was an overemotional actress on a first night, crying and blowing kisses to my public. The driver hooted his horn as they drove away, all their faces pushed up against the glass to catch one last glimpse of the crazy Englishman who had entertained them for a few minutes as they waited for their coach to depart.

I had created a little show out of nothing, and made some strangers laugh. For a few moments we were all happy.

It was one of the most magical moments of my life.

*

On 8 October 1996 the *Sun* newspaper's front page read DI SPY VIDEO SCANDAL, with the strapline 'She's filmed in bra and pants romp with Hewitt'. As it turned out the video was fake. The newspaper had been duped by a man called Nick Hedges into paying him £100,000. Five years earlier he had been directing the National Youth Theatre production of *The Tempest*.

Nick Hedges was a disciple of the avant-garde dancer and choreographer Lindsay Kemp, whose style was for all the performers to white up their face like clowns and move very slowly.* So that is what Nick made us do. It was a very original production, if you had never seen a Lindsay Kemp performance, which most people hadn't.

For some reason Nick had completely missed Matt's towering talent for comedy at the auditions. Therefore Matt was assigned the role of Koken, which in Japanese theatre is the name for someone dressed from head to toe in black with even their face covered who moves the scenery around. As Matt didn't have much to do in the play, he spent a lot of time watching the rest of us rehearse, and if there was one person who could always be guaranteed to laugh at some new piece of business I had added as Trinculo, it was him. Two years older at that age can make a big difference, and I think Matt was perhaps a tiny bit in awe of me. I was at Bristol University studying drama, had already performed at a comedy club

---

* Lindsay Kemp appeared in a few films too, most notably as the pub landlord Alder MacGregor in Anthony Shaffer's *The Wicker Man* (1973).

with Jason, and most importantly been given the principal comic role in the play.

One morning Andrew Denizi, who was playing Caliban, was very late for rehearsals – even later than he normally was. Nick was furious and contemplating recasting the role, even though we opened in a week. Although the NYT is an amateur dramatic company, professional standards are expected of you.

'I'll do it,' said Matt. In his jeans and Arsenal T-shirt and spectacles.

The cast looked around. Some smirked. Andrew was talented and popular and Matt was just . . . moving the scenery around.

'OK,' said Nick. 'You can read the role of Caliban for this scene.'

It was a part of the play involving me as Trinculo, Stephano and Caliban. Matt threw himself into it. Literally. He scuttled across the room, jumping up and down and barking like a dog. Matt wanted the role of Caliban for himself. He was better than moving the scenery around and he knew it. Now Matt had a chance to demonstrate to us all what he could do.

In the tea break afterwards some of the cast muttered disparagingly about how he was trying to take the role away from Andrew, but I instantly respected Matt's fearlessness and ambition. To step into another actor's role like that with no rehearsal and completely go for it was extraordinary. I was impressed, even if Nick Hedges wasn't, and sadly for Matt when Andrew finally arrived he kept the role of Caliban.

The first night of *The Tempest* at the Place Theatre was full of National Youth Theatre members, who all laughed loudly at my scenes. As the days and weeks dragged on, like all NYT productions it failed to find an audience, and the laughter subsided. One afternoon the iconic newsreader Angela Rippon came to a matinee and fell asleep in the front row. The laughter never entirely stopped though, as there was always one person laughing, and that was Matt. The idea that either of us would one day become comedians was still completely fantastical; what bonded Matt and I was our love of comedy. We were both fans.

At last I had found someone whose ecstasies paralleled my own. Both of us had an encyclopedic knowledge of comedy programmes and comedians. We loved *Monty Python*, the Carry On films, Laurel and Hardy, *Blackadder*, *The Young Ones*, Rowan Atkinson. However, there was one show we truly adored . . . V*ic Reeves Big Night Out*.

Even though the second series had just played out on Channel 4, it was for most still waiting to be discovered. This was a series that not only your parents wouldn't like, but your friends wouldn't like either. It was seriously weird. And utterly shambolic. Often it was more per-formance art than comedy. Matt told me that he phoned Channel 4 after the first episode of the first series in 1990 to complain that it wasn't funny. Indeed, *Big Night Out* was so different to anything else that had ever been on television, it was a challenging watch, not least because it seemed an unrehearsed mess. However, after a few episodes you felt part of the club, and this was a club

Matt and I were definitely fully paid-up members of. In the series Vic Reeves and Bob Mortimer created a new way of being funny. They combined Pythonesque surrealism with old-fashioned light entertainment. It remains a towering achievement.

Matt and I probably only sensed the historical importance of the show at the time. For the most part we would bore everyone else in the dressing room by endlessly reciting lines from the programme. What's so important for our story about *Big Night Out* is that our love of it brought Matt and I together.

A couple of years later Bob Mortimer would see Matt's second gig as the ageing thespian Sir Bernard Chumley, declare him 'the most angry man he had ever met' and ask him to be the score master in a new comedy quiz show he and Vic were going to host. My journey would take a great deal longer.

16
Learning to Love an Oddball

My virginity. In summer 1991 I turned twenty and was beginning to wonder whether I would ever be rid of it.

Falling in love had never been a problem. As the years at Bristol passed, Katy Carmichael and I had become incredibly close friends. Katy was everything I wasn't: beautiful, free-spirited, northern. She was from Liverpool, albeit a posh part, and seemed to have experienced absolutely everything by the time she reached university. Katy thought nothing of staying up all night dancing, had a long-standing boyfriend who sailed yachts, and even had a small recurring role in the sitcom *Bread*.*

Dr Gunter Berghaus was a leather-trousered German professor in the Bristol Drama Department. His only sphere of interest was the avant-garde. Once in a tutorial in his office he told us that it was essential we read *Theory of the Avant-garde* by Peter Berger. The next week I told him, 'I looked for it in the [vast] university library, and they didn't have a copy. Nor did any of the bookshops.'

Gunter stood up, his leather trousers squeaking as he did so, and reached for a book on his shelf. 'This is

* Written by Carla Lane, this was the defining sitcom of the 1980s.

actually the only copy in the United Kingdom,' he purred, before putting it back on his shelf.

Gunter prayed at the altar of the avant-garde. 'Some years ago in Berlin,' he claimed, 'I performed a show for forty-eight hours where I was a wolf and all I did was howl and eat my own excrement.'

So he decided we should put on a futurist cabaret.

Even though this was most likely a terrible idea, Katy and I embraced it, as the show was at least a chance to be on stage. We decided we should do an act together, and perform an old song in French we had found about a woman who wanted to marry a millionaire. Katy wanted to come on brandishing a whip; I decided I should wear a rubber raincoat (borrowed from Dr Gunter in a rare moment of generosity) and during the song take the raincoat off to reveal a studded leather posing pouch underneath. Quite what this all meant was beyond us. It hardly mattered. Most importantly it appealed to me and Katy's shared passion for exhibitionism. Despite my sexual confusion there was one certainty: this girl really turned me on. While rehearsing our routine one day, I became so aroused it was impossible for Katy not to notice. Being mature, she ignored it.

The performance was a disaster, and most of the students disapproved of the whole enterprise as futurism had close links with fascism. The day after the last performance Gunter gathered us all into the rehearsal space to discuss the show, and watched smirking as we all started heatedly arguing with each other.

'It's what the futurists would have wanted!' he concluded with a smile.

Katy and I shared a bed when her flatmates were away and she didn't want to be alone in her student flat. In 1991 we went to New York together and for no apparent reason photographed ourselves dressed as Andy Warhol and Edie Sedgwick next to some famous buildings. Yet still I hadn't kissed her. The years of disappointment with girls had given me the feeling that there was something wrong with me that everybody else could see but I couldn't.

By 1992 we were in our final year, and one night Katy and I found ourselves on the sofa of the student house I was sharing with Jason, Myfanwy and Callum Greene (now a film producer for Sofia Coppola and Guillermo del Toro). After a while everyone else had gone to bed and Katy and I were alone.

'I want to kiss you,' I said. 'I need to kiss you.'

Katy turned to face me and we kissed. Soon we hurried upstairs to my bedroom and my passion for her which had built up over years was over in seconds. Katy was kind though. She held me and smiled. We kissed and made love again. I had often wondered whether losing my virginity would be a transformative experience. Would the world appear different afterwards? Would the sun, the moon, the stars look even more beautiful? But this wasn't just sex; this was also love, and for a brief moment the world really did seem different. However, Katy soon decided that she didn't want me as her boyfriend.

'You were an oddball,' she would tell me later. 'I had to learn to love you.'

When we entered the final summer term there was tension between Katy and me. Ten weeks went by as we struggled to recover our friendship. It was not until the night of the final studiospace party that I saw that look in her eyes again. We danced and danced and she came back to my student house. Strange though this may seem, in the early hours of the morning I washed her feet. I partially filled the bath and lovingly bathed, soaped and dried her feet. Soon we were making love again, which went on until it was light.

Katy and I stayed in Bristol after we graduated for as long as we could, never wanting the summer to end, but as autumn drew near we were faced with a question: how on earth were we going to make a living?

I moved back home to Banstead. On the first night my mum came into my bedroom. 'Pants and socks! Pants and socks!' she announced.

'I'll give them to you in a minute.'

'I need them now. I'm going to put the washing on.'

As I heard the washing machine whirr downstairs, my mum came back into my room to tuck me in. She actually kissed me goodnight. It was sweet, but I had just turned twenty-one.

'It's lovely to have you home, son,' she said.

After staying up all night having sex with Katy, it was as if I was twelve again. Much as I loved my parents, I had to escape, but for now I had absolutely no means of doing so. Breaking into television seemed impossible. It was like a walled city. And I didn't have a Trojan horse.

After I failed an audition to be an actor/tour guide in the Museum of the Moving Image in London (just about the lowliest job you could have and still call yourself an actor), I exaggerated my CV and applied to join the actors' union Equity. Equity has a rule that each member must have a unique name, so credits and royalty payments are not confused. My name was David Williams, but there was already an actor called David Williams. My namesake had been in many TV programmes from *Play for Today* to *Brookside* to *Coronation Street*. If I wanted to join Equity – which would help make me seem like a legitimate actor and not just another show-off who had just left university – I had to change my name.

It had to be a spur-of-the-moment decision as I was sitting in the offices of Equity ready to hand over my fifty pounds membership fee.

'So what do you want your professional name to be?' asked the nice lady.

Being young and foolish, I thought it would be great to have a funny name. Recently I had called my university friend Myf at her parents' home. Her mum answered the phone and when I said who was calling, called up to her daughter, 'It's David Wall-iums on the phone!'

A simple slip of the tongue, but when she reached the telephone, Myf couldn't help laughing. So she called me David Wall-iums from that point onwards.

'How about David Walliams?' I suggested to the Equity lady.

'Walliams?!' she repeated.

'Yes, there can't be anyone else in the system called that.'

'No, but just let me check. How are you spelling that?'

'Erm, W, A, L, L, I, A, M, S.'

'No, there definitely isn't anyone else called that.'

'Great.'

'Welcome to Equity, David Walliams.'

'Thank you.'

'Right, where's your fifty pounds?'

So that is why I have a silly name. Still, it's great for Google alerts.

Jason and I regrouped in London and started doing open spots on the London comedy circuit. The listings magazine *Time Out* was the aspiring comedian's bible. Jason and I would flick straight to the comedy pages and scour the columns for clubs that welcomed open spots – unpaid gigs. The hope was if it went well you would be invited back to the club and paid, most likely around twenty-five pounds – £12.50 each.

Having stuck with the name Bunce 'n' Burner we trailed across London playing to drunk people, angry people, and worst of all no people. The most notorious club in London was Up the Creek in Greenwich, run by the legendary compère Malcolm Hardee. Malcolm would get laughs by taking his penis out on stage. It was that kind of club. The object of any open spot or indeed experienced comedian at Up the Creek was to get to the end of the act without being booed or bottled off.

Our act was very studenty.

'I am going to bet that Mr Bunce cannot take a bite of this Mr Kipling Bramley Apple Pie without the crumbs falling onto the floor and spelling out the names of the top five French fashion houses . . . So what's been happening in the news recently?'

I remember one woman in the front row of a comedy club sigh audibly when I delivered that line and say, 'Oh no!'

'Well there's been a lot of talk about whether magnetic crisps should be banned . . .'

In hindsight it was the kind of act that might have ended in a lynching.

Waiting upstairs at Up the Creek to go on, I gazed at the huge oil painting on the wall. It was a re-imagining of *The Last Supper* with Malcolm as Jesus, and comedians such as Jack Dee, Julian Clary and Vic Reeves as his disciples. I noticed a draught and looked across the room. Vic Reeves was standing there in a long black coat and black leather gloves, with his hair slicked back, looking impossibly handsome and glamorous. Completely star-struck I was unable to say anything. Jason was always more confident, bounced to his feet and approached the man who had just reinvented comedy.

'Mr Reeves, my name is Jase and this is Dave. We do a double act together I think you'd like . . .'

Quite presumptuous, as our routine was little more than a poor copy of his and Bob's.

Vic listened patiently as I looked on hopefully from the safety of the other side of the room. This was fate surely. Vic would see us perform, think we were hilarious and instantly put us on all of his TV programmes.

'I'm sorry I can't stay for your act,' apologized Vic. 'I just popped in to see a friend.'

'I'm sorry to hear that, Mr Reeves, but please look out for us. Bunce 'n' Burner.'

'I will,' he lied.

When the first bottle hit, I was so glad Mr Reeves had to leave when he did. People came to Up the Creek especially to boo people off stage. We joined a long list of comedians who never did manage to finish a set. Jason and I barely finished a joke. If we had any.

'Nice guys, but get some jokes!' Mark Thomas told the audience after we had died at the Comedy Store. 'I mean seriously, guys, just get some jokes.'

We listened in the cramped damp dressing room as another comedian got laughs at our expense.

The Comedy Café in east London was kinder to us. On Wednesday nights audience expectations were low as all the acts were open spots. If you won you came back next week and were paid. The same night that Jason and I performed, Matt premiered his ageing actor Sir Bernard Chumley. The Jimmy Savile impression was also in: 'Dear Jim, please can you fix it for me to call you a cunt on live TV?' There was lots of shouting, almost as if Sir Bernard had Tourette's syndrome. The best moment was when Matt dislodged the lady's wig he had been given as a child to reveal the baldness underneath. Despite Matt providing a startling few minutes, the audience that night didn't like it. Strangely they did like the ultimately inferior Bunce 'n' Burner, and Jason and I each looked forward to picking up £12.50 next Wednesday.

In comedy it's the audience that rule. You can never blame them for being wrong. Laughter is an involuntary reflex after all.

'Well done,' said Matt, looking sheepish as the audience that had slow-clapped him were finishing their drinks.

'Well done to you,' I said. 'I enjoyed it,' I added. The writing was unfocused; Sir Bernard did not seem completely original (in 1989 Harry Enfield had written and performed a one-off special as 'British acting legend Norbert Smith'), and yet and yet and yet . . . there was something truly glorious about Matt as a performer. Even in 1992 he had a power and intensity that was rare, especially as he was then still a teenager. Matt was a better performer than he was a writer. I was a better writer than I was a performer. In my opinion that's why we ultimately needed each other to succeed on the scale we did.

Jason and I limped on as Bunce 'n' Burner. He secured us a few moments on regional television children's programmes, but we weren't good. Most importantly we didn't really know what sort of act we were. Soon Jason and I had played all the clubs in *Time Out* for free and no one wanted to pay us to come back. So our double act ended not with a bang, but a whimper.

Fortunately my friends from Bristol University Drama Department hadn't forgotten me. Emboldened by his success as the presenter of the Channel 4 computer gameshow *GamesMaster*, Dominik Diamond secured a comedy pilot called *Trash TV* and invited me and Simon Pegg in to perform a few sketches in it. Sadly the title of the show proved prophetic, and nothing came of it. One sketch featured Simon Pegg and me playing Top Trumps as if we were chess masters, and as we recorded it we were told off by the floor manager for laughing because we found each other so funny.

I did some running work on *GamesMaster* – literally running around bringing more important people tea, etc. The second series was filmed in a water treatment centre, which in the programme was supposed to be the inside of an oil rig. Sometimes the show would have celebrity guests, and one day a pre-hit Take That arrived to play video games and promote themselves to uninterested teenage boys. Dominik and I were weeing and chatting in the Portaloo outside.

'What do you think of that Take That then, David?' he asked.

'I don't think they're going to make it,' I replied. 'They've been around for ages and they still haven't had a hit.'

At that moment the toilet flushed and out of the cubicle walked a chubby man with spiky peroxide-blond hair. It was Gary Barlow. I smiled at him. He didn't smile back.

After the success of *GamesMaster*, Sky One commissioned a five-times-a-week computer games show aimed at young boys. One episode a week was dedicated to giving tips to computer games enthusiasts. Myfanwy Moore had a full-time job at the production company Hewland International and very kindly secured me an audition. Despite seeing the established comedian Roland Rivron go in before me, I was given the job of providing the tips. In the audition I was the only person who put on different voices and was told that's why I was given the job. Also I would have been the cheapest. The truth is I would have done it for nothing.

I created a number of characters for *Games World* suggested by the different games genres. For example for beat 'em up games I was Tony Dolmeo, an accident-prone stuntman in a karate outfit. For driving games I was a tough detective whose catchphrase was 'Get off my manor!' For flying games I was a World War I pilot called Wing Commander Wonker – the outsized flying trousers came from the BBC costume store and bore the name 'E. Morecambe'. I wasn't one per cent as funny as him, but I was at least wearing his trousers. Matt appeared in a brief non-speaking role as a man having a haircut, with me playing a camp hairdresser.

Jet, the sexiest one from ITV's hit series *Gladiators*, was squeezed into a rubber dress as the Gamesmistress, presumably so teenage boys watching would have someone to masturbate over.

After I had finished filming a few episodes, Jane Hewland, who ran Hewland International, brought her twelve-year-old son into the edit suite to see my work. Either he didn't recognize me or didn't care about my feelings because, although I was sitting in a corner of the edit suite, when Mrs Hewland asked her morose only child, 'Is this man funny?' he replied, 'No.' He then added, in case anyone thought that was not definite enough, 'Not at all.' To complete the role of son of a despot he turned his thumb down in the manner of a Roman emperor ordering an execution.

Somehow I kept the job, probably because I was paid a pittance. The series ran for twenty-six episodes, which meant two important things:

- I didn't have to get a proper job.
- I wouldn't have to hand over my pants and socks to my mum every night; I could finally leave home.

I had been spending lots of time at the flat Katy shared with a girlfriend of her's from university, but now was able to rent my own little insect-infested studio flat in London.

Katy was always busy as an actress, and was cast in a play of *The Count of Monte Cristo* at the Manchester Royal Exchange. The nightclubs in Manchester have long been legendary, and we spent many long hot nights dancing after her performances finished on Saturday nights. On Sundays we would head to the bars on Canal Street. One afternoon we saw an older gay man dressed in white shorts sitting out on the grass with a small group of friends. Getting to his feet, he noticed he had shat himself. Everyone nearby noticed too – he was wearing white shorts after all.

Catching all our eyes staring at the brown stain, he announced, 'Every inch a lady!' and waltzed off.

Everybody laughed, but I never forgot the word he used – 'lady'. It was funny.

Games World was revamped for a second series, and a character from the competition night, Big Boy Barry, was given his own show, a sitcom. Or as it turned out, a shit-com. Big Boy Barry was an overweight arrogant child star, a part Alex Verrey was born to play. My role was that of Big Boy Barry's put-upon sidekick, Leslie. It was for the most part miserably unfunny, but I threw myself wildly into it. I added all kinds of strange subtexts, for example that the nerdy Leslie was attracted to men but didn't realize it.

Games World ran for another twenty-six episodes, which meant I secured an agent at the prestigious ICM, now known as Independent and home to some of the biggest British actors in the world from Daniel Craig to Hugh Grant. An audition followed for a new children's programme for the BBC called *Incredible Games*. Again I must have been the best in the price range as I was given the job as the presenter, a kind of Max Headroom character who took kids up and down in a lift and asked them to 'Press my button!'

I remember watching the first episode go out on a Sunday morning with Katy on my tiny portable TV in my tiny studio flat after a particularly late night of clubbing, and then walking out into the streets thinking I was going be recognized. Of course no one did. Not yet . . .

17
Hant & Dec

The head of children's television at the BBC at the in the early 1990s was a lovely man called Chris Pilkington. Having met through *Incredible Games*, he asked me to become involved with a new programme he was developing, *The Ant & Dec Show*. This was in 1994, and Ant McPartlin and Declan Donnelly had played the most popular characters in a children's drama series called *Byker Grove*. Their chemistry on and off screen led to them being given their own entertainment series. I went to a rehearsal room to meet them, having been told that the one who wore a hat was called Ant. So all I had to remember was the word Hant.

Hat + Ant = Hant

The old-fashioned executive producer Peter Murphy wanted them to spoof *The Wizard of Oz*, but I thought how much better it would be if they spoofed contemporary bands and TV programmes. Including me there were three writers (a fourth was sacked as he couldn't come up with anything funny and is now a newspaper television critic, though it would be unkind to say who). I really took to Hant and Dec, and they to me. In boring meetings I would amuse them by drawing obscene pictures on scripts and discreetly showing them. I came up with some funny material: a rap song about Blackpool, a game show called *Beat the Barber* in which kids had their hair cut off if they lost, a spoof of the Take That 'Back for Good' video, and a running serial called *Hollywood Hospital*. I was the star writer, but what I really wanted to be was the star performer, so I would write myself into the sketches. No one seemed to mind until when playing a vicar I took off my trousers for no apparent reason. This was children's television, after all.

At the end of the second series Zenith, the production company, had a party. After a few drinks I sneaked into Peter Murphy's office. Even though he was in his sixties, his walls were covered with posters of Ant and Dec which he had taken out of *Smash Hits* as if he was a twelve-year-old girl. I found a felt-tip on his desk and added huge erect penises to the posters. There were Hant and Dec smiling at each other as their cartoon erections nestled against each other below. It was ultimately an act of self-sabotage, because even though it took Peter Murphy a few days to notice, I never worked for Zenith again.

In 2012 Simon Cowell asked me to become a judge on *Britain's Got Talent*, and I had the pleasure of working with Hant and Dec again. Now Hant has stopped wearing hats, I don't know who's who.

Despite this act of career suicide *The Ant & Dec Show* was a huge success, and I became in demand as a writer for children's TV. In 1996 I was asked to write the links for presenters Andi Peters and Dani Behr for the *Smash Hits* poll winners' party. The now defunct pop music magazine gave out awards voted for by their readers, like Best Haircut (usually rightfully won by Take That's Mark

Owen). This was to be my first meeting with Simon Cowell, and it was a deeply uncomfortable one.

The show took place at the Docklands Arena, and among the artists performing that afternoon in front of ten thousand screaming children were two of my absolute favourites Björk and Pulp, and two of my least favourites, Robson and Jerome.

Robson Green and Jerome Flynn were two actors from the TV drama series *Soldier Soldier*, who had released their version of 'Unchained Melody' from the show. It went straight to number one and kept Pulp's 'Common People' off the top spot. The release was masterminded by Simon Cowell.

I had written Andi Peters the introduction line, 'Wake up, Granny, it's Robson and Jerome,' which as insults go was pretty mild.

In rehearsal Simon saw the script and approached me.

'Are you the writer?' the short man in Cuban heels asked, fixing his eyes on mine.

'Yes,' I replied, a little bit scared of this man, despite the fact that he was half the size of me.

'So you're the problem.'

I had never been referred to as a problem before and was taken aback.

'Follow me,' he said.

'Who are you?' I asked.

'Robson and Jerome are my act.'

I sighed and followed him as he sashayed over to a corner of the stage.

'Sit down,' he ordered.

I did so.

'Look, these guys have had the biggest-selling single of the year; they have the biggest selling album of the year . . .'

'So?' I asked, gaining in confidence now. I loved 'Unchained Melody' but hated Robson and Jerome's version. What was most baffling was why all the grannies who bought it were too lazy to walk a little further into the record shop and pick up the Righteous Brothers' greatest hits instead.

'So, you can't say that about them,' said Simon, lighting a menthol cigarette and holding it between his fingers as if he was a Bond villain.

'I don't think you can smoke in here,' I said.

'I think you'll find I can do whatever I like.'

There was an uncomfortable pause for a moment.

'Look, what's the problem? Grannies do like them,' I offered.

'Grannies like them, kids like them, everyone likes them.'

'I don't like them,' I said proudly.

'Well you are in a minority of one. Why can't Andi say, "Here with the biggest-selling single of the year are the fabulously talented Robson and Jerome"?'

'Because that wouldn't be funny,' I protested.

'And you think what you have written is funny?'

'Yes . . . ish.' I was crumbling now. 'I don't want to change the script.'

'If you don't change it I am pulling Robson and Jerome from the show.'

'But —'

'This conversation is over.'

He put out his cigarette on the floor and *clip-clopped* off in his high heels.

A lighting technician walked past. 'You can't smoke here,' he said to me.

'It wasn't me!'

The script was changed. Simon got his way. As he always does.

Around this time I was summoned to a meeting at BBC TV Centre, to become part of the writing team for a new children's sitcom called *Out of Tune* about a choir. The producer had gathered together around a dozen children's televison writers, and we all sat around a big table and had to say our name and what we had written.

'Hi, I'm Bob. I've written for *Metal Mickey*, *Supergran*.'

'Hi, I'm Phil. I've done *Bodger & Badger* and the Chuckle Brothers.'

'Hello, my name is Mick. I've written on *Crackerjack*, *Rentaghost*, *Seaview*. You name it, I've done it.'

Then it was my turn. 'Hi, I'm David, and I've written for *The Ant & Dec Show*. That's about it . . .'

For a moment looking at those tired faces I glimpsed the ghost of my future. I could make a good living churning out scripts for children's television for the rest of my life, but I knew that wouldn't make me happy.

I had to make a change, and soon.

Meanwhile Matt had been working at the Chelsea FC merchandise shop (despite being a lifelong Arsenal supporter) and had continued to develop his cabaret act as Sir Bernard Chumley. He was invited to do a guest spot in Dorian Crook's Edinburgh show.* Being a close friend of Matt, perhaps the closest at that time, I took the train to Edinburgh to see him. Needless to say, Matt stole the show, and the reviewers agreed.

In addition, Matt played a few supporting roles in the second series of *The Smell of Reeves and Mortimer* and dropped out of Bristol University, where he was doing the same drama course that I had just completed. I had been sending him veggie sausage mix through the post (delicious and cheap – I lived on the sausages when I was a student). Now there was no need, for he was back in London (well Edgware).

Soon Matt and I were free to spend more and more time together. We had been meeting up in Golders Green Park, halfway between where he lived with his mother and brother in Edgware and my flat in Belsize Park. There we would talk and talk about how we would one day make a series called *Sunday Club*. It was meant to be a children's programme from the late 1970s that had never been aired, now unearthed and broadcast for the first time. We made endless notes. Most of our ideas were quite dark – a zoologist would introduce the children to some animals which had all unfortunately died in transit. It would never get made, but we didn't know that and would while away many an afternoon coming up with increasingly bizarre

* Dorian Crook is an old friend of Bob Mortimer, a full-time air traffic controller and part-time comedian.

characters and scenes. So from friendship we were now creating together, albeit a television series no one would ever see.

In the evenings I would either watch Matt play at comedy venues around London, which tended to have wacky names like the Chuckle Club or the Balham Banana, or we would go and see comedy shows together. We were eager to consume any comedy we could find, so one night we might be going to a recording of *Newman and Baddiel in Pieces* at the BBC, the next we were watching Jim Davidson in his adult panto *Sinderella*, during which Matt heckled throughout, pretending to be an overenthusiastic fan, shouting 'JIMBO!' every time Jim stepped on stage. Of course this was far funnier than the pantomime. One blazing hot Saturday night in summer, one when the whole of the country was outside with a cold beer, we stayed inside and watched Roy Chubby Brown's unwatchable film *UFO*.

One night we went to a comedy club in Hampstead. A tall good-looking young man was hosting the night. He had boundless confidence but seemingly no talent for making people laugh. All he did was say to the noisy audience, 'Shut up shut up shut up shut up shut up shut up shut up shut up shut up shut up . . .'

I thought, *If you said something funny they might shut up.* The performance was so excruciatingly embarrassing that we chose to leave, even though Matt knew him vaguely as they had been pupils at the same school.

No one who saw his performance that night would think the young man had any future in comedy whatsoever.

His name was Sacha Baron Cohen. Years later he would find the way in which he was funny. On a smaller scale, so would I.

On another of these nights, on a Tube train to another room above a pub, I turned to Matt and said, 'Why don't we do a show together in Edinburgh next year?'

'As what?' said Matt. 'I want to do it as Chumley.'

'Of course you can be Chumley, and I can come on as various different characters.'

'Who?'

'I don't know yet, but we can write it together.'

Matt wasn't sure he wanted to be in a double act. What's more he was starting to get paid bookings as Chumley on the London comedy circuit so he didn't necessarily need anyone to collaborate with.

'OK,' he said. 'But I might want to go up the year after that on my own.'

It was an uncertain note to start a partnership on, but I agreed. I was desperate to move away from children's television and be in the world he had joined. 'Yes, of course. Let's just do this one show and see what happens.' I had always wanted to work with someone more talented than I was. Matt certainly was, and he had proved it. What's more, we had become like brothers.

However, one night our career together nearly ended before it had even begun. We had arrived at a comedy club early and decided to get some chicken and chips. Matt was a notoriously fussy eater and only really liked chicken and chips, and could conjure it from any menu that included chicken and potatoes in any form.

Crossing the road, Matt was hit by a car and fell to the ground.

I got him inside the takeaway and, panicking a little, asked, 'Are you feeling all right?'

'No.'

'Where does it hurt?'

'Everywhere.'

'You might be concussed too.'

I turned to the man behind the counter. 'Please can you call an ambulance?'

'It's ten pence to use the telephone.'

'Not to dial 999!'

'Maybe it will be quicker to just take a cab.'

I never took cabs, ever. I couldn't afford to. However, this was an emergency. 'You wait here,' I said.

I ran out on the street, hailed a cab then bundled Matt inside.

'Please can you take us to the nearest hospital.'

'What happened?' asked the driver.

'My friend here got run over.'

'Did all his hair fall out in shock?' he enquired.

'Yes, but that was years ago. Sorry, can you just drive, please? He may be concussed.'

The driver sped through London in the early evening of another warm Saturday night. I handed Matt over to the doctors and nurses and called his mother, Diana.

When she arrived at the hospital, we sat in the waiting room for news.

'Thank you for looking after my son,' she said after a

pause. Years later she told me she meant not just on that night.

As it happened, Matt was not seriously injured, and the partnership would of course continue.

Meanwhile, I had been given a slot on a BBC2 yoof comedy called *The Sunday Show*. This is best remembered as launching the career of Paul Kaye as Dennis Pennis, and giving the great Peter Kay one of his first television appearances. I had impressed the producers at an audition, I think mainly for giving rent-a-politician Derek Hatton a massage while I was meant to be interviewing him. However, the producers really didn't know what to do with me, so dispatched me to interview celebrities in the hope of entrapping them into saying something stupid. First was Mandy Smith, the teenage bride of Rolling Stone Bill Wyman, who had recently come out as a born-again Christian. With her I discussed the Second Coming.

'Do you think he'll be driving a Fiat Panda?' I asked.

Remarkably she went along with it.

Sam Fox, the ex-page-three girl who had entered *A Song for Europe*, and darts champion Eric Bristow also played along for a little bit of money and TV exposure. *The Sky at Night* astronomer Patrick Moore did not.

The producers of *The Sunday Show* had decided that the portly xylophone-playing scientist was going to embarrass himself by saying something laughable about alien life forms. A list of 'funny' questions was drawn up, and I was dispatched to meet him.

'So what will alien life forms look like, Pat?' I asked as the cameras rolled.

'Don't call me Pat. My name is Patrick or Mr Moore.'

'Sorry, Pat. So what will alien life forms look like?'

'The idea of little green men from Mars is likely to be wildly off the mark.'

'Thanks, Pat. So what kind of clothes will they wear?'

He snatched my question cards and read through them at speed.

'No, no, no, no. Not answering that. Not answering that. No, no, no.'

He tore up the cards and threw them over his shoulder. 'NEXT!'

'You didn't need to do that, Pat.'

'RIGHT! THIS INTERVIEW IS OVER!'

Patrick Moore pulled off his microphone and, walking out the door, turned to the producer and shouted, 'DON'T LET THAT GOON NEAR ANYONE ELSE!'

I was embarrassed. Even though I do not share his anti-immigration views, I had always liked watching Patrick Moore on television, and now he thought I was a goon, whatever that was.

The Sunday Show ran my three interviews over the last three weeks of the show. By that time Dennis Pennis had firmly and rightfully established himself as the show's star. So I was surplus to requirements and wasn't asked back for the next series.

*

Soon I was back writing with Matt, this time for our first Edinburgh show. The process wasn't easy. Writing never is. Coming up with ideas for our pet project *Sunday Club* was a literal walk in the park, but the Edinburgh show was really going to happen, and soon. The first difficulty was that Matt did not want to start work until three in the afternoon.

'I have gigs in the evening, and it takes me a long time to wind down after all the adrenalin,' he said.

Still three seemed very late, and often I would get a call at 2 p.m., 'Can you make it three thirty?' or sometimes even, 'Is four OK?'

More troubling was that Matt was infinitely more interested in coming up with material for his character Sir Bernard Chumley, rather than any of mine. Both these issues would remain problems throughout our working relationship.

Theatre producer Andre Petjinski's company promoted us, though he once saw our show and hated it so much he wouldn't even talk to us afterwards, which I found hugely insulting. The slot we were given was at midnight at the Assembly Rooms, in a room called the Wildman that sat around a hundred people.

A number of previews were booked in, the first of which was at the Jackson's Lane Community Centre in Highgate. Rehearsals were difficult, as we didn't have a director so were directing each other, which was uneasy. In addition, despite Matt being only twenty-one at the time, he liked to rehearse sitting down. Being brilliant came naturally to him, and he was quite happy for a rehearsal to be little more than a read of the script. However, I always had to work much harder to try and keep up with him, and my way of doing things was to plan meticulously and rehearse again and again and again until it was right.

In our naivety, the hour of comedy we had devised was needlessly complex with hundreds of sound cues, lighting changes, costumes and props, which made the technical rehearsal quite tortuous and the show prone to problems.

For the first night at Jackson's Lane Community Centre we had sold three tickets. It was a miracle that we had sold that many, even though the theatre sat around 200. However, five minutes before showtime the box office received a call.

'There are four people who want to come and see you but are just watching *EastEnders* and would like to catch the end of it,' said the box office manager. 'They asked if you would mind starting five minutes late.'

Matt and I looked at each other.

'We'd be delighted,' I said.

Our audience had doubled.

For some reason the show was called 'Sir Bernard Chumley is Dead . . . and Friends', and the poster featured me in my pants reclining behind Matt as Sir Bernard. It opened with me walking on as a stage manager called Tony Rogers. (This was the name of a friend of my mum and dad and somehow the ordinariness of it amused me.) I entered from the back of the theatre and denounced the performance that the audience was about to see, then, emboldened, Tony started telling his own jokes. Mostly these were incredibly sexist, so he would finish these with the line 'Nice one, lads – sorry, women.'

Tony then introduced Sir Bernard Chumley and we sang a medley of completely inappropriate songs together – inspired by Vic Reeves's entrances on *Big Night Out*. Thereafter Sir Bernard hosted the hour, telling theatrical anecdotes and introducing me in various guises, from performance artist Simon Gieger to Bristol's very own porn star Erik Estrada. On that first night in Jackson's Lane Community Centre we even performed as gay Christian strip troupe Res-erection, though they only featured once. At the end of the show I appeared as the posh university-educated director Chris Neil (named after our agent at the time). I bemoaned the entire performance as a shambles, and we sang an a cappella version of Nik Kershaw's 'Don't Let the Sun Go Down on Me' to finish.

The audience's expectations were low, and we met those expectations. However, Matt and I had at least performed an hour of comedy together, albeit an utterly shambolic one. More previews followed, one of which, it subsequently emerged, was attended by the League of Gentlemen's Steve Pemberton and Reece Shearsmith. Reece later told me, 'We thought it was brilliant, and we thought we'd better get going with our own thing.' That shocked me, as at the time I thought our show was a mess.

In early August 1995 we boarded the train for Edinburgh and watched the landscape out of the window grow harsher as we travelled northwards and anticipated our fate.

On the first night we had sold one ticket.

I thought it would be amusing to print 'Free crèche' on the posters – this was a show on at midnight after all. A disgruntled hard-faced Scottish woman pushing a buggy with a toddler inside confronted me outside the theatre.

'It says, "Free crèche"!'

'I know it does, madam, but it's a joke.'

'A joke! Why is that funny?'

'Well, I, er, thought it might be, you know, as it's on so late.'

'I only chose this show as it had a free crèche. The wee bairn was looking forward to that.'

I peered down into the buggy. The child could not have been two. I wasn't sure there was a huge amount of crushed anticipation.

'I want my money back!' she demanded.

'Well, I am sure the box office can help you out there, madam.'

'Fucking idiot,' she added as she wheeled her long-suffering child out of the Assembly Rooms.

Our audience was now at zero.

The promoter hastily gave out some free tickets to people coming out of earlier shows in the Assembly Rooms and even people walking down the street. Soon zero turned to two, and two to four, and four to ten, and before long we had filled a few seats in our tiny theatre.

Midnight was late for a comedy show, even at the Edinburgh Festival, and the audience had mostly been drinking heavily all day. What was worse, the only way to the toilet was across the stage, so we were constantly interrupted by a parade of drunken men on their way to and from having a piss. Some even had to visit the conveniences more than once during the show. One particularly inebriated gentleman walked across the stage with only a few minutes of the performance left to go.

'Look, it's nearly finished. Can't you wait?' implored an irritated Matt, getting a laugh in the process.

'No, I can't,' replied the man, also getting a laugh.

'Well,' I said, joining in the discussion 'if you go now you can't come back in.'

'Good,' said the man. 'I don't care. The show is shite anyway.'

'Thank you for that wonderful review,' I said. 'Now please just go.'

He left, and Matt and I tried to carry on from where we had left off. After a minute or so we heard the door opening, and in disbelief saw the man trying to catch the last dying moments of the show.

'I wasn't joking!' I said, and attempted to push him out of the theatre. Drunks can have a terrible strength, so Matt joined in and we physically threw him out into the corridor and shut the door behind him.

The audience cheered – they had never seen such anarchy.

On so late in a town awash with inebriates, Matt and I had no choice other than to adopt an aggressive performance style. It was the only way to survive.

One night the comedian Sean Lock came. There was a

moment when I, as disgraced children's entertainer Des Kaye, threw lollies into the audience. To capture the character's mental state, I would throw the lollies harder and harder, and aim above the audience's heads. By accident one hit Sean Lock on the forehead. Unsurprisingly he didn't like it.

'You could have blinded me,' he complained afterwards.

'I'm sorry.'

'It's unbelievable; you could have had my eye out.'

So if you have ever wondered why Sean Lock is so frosty towards me on *8 Out of 10 Cats* you have the answer.

I celebrated my twenty-fourth birthday in Edinburgh. Katy had bought me a Jean-Paul Gaultier skirt. It was a man's skirt, long and black, and I wore it with a pink shirt and black tie. Not since the Hornby Mallard train set that my granddad had bought me in 1979 had I loved a present so much. I wore it that night, and as we walked the streets of Edinburgh to a party two rough-looking Scots youths confronted me.

'Why are you wearing a skirt?' demanded one.

'Because I've got some imagination!' I said, before flouncing off. I was quite lucky I wasn't beaten up.

Another night, in an effort to help Matt come out, Katy and I took him to a gay club called CC Bloom's. It was customary for Katy and I to go to gay clubs as we preferred the music and the people. Gay clubs always have a party atmosphere.

Everyone who knew Matt assumed he was gay. Not that he was camp; he isn't really, and is actually a lot more blokey than me. However, as he never had a girlfriend or seemed to want one, it seemed a strong possibility that he was gay or at least confused about his sexuality. I never asked Matt if he was gay; I felt he would tell me if he wanted to, but one night Katy and I thought it might be enlightening for him to go to a gay club. This proved to be a mistake.

As Katy and I drank and danced with a roomful of gay Scots I could see Matt was not enjoying himself. He stood holding a bottle of beer, with his back firmly pressed against the wall.

'Are you having a good time?' I shouted in his ear hopefully.

'I don't like this,' he muttered. 'I don't like this at all.'

'Why don't you come and dance?'

'I'm going to leave.'

'We've only been here ten minutes.'

'I'm leaving now . . .'

'We'll come too.'

I found Katy and we walked in silence through the streets of Edinburgh to the flat we were sharing. Matt just wasn't ready.

Over the three weeks the audience numbers for our show steadily grew. The word of mouth was good, and on the final Saturday night we sold out. Although we received some positive reviews, the show was too rude and anarchic to appeal to any TV executive. Except one. Myfanwy Moore. Yes, her again.

18
Mash 'n' Peas

Myfanwy Moore, my official guardian angel, was now a producer with the Paramount TV channel. It was still the early days of Sky, and although Paramount only showed reruns of American sitcoms, it wanted to make its own programmes. Myfanwy asked Matt and I to put together a show called *Spoofovision*. This would be a dozen collections of original sketches, all spoofing television series. Largely though, we could do whatever we wanted. And did.

Edgar Wright (who would later direct *Shaun of the Dead* and *Hot Fuzz*) had approached Matt at a gig one night. Edgar had seen him in *Shooting Stars* and wanted him to play a role in a low-budget film he had written called *Crawl*. He was only twenty but looked twelve, and already had made a film showing at a cinema in London, a western spoof called *A Fistful of Fingers*. One night I took Katy to see it, and I could see immediately that Edgar was someone who really understood the genre, knew comedy and could direct. In short, he was a child genius.

So when Myfanwy asked, 'Who would you like to direct?'

I said, 'Edgar Wright. You have to go and see his film. It's not the best film ever made but you can see he is a

18. (*above left*) With Hant and Dec.

19. (*above*) *Incredible Games* had some amazing guest stars. Yes, I met Mr Blobby.

20. (*left*) A sketch that, fortunately for us, was never shown: 'I am black and my dad's in the Klan.'

21. (*above*) The so-unfunny-they-were-funny double act Mash and Peas.

22. (*left*) *Take Heart* Lucas and Walliams style.

23. (*left*) With my real dad Peter Williams.

24. (*below left*) With my pretend dad Paul Kaye. 'Beat me on my bare bottom, Daddy.'

25. (*below*) Everyone at the time asked me if I was wearing a chest wig. The answer, sadly, is no.

26. With Edgar Wright and *Doctor Who*'s Brigadier Nicholas Courtney filming *Sir Bernard's Stately Homes*.

27. (*left*) Backstage at *Shooting Stars*. We both look incredibly gay.

28. (*below*) From the genius of Vic and Bob, the Labour Party Band. I was Peter Mandelson, apparently.

29. 'My Gay Dads' with Simon Greenhall.

30. (*left*) Keith Harris and Björk.

31. Happy times with the comic genius Caroline Aherne.

32. In Paris.

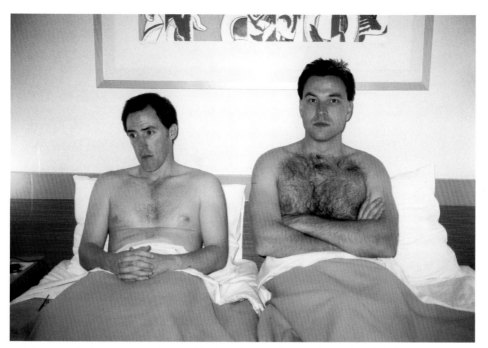

33. Sharing a bed on an ocean liner with Rob Brydon. Some of my chest hair is now on Rob's head.

34. In Venice with my Rob.

35. Lurking behind him in character in *Cruise of the Gods*.

36. (*right*) As Michael Jackson in *Rock Profile*, with Edgar Wright. I didn't do the voice.

37. (*below*) With the long-suffering Jamie Theakston in *Rock Profile*. We are Howard and Jason from Take That.

38. With Steve Furst as the Bee Gees. I am the lion one.

39. ABBA, of course.

40. Sir Elton John and My Partner
David Furnish.

41. Simon and Garfunkel just before they fell
out again.

42. (*left*) With the comedy pope Graham Linehan, in Dublin.

43. (*above*) Robin and me with a man with abdominal muscles much like my own.

44. (*below*) The very funny and ever so naughty Mark Gatiss.

giant talent.' Never have I been surer of a friend's future success than Edgar's.

'How would you feel about a gay man producing you?' asked Myf.

Matt and I looked at each other, puzzled. We were sitting in a coffee shop in Soho, just down from the Paramount offices in Rathbone Place.

'Well, we don't mind,' said Matt.

'We don't have to have someone gay,' I added. 'We don't mind either way. Why?'

'Well, I think you would be really good with a gay man producing you.'

It was if she was trying to force us or our work out of the closet.

A week later we met Johnathan Rawlinson, who took an instant dislike to us and us to him. Unfortunately he still became our producer, and contributed less than nothing. He acted as if he was our headmaster. When Matt and I mucked around on the walkie-talkies one day he said, 'I am reporting you to your agent.'

We really had no idea what the show was going to be. All we knew was that we had to do spoofs. We invented two appallingly unfunny hosts called Mash 'n' Peas.

'I'm Danny Mash . . .'

'And I'm Gareth Peas.'

They were two desperately immature men who openly squabbled. Their catchphrase was 'Get knockin'!' and they introduced a series of thematically linked sketches. The themes included American sitcoms, the making of a boy-band documentary spoof and children's TV.

Perversely minded, Matt and I wrote a spoof of *Diff'rent Strokes* called 'I'm Black and my Dad's in the Klan'. Matt appeared on his knees and in blackface, and I wore Klu Klux Klan robes and a hood. Fortunately for us and them, Paramount decided not to broadcast it. Ones that were shown included the 'Take Hart' sketch, in which Matt played the children's artist Tony Hart, while I was his comedy sidekick Mr Bennet with a bucket on my foot, and our friend the always inventive comedy actor Paul Putner took the role of a beer-swilling Morph; and a spoof of Mariella Frostrup's film review show with Matt as Mariella and featuring me as Cockney Film Star. With his leather jacket, glasses and lisp, Cockney Film Star later morphed into Lou Reed in *Rock Profile* and finally into Lou from Lou and Andy in *Little Britain*. The best sketch was a spoof of the American alien sitcom *ALF* entitled 'There's a Puppet in My House'. I played a man who unsurprisingly had a puppet in his house.

'The boss is coming round for dinner tonight. I hope that pesky puppet doesn't mess things up for me!'

Matt was the boss, and Jessica Stevenson played my wife.

When I asked, 'Why are you twitching?' she replied, 'I'm playing her as if she had come back to the series after a really bad car crash.'

Genius.

However, even the best ones were more funny-peculiar than funny, and after our relationship with the producer went from bad to worse and lawyers wanted to change every word that we wrote for 'legal reasons', we started to resent doing them. It is hard to do a spoof without making a joke about someone.

Dominik Diamond had a live chat show on Paramount called *Dom 'n' Kirk's Nite o' Plenty*, and Matt and I were booked to appear to promote *Spoofovision*. We waited backstage in our Mash 'n' Peas sweaters with the realization slowly dawning on us that we had no idea of what we were going to do. I was beginning to panic.

'What shall we do on the show tonight?'

'Don't worry, Dave,' said Matt. He always called me Dave though no one else did. 'We'll come out as Mash 'n' Peas and sing a song.'

'And then what?'

'And then we'll just see what happens.'

'OK.'

It was to be the worst night of our careers.

Kirk wasn't there for some reason, so co-hosting was the winner of *Gladiators* in 1994, Eunice Huthart. Dominik introduced us; we sang a deliberately annoying song, Gary Glitter's 'It's Good to Be Back', and repeated the lyric 'Hello hello' again and again and again.

Matt and I thought we would be so unfunny that we would be funny.

We were wrong.

Soon after we finished our song Dominik said something on screen to us that you must never say to comedians: 'You're not funny.' It's the worst insult imaginable.

While his statement was true, Matt and I decided, without exchanging a word, that we would get our revenge by ruining Dominik's show. Which was live on TV, even if watched by only a few thousand people.

We answered every other question he asked with 'Dunno.' Then we suggested Diamond had been sacked as presenter from *GamesMaster*, which was grossly unfair as he had actually left the series for completely honourable reasons, in protest at the McDonald's sponsorship of series three. Dominik was a highly principled man.

Needless to say, things took a turn for the worse from there on in. Matt and I repeatedly shouted the wrong answers in a telephone quiz, which managed to put off most of the callers. The times the callers answered correctly, Matt and I each had to throw a dart to give them a score. Neither of us tried to hit the board, and one of my darts narrowly missed Dominik's head.

As the credits rolled I put my finger between the cheeks of Dominik's bum. That I think was the final straw in a huge blazing pyre of final straws.

When the show finished Dominik's face was white with fury. 'I am going to fucking kill you!' He wasn't joking. I ran and hid in the toilets. Dominik followed me in and pounded on my cubicle door, shouting, 'Come out of there, you cunt! I am going to smash your fucking face in. You cunt! You cunt!'

'I'm sorry, Dominik!'

'After all I've fucking done for you. CUNT!'

He had a point. Dominik had helped me over the years, and I had repaid him by sabotaging his chat show.

'I am going to smash this fucking door down!'

Unseen by me, Dominik then pinned Matt to the wall

by his throat and had to be pulled off by a security guard. He was angry at Matt, but he was a hundred times angrier at me. Matt escaped, and Dominik was pulled out of the toilet. Still inside the cubicle, I unlocked the door and sprinted out of the fire exit. I ran down Rathbone Place and hurled myself down the escalator of Tottenham Court Road Tube station still in my Mash sweatshirt. Looking behind me all the way, I jumped on the first train, sat down on the dusty seat and cried. I had ruined my first appearance on a chat show, and more importantly destroyed my friendship with Dominik. We would never speak again.

I'm still ashamed about what happened that night.

19

'An anal misogynist cul-de-sac'

'Lucas and Walliams have torn free of their satirical moorings and are skating headlong into an anal misogynist cul-de-sac' was the respected comedy critic Ben Thompson's review of our second Edinburgh show in 1996. I wasn't sure what an anal misogynist cul-de-sac was, though I was pretty sure it was not somewhere you wanted to be skating headlong into. Ben had reviewed us really well the year before, so this felt like a huge step back. Being on at midnight had pushed us too far towards rude jokes, and we were turning into Derek and Clive before we had been through the warmer and funnier phase Pete and Dud had in their *Not Only . . . But Also* period.

Shooting Stars had just started on BBC2, and although not an instant hit, Matt's turn as the score master George Dawes was enough to guarantee us selling some tickets. That year our production was called 'Sir Bernard Chumley's Gangshow', and it had a vague Scouting theme. In Edinburgh I went to see a show that proved another epiphany. At first the poster had really put me off – three men in dinner suits, one with a dagger in his mouth. To me it looked like a magic act, and I hate magic. However, it was in fact one of the greatest sketch groups of all time, the League of Gentlemen.

Despite this being their first Edinburgh, their hour of comedy was infinitely more assured than ours. The simple presentation with a minimum of props and costumes combined with excellent writing and performances made for a masterful show. Like us the League went into dark areas of comedy, but unlike us they did it without being obscene. We had a piece in which Sir Bernard Chumley sang the word cunt repeatedly to the 'Dance of the Sugar Plum Fairy' from Tchaikovsky's *Nutcracker*. It never failed to elicit laughs, but it was juvenile. Their characters and ideas were much more grown-up, and crucially they were performing sketches.

Considering Matt and I later became famous for a sketch series, it may seem odd to learn that our live performances were essentially cabaret shows, with the characters talking to the audience. The problem was the cobbled streets of Edinburgh were littered with flyers of pasty-faced posh student types who, not being that funny on their own, had sought safety in sketch groups which would never be heard of again – The Dutch Elm Conservatoire, Curried Goat, The Cheese Shop – the debt to *Monty Python* sometimes even evident in their names.* So Matt and I didn't want to do sketches. Matt especially didn't, as he had developed Sir Bernard Chumley as a stand-up act. But the League was different. Most of their

* The 'Cheese Shop Sketch' is one of the most famous pieces from *Monty Python's Flying Circus*.

sketches were character rather than concept led, which was unusual at the time. And instead of having members surplus to requirements, all three performers were potential stars.

The League nurtured an army of fans that year; Matt and I had just one. That Edinburgh we met our first super-fan. A large Scottish gentleman came to see our performance every night, and had his picture taken with us every night. Of course when he first approached us we were incredibly flattered, and we talked to him for hours. But as he came time after time we realized he must be a little bit nuts. One night he gave us a script he had written for us. On the cover page was the picture of us with him he had taken the first night we had met. The title was 'An Evening of Bad Taste', but he had crossed out 'Taste' and written 'Breath' instead. Eight *hundred* pages . . .

'I stayed up all night and just wrote and wrote and wrote. It can be your next show . . .'

'Thank you so much,' we said.

It was not unlike the end of Stanley Kubrick's film *The Shining*, when it is revealed that Jack Nicholson has written 'All work and no play makes Jack a dull boy' over and over again. Except the word our Scottish super-fan had written over and over again was cunt. Maybe he was trying to tell us something.

Later that night Matt said to me, 'If we ever make it really big, and the head of the BBC or whoever says, "Guys, you can make any show you like now," we should give him this script and say, "This is our next project."'

That year I spent a lot of time with the League – Steve,

Reece, Mark and Jeremy (who only wrote). They were all fiercely intelligent and I learned much from each of them. Reece had a question by which he would judge any comic idea: 'What is the thing of it?' In other words, what is the joke of the piece? This became a mantra for me when dreaming up characters or sketches. Each one had to have a strong central comic idea driving it. It was never enough just to put on a wig and affect a silly voice.

Mark Gatiss was by far the naughtiest member of the group, and I instantly adored him. I went countless times to see their performances in the sweltering afternoon heat of the Pleasance. The League's show could clearly transfer immediately to television, and some of their most celebrated sketches – those in the local shop or Pauline with her job seekers – made it from stage to screen with barely a word changed.

'Maybe we should do sketches?' I said to Matt as we were laying out our props in the Wildman Room and saying goodbye to a certain Graham Norton, who was on just before us.

'Everyone does sketches,' said Matt. He was right. 'And the audiences love Chumley.' He was right there too.

That year we had written a long monologue for Chumley about his fifty years in show business, which was crammed full of jokes – fifty in fact. However, there were an increasing number of performers doing old show business types in Edinburgh, including Steve Furst's Lenny Beige, Steve Delaney's Count Arthur Strong and a young pre-*The Office* Mackenzie Crook as Charlie Cheese. For comedians just appearing at the Fringe means entering a competition. Not only for the Perrier Award (which eluded us but the League inevitably won in 1997) but more importantly to be chosen to develop your show for television. Thousands of performers go up every year. One or two might end up with a television pilot. More often than not, no one does.

'Sir Bernard Chumley's Gangshow' was too rude for television, although a charming producer named Richard Wilson (not Victor Meldrew) from BBC Radio 4 approached us after a performance, and soon after we piloted *Sir Bernard's Soirée*, in which Chumley hosted a party in his flat. We must have been influenced by *Noel's House Party*, which was towards the end of its torturous 169-episode run, as the concept was very similar. Letitia Dean (Sharon Watts in *EastEnders*) came to one of our live performances in Edinburgh. We had one famous fan, so we asked her to be in it. The best bit was when Matt as Sir Bernard asks her question after question about the soap she stars in.

'What happens to Pat in the end?'

'I don't know.'

'What happens to Ian Beale in the end?'

'I really don't know.'

'What happens to Dot in the end?'

This went on for ages. Matt is a master of repetition and as a performer has little or indeed no fear. He was prepared to say 'in the end' enough times that it would start off funny, become unfunny, then become funny again. It was such a great piece of material, I suggested we re-use it for *Little Britain*, when Marjorie Dawes has a noooo member in

EastEnders actor Derek Martin (Charlie Slater). And of course recycling is good for the environment.

Despite its moments, our Radio 4 pilot was scrappy and only intermittently funny. A year came and went before the station finally told us it wasn't going to be a series.

It was a difficult time for Matt and me. Our contemporaries were overtaking us at speed: Simon Pegg and Jessica Stevenson were developing *Spaced* for Channel 4, and the League was recording what would be the precursor to its TV series – *On the Town* for Radio 4. What was worse for me was that Matt was increasingly in demand on his own. *Shooting Stars* was becoming wildly popular, and Matt was its breakout star. He appeared in a BBC2 sitcom called *Sunnyside Farm* with Mark Addy and Phil Daniels; earned what most people would consider a fortune doing Cadbury's Creme Egg adverts on TV, and received the biggest cheer on his entrance in the *Shooting Stars* live show. I was starting to feel like an albatross hanging around his neck.

In the midst of all this something happened that made all this seem unimportant. Matt's father died. John Lucas had had a difficult life. He had served a short sentence in prison for fraud, and ended up divorced from Matt's mother. Now at just fifty-two, he was dead. Matt and his brother Howard were devastated, as was John's second wife Andi and her two children.

Matt was on the *Shooting Stars* tour at the time, and rang me early in the morning to tell me the news. The night before the funeral we sat in my tiny one-room rented flat in Hillfield Court in Belsize Park to watch *The British*

Comedy Awards. Matt had sensibly decided not to go. *Shooting Stars* picked up an award, and Vic and Bob took to the stage to massive cheers. It struck me how this moment of public triumph had coincided so cruelly with his private grief.

As Matt left I hugged him and said, 'Everything is going to be all right tomorrow.'

He looked at me without saying a word and then turned to go.

The door closed behind him and I instantly regretted what I had said. Everything was not going to be all right tomorrow, or the day after, or the weeks and months or even years that followed. Poor Matt. He gave up on religion after his father's death. For him it confirmed that there was no god. Something that I had realized many years ago.

Around this time my relationship with Katy finished. We had spent a lot of our time together staying out all night clubbing, and in that haze we had lost sight of the friendship that initially brought us together. Katy was much more of a party monster than I was, and had begun renting a flat in Soho. Every time I went round to see her it was full of strangers wanting to stay up all night and get drunk, or whatever. I still loved her, though she was making it increasingly hard for me to do so.

Katy initiated the break-up by inviting me to Bristol, where she was acting in a Restoration comedy at the Old Vic Theatre, and then completely ignoring me when I arrived. I was going to stay with her in her digs but she was so dismissive of me, humiliating me in front of her friends, I had to wander the streets of Bristol and find a hotel at midnight. I took the first train I could the next morning. Soon after, it emerged that she was dating an actor in the play. She had forced me to break up with her. However, I don't begrudge them their happiness because fifteen years later they are still together and have three beautiful children. So Katy made the right choice.

For many years afterwards the only love I knew was of the unrequited kind. I fixated on a girl who sold newspapers . . .

Thursday 21/6/1998

Once every six months the daughter of the news-stand vendor at Belsize Park Tube sells the papers. I really really fancy her. She has a kind face and can sense my attraction and smiles back. Whenever she's there I buy a paper whether I want one or not. Last time I bought an *Observer* I never read, today an *Independent*. All I've been able to do is mutter a few words like some voice-breaking acne-riddled schoolboy. Today I surprised myself by striking up a conversation. I was still nervous but at last we spoke to each other. I learned that she works for a music management company. But as more and more people were demanding their *Mails* and *Telegraphs* I became embarrassed and left her to it. I wish I was more of an operator. Then I would have taken her number or given her mine. Or at least learned her name. But I am a fool. And will have to wait another six months until I can move things on. My life is like *The Remains of the Day*.

20

'Asleep in yesterday's suit'

In 1997 Matt and I were presented with a huge opportunity. Vic and Bob were producing a programme for Ulrika Jonsson, the ex-weathergirl who had been such a surprise hit on *Shooting Stars*. It was to be called *It's Ulrika!* and Matt and I were to be her co-stars in the sketches. Vic and Bob were so busy with other projects, they wanted us to (kind of) be them in this spin-off. At that time Ulrika was one of the most famous women in the country. Everything Vic and Bob touched turned to gold. What could possibly go wrong?

I recorded the whole experience in my diary.

Monday 23/6/1997

At 10.30 a.m. I arrived at the American church on the Tottenham Court Road to rehearse *It's Ulrika!* At 11.30 a.m. Vic Reeves arrived and we started. Today I rehearsed a couple of sketches in which I play small parts. Sir John Birkin is the director and a grand master. He calls Vic and Bob 'Gentlemen' and Ulrika 'Miss Ulrika'. Matt was there until about 1 p.m. but I had to stay until 3.30 as I was cast in a *Watchdog* spoof he wasn't in. I was concerned about being left 'alone' without Matt, as he is of course now really such a big part of Vic and Bob's world.

However, I didn't need to worry. Ulrika was wonderfully friendly and not the least bit starry or patronizing. We got on very well and I immediately understood why this whole show is happening. She has real charisma. You can't help but warm to her. She is part teenage girl and part middle-aged bloke down the pub.

I had to play a man who has been murdered by his own pullover to Ulrika's Alice Beer in the *Watchdog* spoof. I gave quite a naturalistic performance that had Vic 'n' Bob laughing generously. This made me deliriously happy! To have these two icons that I have adored for years (I'm looking at a picture of them on my wall right now) laugh at me. Wow! It's the stuff dreams are made of. And without my comedy partner there I was forced to talk to them as me rather than as Matt's mate. So I left the rehearsal rooms with a definite spring in my step.

Tuesday 24/6/2007
The first day of filming on *It's Ulrika!* The studios were at Wembley Park, and as the production company Channel X are too mean to send a car I had to get three buses and the Tube. Much of the day was spent filming a Las Vegas nightclub scene. The director John Birkin is very thorough and the process was painstaking but never boring. The highlight of the day for me was recording a short scene for the

Watchdog spoof. Ulrika as Alice Beer was interviewing me as a murder victim/murderer. It felt very funny. It wasn't gaggy but it just had a comic feel. So much so that Ulrika had a fit of the giggles which halted filming for about fifteen minutes. The worst thing about getting the giggles is that after a while you don't know why you're laughing and that makes you giggle more. Vic and Bob were very encouraging of me with their laughter. I was completely at ease with them and felt privileged to be part of their world. It is a very special place.

In the Las Vegas scene Vic played a nightclub host. For some reason he was dubbed 'The Chimp' and the lulls in recording were filled jamming scenes with this new character. It was hilarious. He would wander over to the rest of us and open with 'I got a great deal. Three hundred coconuts are coming into town tonight. Are you in?' I hope they develop this character further; it was brilliantly funny. He became 'Kinky' John Fowler in *Bang Bang, It's Reeves and Mortimer* and *Catterick*. And what a joy to see the two funniest men in the world create something new, right in front of my eyes. I will never forget that.

Friday 27/6/1997
During the day I rehearsed *It's Ulrika!* at the American church on Tottenham Court Road. Vic and I amused ourselves looking at the bizarre religious children's drawings that adorn the walls. In the morning I had to stand in for Gloria Hunniford in a sketch with Matt

and Ulrika. I did it so well it was decided that I should play the role instead, even though Ulrika still has to say the line '. . . aren't you Gloria Hunniford?' to me. The whole sketch had metamorphosed into something very peculiar by the time we had finished with it. Bob was not so keen on me being in the sketch so I had to squirm in silence as my fate was discussed by these show business legends. Surely I'm funnier than Gloria Hunniford! This week I was lulled into believing that Vic and Bob are really friendly, but when rehearsals ended they virtually ran out – barely even saying good-bye to Ulrika. They are both quite unknowable.

Tuesday 1/7/1997

The *It's Ulrika!* rehearsals went well today. As each day passes I become more and more convinced that Vic Reeves is the living embodiment of comedy. Pet Shop Boy Chris Lowe said to me, 'You only had to look at him standing at the bar and you laugh.' Vic has that rare quality that Eric Morecambe and Tommy Cooper had. Impossible to describe, but if I had to I'd say it was pure absurdity. Anyhow Matt and me ran through our Ulrika lookalike sketch and it got funnier each time.

Wednesday 2/7/1997

Today's *It's Ulrika!* rehearsal was very strange. Vic was asleep in the rehearsal room in yesterday's suit. Matt said he rolled in drunk but insisted on staying and then fell asleep! So the producer made up a bed for him in the corner of the room. And as I was on the phone to a friend in the corridor Ulrika flashed her tits at me. Back in the rehearsal room she kept on attacking me, or drawing on my arm for no apparent reason. Very difficult to know how to respond, so I ignored her. However, that just made her do it more! My grandma said of Ulrika, 'Don't let that woman get her claws into you!' I think she flirts with every man she meets.

Thursday 3/7/1997

Oh no. No no no no no no no no no no no no no. I am in pain. At 9.20 p.m. a car ran over my foot. At 12.00 a.m. I got back from the Royal Free Hospital. The day was long. Eleven hours at Fountain Studios in Wembley waiting around to do a handful of reaction shots for the Las Vegas sketch in *It's Ulrika!* Racing home I stepped off the 268 bus in Belsize Avenue. As I tried to cross the road in front of it, I didn't see the car overtaking and leaped out of the way. Unfortunately my left foot was run over. The driver was quick to abdicate responsibility and showed no sympathy: 'I've got to be at work in ten minutes.' However lots of local people came to my aid, especially an older Eastern European lady who came from the old-fashioned school of first aid, asking, 'Would you like a cigarette?'

I felt like quite a star – an ambulance and the police arrived. As I was travelling by ambulance I expected not to wait long to be seen at the Royal Free. It was

11 p.m. by the time an inaudible doctor prodded my foot. An X-ray revealed a small break in one of my toes. So I have been given painkillers, and two of my toes have been strapped together. The hospital was full of mad drunk people. Perversely the nurses seemed to enjoy dealing with the nuts more than the patients. I listened in pain as out in the corridor groups of three or four nurses would wind them up: 'You can't sit there . . . Give me that bottle . . . If you come back again tomorrow night . . .' Etc., etc., etc.

Friday 4/7/1997

I got through it. It's 12.42 a.m. and the *It's Ulrika!* recording is finally over. I regret to say that the evening was a little embarrassing. It took four hours to record, and suddenly having to carry a whole show, Ulrika was more than a little out of her depth. Poor woman. It was just all too much pressure on her. She just couldn't communicate with the audience between takes, and ended up being negative and apologetic. And she kept on swearing, which turned a lot of people in the audience against her. Vic and Bob's humour might be a little crude at times, but they never swear.

As for me, I relished working alongside Vic and Bob. People laughed and they enjoyed the look-alike sketch, and Matt and I carried our roles off with aplomb. Matt made a couple of wisecracks in the recording breaks, which delighted the audience immensely. What a pro he is. I don't have the confidence to do that yet. As for Vic and Bob, even though I have now spent a couple of weeks solidly with them, I'm not sure I know them any better now than before. They are really distant, Bob in particular. Vic is more approachable, and we had an interesting chat about art. He definitely tries to draw a veil over his intellect, even though he is seriously bright. Matt has been very supportive and protective of me over the last fortnight, and for that I am very grateful. Like a big brother. Even though I am bigger and older.

Of course the one-off programme never became a series. I was disappointed, as Matt and I could have both really shone supporting Ulrika. However, the experience gave me some much-needed confidence. Your comedy idols laughing as you rehearse a scene – at that time it felt like the absolute peak of my career – but Matt and I were still desperately searching for a TV project of our own. Matt as George Dawes had been for many the most popular element of *Shooting Stars*, but it was still Vic and Bob's show.

As luck would have it, a friend of mine from Hewland International, Richard Osman – brother of Suede bassist Matt Osman – had landed at job at Hat Trick Productions. Hat Trick is a brilliant company which specializes in comedy (it produces *Have I Got News For You*). Richard is fantastically clever, but it was a huge endorsement for him to get a job at Hat Trick, albeit in development. I would often go and visit Richard at the company's office

in Soho to talk about ideas – I was, after all, up and coming. Once I sat in reception with Peter Cook, who was
preparing his legendary Clive Anderson chat-show special in which he played all the guests. He was flirting with
the pretty receptionist, showing off his bowling skills by
getting a paper cup into the bin.

'Girls can't bowl overarm,' he told me.

'Only underarm,' I offered, trying and failing to improvise with this comedy god.

'When a girl throws it's like this . . .' he said, miming a
cack-handed delivery. I laughed, not wanting the little
private performance ever to end.

Having subsequently met other comedy people who
knew him well, including David Baddiel, Jonathan Ross
and Graham Linehan, I now know that Peter Cook didn't
save his comedy for an audience or when he was getting
paid; he liked to make everyone he met laugh. I was so
glad to even sit in the same waiting area as him.

Richard had seen the spoof boy-band documentary
Matt and I had done for Paramount. Boy bands were everywhere at the time. Take That dominated the charts, and in
their wake many lesser acts followed. There had been
an unintentionally hilarious documentary on TV called
Making the Band about the creation of the group Upside
Down, which had inspired Matt and me. Two middle-aged
gay men who had made a fortune in business had decided
they wanted to be pop Svengalis. Writing the script for
our Paramount spoof was a case of watching the documentary over and over again, and identifying the funniest

parts (of which there were many). Some of it you could put in the script verbatim.

Richard Osman thought there might be a Channel 4 series in the idea, so Matt and I met up with him. This was a huge break – to star in a series made by the best comedy production company in the country, a series that would be seen by millions, rather than thousands on Paramount. But Richard and Matt instantly disliked each other. There was mutual mistrust, and perhaps jealousy, as they were both friends I wrote comedy with.

'So shall we start here in the office at 10 a.m. every day?' suggested Richard.

'I want to start later,' said Matt. 'That's rush hour and I want to get a seat on the train.'

'But you get on the Tube at Edgware, which is the start of the line. That means you're guaranteed to get a seat!' Richard was laughing but Matt was not amused.

Being caught between these two undeniably talented people became increasingly uncomfortable.

Wednesday 9/7/1997

There was tension at the end of the day when I suggested we start half an hour earlier tomorrow, 10.30 a.m. instead of 11. This didn't go down well with Matt. He really hates having to get up early and will do anything to prevent it. Richard had previously idly suggested that anti-Semitism wasn't as widespread as racism against Afro-Caribbeans, which was a mistake. Against overwhelming evidence to the contrary, Matt completely refuted it.

Thursday 10/7/1997

An eventful day. Hat Trick at 11 a.m. Matt huffed and puffed his way in at 11.15. He said he refused to work any earlier because he won't travel on rush-hour trains. He told me and Richard this as if we had never been on a busy Tube before. When I remarked I was writing a diary, he reacted very badly: 'Oh no. I'm gonna have to write a counter-diary denying everything!' And he wasn't joking. At the script meeting today, 'Put this in your diary. Me and Richard having a bet about whether Ben Folds Five are on Nude records or not.' Both of them can be Professor Neverebberwrongs at times. But every day they work together they become increasingly antagonistic. At one point when Richard left the room Matt complained that Richard had not made enough eye contact with him when he was talking. 'Did you see? He was looking at you the whole time I was speaking.'

With Matt sometimes unavailable or unwilling, Richard and I pressed on with the project without him. We wrote the first episode together, and I was really thrilled with it. Matt did not share our enthusiasm, and as subsequent episodes arrived in which the world of the series opened up, Matt counted his lines and grumbled that there weren't enough.

Despite all this my allegiance was always to Matt. Working with Matt could be difficult, but we were infinitely closer than Richard and me. Of course Matt is also an undeniable comic genius, something Richard is not. As the weeks and months passed, and Channel 4's interest grew, Richard started behaving strangely towards me too. I would turn up for a writing session at the Hat Trick offices, and he would be distant and silent. Or Richard would say he was busy, and having cleared the whole day to write with him I would end up going home after half an hour. I began to get the feeling that he wanted not just to produce but write the whole series on his own.

Friday 21/11/1997

Lunch with Richard Osman confirmed my worst fear: he hates Matt. That is the essential truth behind our contractual nightmare over *Boys R Us*. And although he hasn't said it, I am sure Matt hates Richard too. And unfortunately the deck is stacked in Richard's favour. 'I know Matt can be difficult, but as a comedy actor few can match him. No one could play Gareth, the fat singer/songwriter better than him. Can you not at least concede that?' Richard dismissed this. But we did do some great work on script four. It's going to be brilliant and it would break my heart for Matt and I not to be part of it. But my loyalty is to Matt, and always will be.

Thursday 5/2/1998

The day spent writing with Matt was disrupted by phone calls from our agent Samira. Apparently Kevin Lygo (anagram of King Lovey), who is head of

Channel 4 comedy, doesn't think Matt and I should play Gareth and Scott. Why? Even more unbelievable than that, neither does she! And she is our agent! When she said that I thought, *You're not my agent any more*. The only flicker of hope rests in the fact that between us, me and Matt own two-thirds of the format and maybe could 'pull' the show. But I doubt this. Later I spoke to Matt on the phone, who had been talking to Bob Mortimer about the Hat Trick situation. Bob came up with the completely maverick idea of me and Matt doing our own boy-band spoof on the Channel 4 sketch series *Barking*. I am doing to show the world it was our idea and piss off Hat Trick. But I doubt the bigwigs at Channel 4 would let it happen. 'What doesn't kill you makes you stronger,' I said to Matt. Maybe we'll bow out of TV for a year and concentrate on live work.

As I noted in my diary, Richard was forgetting something very important: Matt and I were the creators of the show. Although a spoof documentary about the creation of a boy band was not something you could patent, we were the first people to do it, and most of the characters and situations in the Channel 4 series had their origins in our sketches for Paramount. We were summoned to a meeting at Hat Trick's offices with its boss Jimmy Mulville and Richard Osman. We thought it was to resolve our differences; it was more of a military coup.

Friday 12/12/97

A devastating day. From 10 until 11 a.m. in the Hat
Trick meeting room with Matt, our agent Samira
Higham, Jimmy Mulville, Richard and his agent. We
were characterized by Jimmy as talentless fools who
had left Richard in the lurch by going on tour and
who should not be allowed to ruin his brilliant scripts.

Richard said nothing, not a word, as Jimmy Mulville
shouted at us for half an hour.

'Richard has worked so hard on these scripts,' he
snarled. 'I am not having you two ruining this show!'

'But we created it,' I said, shaking with anger.

'I have seen your sketches. They are nothing. Nothing.
Do you think you have a monopoly on boy-band spoofs?'

We didn't of course, but if Hat Trick didn't need our
permission to take our idea Jimmy Mulville wouldn't be
wasting his breath screaming at us.

I tried to catch Richard Osman's eye. He just sat there
and smirked.

'You are going to sign this contract,' said Jimmy. 'Count
yourself lucky we're giving you anything for it. Now get
out of here.'

I have never been treated with such disrespect. Samira
crumbled and I had to take it upon myself to fight our
case. It was a valiant effort but ultimately in vain.

Matt and I walked out into the streets of Soho. We
couldn't believe that Jimmy Mulville – who we had
vaguely enjoyed watching on the comedy sketch show
Who Dares Wins – had screamed at us. Matt said, 'I hope

Jimmy Mulville drops down dead.' And that Richard, like a guilty man on trial who did not want to incriminate himself, had chosen to say nothing. 'I told you we shouldn't have trusted Osman,' said Matt. He couldn't even bring himself to say his first name any more. I felt so bad that I had trusted him and so helped create this awful mess.

Increasingly bad news came via Samira Higham at ICM. 'Neither of you are going to be in it.' We were incredulous. 'But you do need to sign a contract so they can make the series.'

'I am not signing it,' said Matt.

'If you don't sign it neither of you will ever work in television again,' hissed Samira.

'Why?' I asked.

'Because you will have stopped Hat Trick producing a series with Channel 4, and people in the business will talk, and you will have such a bad reputation that no one will ever want to work with you again.'

'I am not signing it,' said Matt again.

But in the end he did. It felt like we had a gun to our heads. The contract netted us a small amout of money each, and the show went into production with the title *Boys Unlimited*. A young James Corden was cast in Matt's role, and although he was good, I can't help thinking that Matt would have been better in what was really an extension of his performance as Gary Barlow on *Rock Profile*, which was masterful. Needless to say, Matt and I were delighted when the series bombed. It sank without trace and was not recommissioned.

Nearly a decade later Matt and I were walking down Old Compton Street in Soho with our *Little Britain* producer Geoff Posner. We were stars now, and *Little Britain* was undeniably the biggest comedy show in the country. Lovely Geoff, who is a friend to everybody, knew nothing about all this ancient history. Walking towards us was Jimmy Mulville, shockingly thin as he was recovering from cancer, and Geoff introduced us. Matt and I both bristled. I really really didn't want to shake the hand of the man who had shouted at us in his office that day, but I didn't want to embarrass Geoff, so reluctantly I did. I looked out of the corner of my eye to see what my comedy partner would do. Matt was more inclined to harbour a grudge than me, but after a while he shook Jimmy's hand too. When we walked away I was shocked at how raw the anger in me still was.

Not long after that I met Jimmy again by chance at a dinner party and he finally apologized to me.

'You could have had *Little Britain*,' I said, 'if you had stuck with us.'

'I know,' he said. 'Don't think I haven't thought about that.'

'You would have made a fortune.'

'I know. Look, tell Matt I'm sorry too.'

'No, that's not good enough. You have to write to him.'

'Write to him?'

'Yes. He deserves a proper apology.'

'Oh OK. I will.'

'Then we might, we just might, consider appearing in a Hat Trick show.'

Both of us had refused to appear in anything made by the company, and we had been asked countless times to appear on *Have I Got News For You* after the success of *Little Britain*.

Jimmy wrote his letter. It is strange how healing a simple apology can be. Now I rather like Jimmy Mulville. He is a funny and intelligent man. In fact he told me one of my favourite show business anecdotes.

A friend of his attended an avant-garde Polish mime act at the Edinburgh Fringe in the early 1980s. A man came on the stage naked covered head to toe in white paint. The audience went with it, thinking, *Ooh, very experimental.* The man bent down and shat on the stage. The audience stayed with it: *Very interesting.* At the interval an announcement was made: 'The performance cannot continue because of the ill health of our leading performer.'

Richard Osman never said sorry.

Now I switch on the TV waiting for the news to start and see that he is dispensing facts as Xander Armstrong's sidekick on the daytime quiz show *Pointless.* So the story does have a happy ending. For Matt and me.

A Surprise Guest Star

In the autumn of 1997 Matt and I put together the best of our Edinburgh shows and entirely on the strength of Matt's success in *Shooting Stars* went on the road. We called it 'Sir Bernard Chumley's Grand Tour'. The show played arts centres, small theatres, even a nightclub. A decade later Matt and I toured *Little Britain Live* through the UK, Ireland and Australia. We played to a million people in total, often at arenas where the audience topped 12,000 each night. Fewer people saw us over six weeks in 1997 than they did on one night on the *Little Britain Live* tour. However, it was one of the most important experiences of our lives.

Matt was already a very seasoned performer, having 'done the circuit' for years. I was much less so. At the Edinburgh Fringe Festival the audience is pretty middle class, akin to a theatre crowd; a comedy audience is much less forgiving. If they don't think you're funny they don't sit in silence like a the theatre audience, they let you know.

As 99.9 per cent of the audience had bought tickets because they had seen Matt in *Shooting Stars*, when I came on at the start of the evening as stage manager Tony Rogers, most people thought I was the real stage manager.

Being almost completely unknown could be a blessing or a curse. Sometimes the audience were pleasantly surprised that there was someone else funny in the show other than Matt; at other times they were restless because the person they had come out to see wasn't on stage yet.

For me it was a really important challenge. To be able to make the audience laugh for ten minutes on my very own at the start was never going to be easy. Mostly I succeeded. Sometimes I failed. When I failed I just had to go on stage the next night and try again.

Matt's friend Tim Attack joined us to play keyboards. In 2011 Matt fulfilled his ambition of appearing in *Les Miserables*. Until then he had been something of a frustrated musical star, and in my view there were far too many songs in the show. Our great friend the comic actor Paul Putner toured with us too. Paul played the manager of whatever venue we were playing, and as he did not have a high TV profile the audience usually believed he was the real thing. Paul would come onto the stage unannounced and threaten to stop the performance as it had become too rude. Often the audience would boo him, and of course most comedy audiences like their entertainment rude. Using a successful sequence from our Edinburgh show, Matt as Sir Bernard Chumley would dance around him singing 'Cunt cunt cunt!' to the tune of the 'Dance of the Sugar Plum Fairy'.

One night Matt came off stage furious that the audience hadn't laughed much, and listed the jokes that hadn't received the response he felt they deserved.

'Clive Dunn? Russ Abbott? Nothing! Cunt cunt cunt? Nothing!'

It wasn't meant to be funny, but it really made me laugh.

Sometimes Matt would announce after a show, 'Right, I've got notes for all of you.'

Despite that fact that I had co-written the show, Matt could often treat me as an employee, allowing me no more status than Tim and Paul. Though of course it was Matt's creation Sir Bernard Chumley who hosted the show, and Matt (or George Dawes as most people who recognized him called Matt at that time) who was the draw. As a result, confusion reigned (within me at least) as to the equality of our partnership.

At the end of the show there was a three-way struggle between Matt, Paul and me that led to a blackout. In the darkness I would drop to my knees with Matt bending over trying to strangle me. Paul would bend over behind him and Matt's trousers would come down. The lights would then snap back on and it would look like we were having some kind of gay orgy. We would then turn to the audience and say, 'How embarrassing!'

This was a great finish to the evening, a visual joke that could have been from a bedroom farce which meant the audience would go out on a high. However on Thursday 30 October 2007 the audience at the Swindon Arts Centre got more than they paid for. As I wrote in my diary at the time, 'There was a surprise guest star in the show tonight. Matt's penis. It poked out of his boxer shorts and said hello during the trousers down sequence. Needless to say it received the biggest laugh of the night.

As I was on my knees right in front of Matt's crotch it came dangerously close to touching my face.'

My diary entries at the time give a flavour of the six-week tour . . .

Sunday 19/10/1997
On the way to Hull we shared a very dreary and expensive lunch at the Little Chef. Why do they call their fish and chips 'Good O' Fish 'n' Chips'? Photographs of plates of food illustrated the menu; England at its crappiest. We half-filled the Hull Truck Theatre but thankfully the audience really went for it. I slipped over quite badly getting on stage as Tony Rogers and when everyone laughed I said, 'I don't find it very funny.' A line I had improvised on the occasion of a similar accident ten years before in a school reading competition.

Saturday 25/10/1997
An 11.30 a.m pick-up in the *A-Team* van bound for Liverpool. Yes, we are travelling everywhere in the back of a black Transit van. The Neptune Theatre tonight. A 500-capacity sell-out and the scallies loved it. I felt really in control of my performance and rather triumphant as the lights dimmed for the curtain call. Katy's parents Peter and Sue came to see me perform. I greeted them backstage in my underpants as all actors do. After having split up from their daughter I was glad they had seen me on top form.

I was feeling pretty anxious for most of the day because to fail in front of them only for that to be reported back to Katy would have been humiliating. After some altercation about where we would eat dinner, Paul said he didn't like Chinese. Aside from fish and chips, Matt only likes Chinese – we went to a Chinese and had an enjoyable meal. The promoter Mike Leigh and I went off for a walk afterwards but it became clear his motivation was to chase some skirt. Liverpool on Saturday night is something to behold. Blokes in lime-green polo shirts with girls in plastic dresses and knee-high boots tucking into burgers and chips at 2 in the morning, not a coat in sight. Needless to say, no skirt was chased. I voted to retire early and my thoughts were nostalgic ones for a place where the girl I loved came from. I am now lying in the most average hotel in the world – The Gladstone. I would call it the most hoteliest hotel. Right now I am toying with the idea of crossing out the Leviticus verse in the Gideons Bible about homosexuality . . .

'18:22 Do not lie with a man as one lies with a woman; that is detestable.

'20:13 If a man lies with a man as one lies with a woman, both of them have done what is detestable. They must be put to death; their blood will be on their own heads.'

I just did. And I feel all the better for it.

Years later I refused to take the Bible with me on *Desert Island Discs*, which provoked a flood of letters from

Christians urging me to turn towards the Lord. I would always write back.

Dear Sir/Madam,

Thank you so much for your kind letter and the gift of a Bible. I have read it and am pleased to tell you I am now a committed Christian.

Yours Sincerely,
David Walliams

Sunday 26/10/1997

We arrived in Oldham at 4.30 p.m. and the omens weren't good, cold deserted streets and the set of the play *Dead Funny* still standing on the stage. But 403 punters came and as Matt said to me afterwards, 'Tonight the audience saw as good a show as they'll ever see.'

I may have thought it, but I would never say it. But Matt was right to be confident, as he is such a special performer.

I took some of the scenery down with me with my fall on stage at the end after the our self-penned 'Elf Song',* which obviously delighted the crowd. Matt

---

* It was a song in the style of a children's record, like 'Right Said Fred'. I was on my knees with a sign round my neck which read I AM A ELF. Matt as Sir Bernard Chumley would sing about putting a book on a shelf, it falling off, and hitting me on the head. Every time he did so, he hit me on the head with a book. The song would break down in an explosion of revenge violence from me.

was mobbed in the bar afterwards, and in that way people can, when they have had a few pints they turned a bit hostile towards him with comments like 'Ooh, he's a bit abrupt' – and we left.

Tuesday 4/11/1997

Tonight felt like work. Which is what it was. We were playing York Arts Centre, which is an absolute pit. We had to almost build a theatre or at least take a 'Let's do this show right here in the barn' type attitude. Thank God what we wrote was good because we really needed those big guaranteed laughs to carry us through. A couple of obsessive *Shooting Stars* fans fawned over Matt and even me afterwards. One was quite badly disfigured, and without wanting to fall into sentimentality her smile and joy at having her photo taken with Matt made the whole night seem worthwhile.

Friday 7/11/1997

The show in King's Lynn tonight was a success, though some bits went over their heads. One bizarre individual was so overexcited at the start of the evening I had to say, 'Please try and remember you're not *in* the show.'

It was the one of the funniest pieces in our live show at the time, and captures the spirit of juvenility and anarchy that pervaded our work at the time.

Monday 10/11/1997

Another day on the road. A long journey to the Chester Gateway Theatre The show was a sell-out and a huge success and proved a brief respite from another four hours in the van. This time Matt was in a real mood about the Belfast gig this coming Saturday. He decided to pull it without talking to any of us and threw himself into a sulk when I said I'd prefer to honour the booking. He ignored everyone and got out of the van without saying goodbye.

Friday 14/11/1997

Eight hours in the van. The M1 was closed. Travellers and police had caused a blockage on an A road. We left my house at noon and arrived at the Newcastle Theatre at 8.30 p.m. half an hour after the show was supposed to go up. We went up at 9 and all was going well for me as Tony Rogers at the start of the evening's entertainment until I managed to pick some psychopath out of the audience. He took his trousers and pants off on stage. Sure I asked him to, but I didn't think he'd do it! An important lesson with audience participation was learned. They don't always do what you want.

Saturday 15/11/1997

A terrifying plane ride took us to Belfast. The show went up at about 11.15 p.m. and we came down at 1 a.m. The audience were really rowdy at first, but by the end were so drunk and tired they couldn't really laugh any more. I had accounted for their rowdiness but not their eventual apathy. Matt came into my hotel room after the performance. I told him he needed a rest and should go on holiday. 'I've got no one to go with,' he said. Which made me sad. We talked way into the night, just as we had when we first became friends.

Sunday 23/11/1997

The last show of the tour. Bristol Old Vic Theatre. Sell-out. The last time I was there I lost the love of my life so I found the journey quite unsettling. Walking into the building, I remembered more than I wanted to. I arrived on stage lacking concentration but fortunately no one seemed to notice. We were a hit tonight. We've made a lot of people laugh over the last six weeks. That's something to be proud of.

Every night we would pull someone out of the audience to play musical chairs with Sir Bernard Chumley. My task was to find a 'volunteer'. I spotted a young man with funny glasses sitting in the second row and pulled him up. When I got him onto the stage I realized he suffered from cerebral palsy. The game involved running round and round these chairs. I had a split-second decision to make. Do I return this man to his seat or not? I decided it was an equal opportunities show and there was no reason why he shouldn't be part of it. Although the audience was tense, our volunteer loved it. The sequence would end with the audience member posing for a Polaroid picture with Sir Bernard. As the camera flashed Sir Bernard would hold up a sign behind the unsuspecting man, which read simply TWAT. This night Matt was too embarrassed to hold up the sign. He was right: the audience may have lynched us.

Looking back, the most important aspect of this tour is that Matt and I really bonded. We spent hours in the back of a van together. We had to put up the set ourselves. We had to deal with drunks, hecklers, overenthusiastic fans, poor ticket sales, terrible food, even Matt's penis very nearly falling into my mouth live on stage. We shared success. And we shared failure. And we nearly shared bodily fluids. Little did we know there was much more failure to come.

The next year Matt and I were invited to appear at the prestigious comedy festival in Montreal, Just for Laughs. The dream is that you perform there; an executive from a major American network sees you, and you are given your own TV series. Of course, like at the Edinburgh Fringe Festival, this rarely happens. Another British act performing that year was Michael Pennington aka Johnny Vegas. At one cabaret night Johnny hauled a man in a suit out of the audience and asked him what he did,

'I am a vice-president at CBS,' was the reply.

'Give me a series,' implored Johnny, before mock-whispering, 'I'll give you a blow-job.'

Despite this offer, like us, Johnny Vegas failed to land a US deal.

The lovely Graham Norton was also performing, and having met him in Edinburgh Matt and I had lunch with him. In the warmth of the afternoon sun the conversation turned to sexuality. Having had my sexual awakening as a boy with other boys, a confusion had swirled within me.

'Look,' said Graham, his lovely Irish lilt dancing on his words, 'I could enjoy sex with a man or a woman – it's all the same really. Sexuality is more about the emotional than the physical side of things. What really matters is whose arms you want around you.'

'A woman's,' I answered without hesitation.

'Well, you're not gay then,' said Graham.

And I never worried about it again.

'An Old Pile of Rubbish'

While we were touring Matt and I were also developing a tiny TV series which would be a flop of epic proportions, *Sir Bernard's Stately Homes*. It seemed like the perfect vehicle for us.

Not being deemed ready by the BBC for a full series of six half-hours, we were offered a series of six ten-minute episodes. Bizarrely our agent's brother gave us the title. From that we wrote a series of convoluted adventures involving Sir Bernard Chumley and the psychotic stage manager Tony Rogers. We hoped we would recapture the magic of those Edinburgh shows, but somehow we completely failed. Our writing at the time just wasn't good enough, and our ideas still woefully immature. The conceit of the series was that Sir Bernard had an ulterior motive in making the series – he was hunting for a golden potato. Hidden at a stately home, this was a prize offered by a crisp company to promote their brand. Someone should have stopped us. Unfortunately for us they didn't.

The script editor was the legendary comedy writer Barry Cryer, though I actually never met him. That's because I was struck down with hepatitis and hospitalized.

For three or four delirious days I had been unable to

leave my one-room flat. Drinking just the tiniest sip of water would make me throw up. I hobbled to the doctor's, the stoicism my parents had taught me preventing me telling the receptionist how ill I was. Dr Bostock took one look at my yellow skin and bloodshot eyes and said, 'You have hepatitis. You need to go immediately to Coppett's Wood Isolation Hospital. This is an emergency.'

It was a hospital for infectious diseases and looked like a World War II POW camp. As soon as I arrived I was injected to stop the vomiting and put on a drip. There I had to stay for ten days. Despite the hospital being in an obscure corner of north London, I had many visitors.

'I have never seen anyone sent so many bunches of flowers,' said one nurse. That made me feel a little better. My parents took three days to come and visit me, which, considering this was the most serious physical illness of my life and potentially fatal, was a surprise. My mum would have wanted to come immediately, but my father must have made her wait.

One day towards the end of my stay a big black nurse came into my room, not unlike Precious Little in *Come Fly With Me*. I could hear the squeak of her food trolley coming up the corridor and then stop outside my door.

'Good morning! Good morning to you!' she exclaimed in a thick Jamaican accent. 'What you want for breakfast?'

'What have you got?' I asked from my sickbed.

'Everything!' she pronounced joyously.

'Everything?' I asked.

'Everything!'

I hadn't eaten a proper meal for a week and was starting

to get my appetite back. 'Two poached eggs, bacon, mushroom, baked beans. Brown sauce on the side.'

'Just toast or cereal.'

'Oh sorry, I'll have some Rice Krispies then.'

'Cornflakes only.'

'I'll have cornflakes then.'

It still makes me laugh how she said 'Everything,' almost singing it as if in a gospel choir. And how if I had just asked for cornflakes in the first place, the illusion would have remained intact.

The first person I saw when I left hospital was Matt, as we had to start writing together as soon as possible. The first thing he said to me was, 'Oh I've been ill.' Quite an extraordinary sentence to say to somebody who has been lying in an isolation ward in a hospital for a week with a drip in his arm. I was still painfully thin and my skin yellowish in colour.

Matt had a cold. Whatever he had, he always had it worse than you.

Against his better judgement, Edgar Wright agreed to direct *Sir Bernard's Stately Homes*. On the first day of filming I remember arriving early and seeing all the vans and trailers that come with any TV programme or film.

Saturday 17/10/1998

SBSH shoot day one. I couldn't sleep of course. So anxious. Only compounded when we arrived at the location to see all those lorries and people there for us. Weird. 'They are all here for us,' I said to Matt. 'We better be good.'

An actor we had met on the set of the film *Plunkett and Macleane*, David Foxxe, played a different part in each episode. We both instantly adored Foxxey, not least when he had an argument with an airline stewardess on the plane home from the Czech Republic and told her, 'Less of the personality, dear.' He was the living embodiment of the camp old actor, a real life Sir Bernard Chumley.

Despite being directed by Jake Scott (the son of Ridley Scott), and starring Robert Carlyle and Jonny Lee Miller, both fresh from *Trainspotting*, *Plunkett and Macleane* was a flop. Our roles were too small for it to matter. The abiding memory I have of the film is seeing Liv Tyler skipping through the Czech countryside wearing a long white dress, like an angel who had fallen from heaven. Years later I danced with her at Elton John's sixtieth birthday in New York, and was so overwhelmed by quite how lovely she was, I had to stop.

We asked Tom Baker to play a bishop in one episode of *Sir Bernard's Stately Homes*, but he turned us down. Nicholas Courtney, who played the Brigadier in *Dr Who*, accepted a part – as a policeman. He was a brilliantly entertaining man. When asked how he liked his coffee he replied, 'Shirley Bassey. A little bit of black, a little bit of white.'

Nicholas was not at all precious about being known only for playing the Brigadier. In fact he was full of stories with punchlines like, 'So the director asked us all, "Has anybody got any questions?" And Jo Grant, who was sat on my lap said, "Yes. Why has the Brigadier got his hand up my jumper?"'

When he needed the toilet, he announced, 'The Brig needs a shit.'

Our writing for *SBSH* was childish. For instance we were convinced that re-enacting a scene from *Jim'll Fix It* when some Cubs ate their packed lunches on a roller coaster would be hilarious.

Wednesday 21/10/1998

I spent the day dressed as a Cub at Chessington World of Adventures. Strangely, it wasn't that much fun. I worried too much about everything and I could sense that the episode was turning into *Chucklevision*. Matt seemed keen for that to happen and I started to become very tense.

After the two-week shoot finished, Matt turned to me in the car home and said, 'That's as long as I ever want to film for in one go.'

'Then we'll never make a proper series then,' I replied, flabbergasted. 'Because to make six half-hours that's at least six weeks shooting.'

When Matt said things like that, I wondered if we really did have a future together. My parents had drilled a very strong work ethic into me, but it wasn't shared. And of course, Matt was overweight, suffered from asthma, and presumably had a lot less energy.

Watching *Sir Bernard's Stately Homes* now (we refused to put it as an extra on one of our *Little Britain* DVDs but unfortunately it is on YouTube), I'm horrified at quite how dreadful I am in it. I try so desperately to pull as many faces and include so many mannerisms as Tony Rogers, my performance is painful to watch. However, Matt is really rather good, and had already learned how to act for the camera.

Victor Lewis-Smith was then the TV reviewer of the *Evening Standard*, still the most read newspaper in London. He devoted a whole page to quite how awful the show was and launched a personal attack on me in the paper on 13 May 1999.

WHAT AN OLD PILE OF RUBBISH

It's typical that none of the recent obituaries for Johnny Morris mentioned one key fact about the man: that the loveable 'voice of the animals' once roundly insulted me. 'You're a cretin,' were his exact words – and all because I'd confided to him my childhood theory about those stags' heads you often see mounted on the walls of stately homes.

As an infant, I'd always assumed that the unlucky animals must have been involved in freak, high-speed accidents, and that their antlers had somehow smashed holes right through brick and plaster. Indeed, I'd often check round the back of the house, to see if the body was dangling there, but it never was.

However, as I told Johnny at the time, it seemed a reasonable assumption to make, because who (except possibly a member of the clergy or the Metropolitan Police) would want to mount an animal? Now he's gone, but I understand that Johnny Morris was impersonating animals right to the end. In fact, during his final moment on earth, he croaked. Sadly missed.

There were stags' heads aplenty on the walls of the fictional Baxter Grange, the setting of last night's episode of **Sir**

Bernard's Stately Homes (BBC2). Theatrical raconteur Sir Bernard Chumley is the creation of Matt Lucas (better known as Vic and Bob's bald sidekick George Dawes), and he's noteworthy for three things: a dreadful rug, an accent that veers between Belgravia and Bermondsey (sometimes intentionally, sometimes not) and a visceral hatred of other, more successful thespians.

Last night's tour around 'the ancestral home of Lord Nelson' began promisingly enough, although the deliberately crass message from his sponsors ('in association with Allen's crisps, the *cheaper* crisp') was a little too close to the truth in Mr Lucas' case.

Sorry, but it ill-behoves a man whose career to date has peaked with a series of Cadbury's Creme Egg commercials to point the finger at actors who shamelessly exploit their fame for money.

'Work started on Baxter Grange in 1805, and in 1805 Nelson took up residence until his death in 1805 . . .' he began, neatly parodying the jumble of unmemorable and unremembered facts with which visitors to stately homes are invariably assaulted by tour guides.

But oh dear. Just as I was delighting in the fact that Lucas had finally divested himself of partner David Walliams, the dismally untalented man popped up in the role of a jobsworth gardener.

Living proof that you *are* only young once, but you can stay immature indefinitely, he persistently interrupted the filming in the mistaken belief that he possesses the stroppy charm and immaculate comic timing of a Michael Palin (he doesn't).

From then on, the programme speedily went down-market, from mansion to pre-fab, relying on puerile jokes that were reminiscent of Trevor and Simon with a couple of A levels (and we know how easy those are to get nowadays). Indeed, I doubt whether even Punt and Dennis (the world's unfunniest typing error) would even agree to perform such abysmal material. No, on second thoughts, I take that back. I've heard The Now Show on Radio 4. Punt and Dennis will perform *anything*.

As regular readers know, I'm all in favour of scatology (although at university I confused it with eschatology and inadvertently spent three semesters studying 'apocalyptic theology'), but double entendres like 'Lord Nelson entered Lady Hamilton from behind when he got caught in her bush' fell hopelessly flat through the sheer ineptness of the set-up and wording.

A plot about finding the location of a mysterious 'golden potato' hove fleetingly into view late in the day, but such a flimsy premise cannot possibly bear the weight of six episodes, and by the end of this first instalment Lucas was already reduced to dressing up like a pirate with a plastic parrot on his shoulder, and shouting 'Aaah, Jim lad.'

Not only was it desperately unfunny, but it was tragically similar to a dire routine that Tony Hancock used to perform in the Galton-and-Simpson-less twilight of his career. But at least he had the decency to commit suicide afterwards.

A spoof documentary about stately homes is a potential gold mine for a keen-eyed comic. The hilarious conflict raging within the soul of every aristo who opens his house to the public (hating the rabble, yet needing their money) could keep any half-decent writer busy for a lifetime, yet this was unobservant, badly-scripted, semi-improvised tosh.

That comic genius Peter Cook used to extemporize superbly on the topic (having wisely perfected his ad libs in advance), but sadly, like Johnny Morris, he's no longer among us.

Indeed, with so many media deaths, and the plethora of respectful minute silences that have followed, perhaps Lucas and Walliams could learn a valuable lesson. Having died on our screens last night, why don't they host a televisual first next week, by offering us a 10-minute silence during their next 10-minute show.

It actually took longer to read his review than watch the programme. Matt was becoming more and more famous for his work with Reeves and Mortimer, but I was almost unknown and quite taken aback that someone had written 1000 words about quite how appalling I was.

Years later, Rob Brydon showed how you could make a ten-minute programme a huge success with the sublime *Marion and Geoff*.

Amazingly, still more failure awaited Matt and me.

Gorgeous producer Nira Park, who went on to make *Shaun of the Dead* and *Hot Fuzz*, wanted to create a TV series with some of the biggest names in comedy at the time. Who wouldn't? Nira had the connections. Keith Allen happened to be her fiancé, but she also knew John Thompson, Sally Philips, Peter Serafinowicz and Paul Kaye. The problem was Nira didn't know what the programme should actually be. So it was up to us to suggest characters and then write a TV pilot in which they all meet. I brought in Matt, and we started writing a script with two very talented men who would both become lifelong friends. They were Robert Popper (who created *Look Around You* with Peter Serafinowicz and *Friday Night Dinner*) and Mark Freeland, now head of comedy at the BBC. A year later the four of us were still writing the pilot episode.

We wrote draft after draft, and after a while (like Scientology) we were so deep into it we couldn't get out. The idea we had was the first idea that anybody who wants to do a sketch show without actually doing a sketch show has, that the characters all live in the same place. That is not to detract from *The League of Gentlemen* TV series, which was a work of utter brilliance. They had the good sense for their characters not to meet each other; unfortunately we did not.

Finally a script emerged, though after a year all four of us had become totally blind to what was good and what wasn't. A childhood hero, Nigel Planer from *The Young Ones*, also joined the cast, as did Paul Putner and Kate Robbins. There were a few good ideas. Matt would play the part of Pat Magnet, the town's unofficial ruler, who invented the magnet and was of indeterminate gender. Paul Putner and I were brothers. Our mother had died, and I hadn't told him so I could manipulate him into doing things for me.

Matt didn't turn up for the cast read-through. We waited and waited, but he didn't arrive. As his comedy partner everyone looked to me for an answer.

'David, where is he?' asked Nira.

'I don't know.'

As it was the morning I thought Matt was probably still in bed, but I didn't want to say. Unlike Morecambe and Wise we never shared a bed. Matt had indeed simply overslept. But by a few hours. So we reluctantly carried on with the read-through without our lead actor, which was not idea. Also, the script was overlong and overcomplicated, trying as it did to incorporate everyone's disparate ideas.

We all decamped to a small rural village to film it. Matt, normally so brilliantly funny in every role he plays, made some very bizarre choices for Pat. He was strangely stiff as the genderless mayor, which meant his character was not as funny as it had promised to be while we were writing it together and he was acting it out in the office. A few scenes worked, one in particular when Paul Kaye's character bought an iced bun from Nigel Planer's, but mostly it was the worst thing comedy can be, boring. On the penultimate night . . .

Sunday 9/5/1998
Keith Allen and Paul Kaye never went to bed. So there was much devilment this morning. They had amused themselves all night by phoning live sex lines from the hotel until 6 a.m. On whatever he was on Allen became a monster. We were all dressed in medieval costume for a flashback scene. Keith raced up and down the hills and dales in green velvet with a warlock hair-do exposing his genitalia like some demented gorgon.

With no promotion, *You Are Here* limped onto Channel 4 late on 30 December 1998, and was never seen again. Now the possibilty of Matt and I making our own series on terrestrial television was non-existent. Nobody wanted us.

23
Goblin or Hobgoblin?

So to make a living I accepted small parts in other people's TV shows. They stopped me having to get a proper job.

I played Soft Alan: the Biggest Fruit in the World for ten seconds in *Shooting Stars*. 'I didn't want to do him,' said the producer, Charlie Higson, when I arrived. 'That's why you're here.' Despite that inauspicious start to the day, I was dressed as Quentin Crisp and flown through the air into the arms of Scottish singer and actress Clare Grogan, so all was not lost. And I got paid fifty pounds.

That led to other supporting roles with Reeves and Mortimer. On their sketch show series *Bang Bang, It's Reeves & Mortimer* I made up the numbers. If there were four or five people in a sketch, I would play the fourth or fifth person. We stayed in the sleepy seaside town of Eastbourne to film it. There I witnessed how weirdly some folk behave around famous people.

'I'm good enough to sit here!' said a drunken lady as she squeezed herself between Vic and Bob in the hotel bar. 'I'm good enough to sit here!' she repeated, as everyone had ignored her first time around.

'You two! "Dizzy"! Now!' shouted a man in an effort

to cajole the two stars to reprise their number one single at the wedding next door.

'I'm sorry, but we've been working all day,' said Bob, 'and we're just having a quiet drink.'

'I SAID, "DIZZY" NOW!' repeated the man aggressively.

I also saw the upside of fame too. Vic arrived at the hotel in a beautiful 1960s E-type Jaguar and took one of the prettiest girls on the production up to Beachy Head to 'look at the view'.

Wednesday 29/7/1998

Today we shot a sketch in Dungeness. I played Laurence Llewelyn Bowen (the flouncy one from *Changing Rooms*) – with my trousers round my ankles, a prisoner of Vic's Hick. (Bob, Charlie and Matt were also prisoners as Jimmy Nail, and from *EastEnders* Pat Butcher and Mike Read.) I have yet to work out the rules of Vic and Bob's writing. Maybe there aren't any, the sketch was certainly bizarre. Little logic, even less reality but definitely funny. And what a joy not only to be in their work, but to watch them work and piss about with them in the recording breaks. And their humour is so generous. It's not about putting people down or being witty or scoring points in a competition for who can be the funniest. Rather it's another world they invite you to be a part of. The most magical part of today for me was being installed in the back bedroom of the house we were filming in with Vic. We were pretending we were at a car boot sale and picking up everything in the room — a barometer, a CD, a pair of shoes, and looking at their undersides and weighing them before making a decision whether to buy them or not. In the costume van afterwards Bob was whispering how Vic always forces him to visit museums and places of interest in the local area when really he would prefer to watch telly all day.

A few years later I would be invited back into their world to play Browning, a goth ghost hunter in an episode of their re-booted *Randall and Hopkirk (Deceased)*. Again the funniest moment would be off screen.

Monday 4/12/2000

In a break from filming today Vic enlisted my help in preparing a list of little fairy-tale people in order of goodness. We pondered whether the hobgoblin was worse than the goblin. Later I saw he'd prepared the following list, which I kept.

GOOD

1. Fairies
2. Sprites
3. Elves
4. Imps
5. Pixies
6. Goblins

7. Hobgoblins
8. Trolls

BAD

Amazingly I still have it.

One of my best friends at the time was the League of Gentlemen's Mark Gatiss. We became inseparable for many years. He took me to see Eddie Izzard perform a stand-up show at Wembley Arena for the Prince's Trust. We sat a few rows behind Prince Charles, and when he got up to leave I shouted, 'GAWD BLESS YOU, SIR!' in a mock cockney accent. Prince Charles turned around, nodded at me, smiled and straightened his tie, unsure whether I was an overenthusiastic subject or not. Mark and I laughed about it for weeks. This next diary entry is typical of how Mark and I would spend our days . . .

Saturday 26/07/1997
Mr Gatiss came round for lunch. He spent most of the afternoon jokingly scouring the personal ads in gay magazines *Boyz* and the *Pink Paper* for me. The only remotely suitable one we found read 'Flatulent men wanted. Me: young, cute and slim gas lover – at the receiving end. You: outrageous, macho and raw with a lot of gas.' It's nice to know there's someone for everybody! We sat on the sofa together and watched episode five of the Tom Baker *Dr Who* story 'The Seeds of Doom'.

Yes, we were and are big *Dr Who* fans. Mark has of course been very much involved in ensuring the programme's recent triumphant comeback, so when in 1999 the long-running sci-fi series had a night devoted to it on BBC2, he and I were asked to write and perform in a series of sketches. These would be interspersed between the documentaries and repeated episodes. We wrote three, one of which involved Mark playing the Doctor (a lifelong dream of his), another where we played two sexually confused fans who had kidnapped Peter Davison so we could molest him, and a final one in which we re-imagined the pitch from the producer at BBC to make the original series.

The sketches were very well received, but when I asked my dad whether he had seen them all he said was, 'That Mark Gatiss is very talented.'

It was sad for me because all I ever wanted was to make my parents proud, but he always withheld praise, or in this case gave it to others. At this time we were clashing a lot. My father was right wing and could have pretty intolerant views.

Sunday 8/8/98
The death of Enoch Powell sparked a debate of sorts over lunch at my mum and dad's house. I had to listen to a river of disgusting second-hand racist rhetoric from both Nannies and Dad. Just revolting. And heartbreaking. A few years ago I would have had to cry and scream and leave the table. Today I listened and chose my words. But I didn't mince

them. 'You're speaking from the point of view of rac-
ists,' I concluded. They defended Enoch Powell, and
could not even accept that history has proved him
wrong. And on the subject of Asians I said, 'You're
complaining about someone from India opening a
shop when only a hundred years ago we as a nation
were committing genocide in their country.'

'I don't believe that,' said Dad.

Ultimately it's no use arguing with him, but I
couldn't listen to him either. I was proud of Mum,
who came down on my side in a quiet way. The worst
of it all is that I am talked to as if I'm some kind of
naïve innocent because I am not against 'the blacks'.

'I could never love a racist,' I said, looking at my
dad. And for a moment he fell silent.

As I matured I realized I could never change my father
or his views, and I learned to love him as he was. Thank
God we even hugged before he died of cancer in 2007.

I made a huge number of minor appearances in TV
shows in the late 1990s and early 2000s. Most actors have
either *The Bill* or *Casualty* or *EastEnders* on their CV; I
have all three. I had two lines in the Dylan Moran sitcom
Black Books. I appeared in an episode of a long-forgotten
ITV sitcom entitled *High Stakes*. However, I was learning
all the time and never more eager to learn than when in
the presence of someone I really respected. The star of
High Stakes was Richard Wilson. In rehearsals there was a
scene where my character locked himself in a cupboard.

To make the other actors laugh I did a high-pitched voice from inside. In the tea break Richard Wilson gathered the cast.

'Now the first rule of comedy is do not play for laughs. Play it for real, and the laughs will come. Everyone should be giving a completely real performance . . .' I felt well and truly told off, before he added '. . . except me!'

That made us all laugh and put us at our ease. He was right of course. *High Stakes* was meant to be a two-hander between Richard and the great Jack Shepherd, best known as the TV detective Wycliffe. Richard was of course already greatly loved for playing Victor Meldrew in *One Foot in the Grave*, and he went out and talked to the audience before the recording. As a result the audience laughed at every line he spoke. Jack Shepherd got very few laughs at all. I made a mental note to self: *always* talk to the audience before a recording.

Sunday 22/10/2000

At 7.30 p.m. we put our episode of *High Stakes* in front of the audience. They had come to see Richard, and it was Richard they laughed at. Sadly not Jack. They laughed enough at me, but it took the audience a while to work out I was supposed to be a funny character! Richard was a star after the recording too, pouring everyone champagne and introducing people to people. I held his hand and thanked him.

'You were very good,' he said.

'Thank you. When I grow up I want to be you,' I replied.

Now I am rarely embarrassed. However, I was when I landed a role in Rob Grant's sci-fi sitcom *The Strangerers*. Rob was the co-creator of *Red Dwarf* but he had fallen out with his co-writer Doug Naylor over how they were going to buy houses near each other to make their writing more convenient. One of them didn't. Unfortunately the break-up was so irreparable that Rob wrote a series on his own. It was on Sky at a time when no one watched Sky. *The Strangerers* was probably watched by two people, Rob Grant and Doug Naylor on the quiet. I have never ever seen it because at the time I didn't have Sky. Mark Williams and Jack Docherty were the stars, playing two aliens who come to earth and try to pass themselves off as humans.

I didn't get off to the most promising start with my co-star Paul Darrow, who's best known for playing Avon in the 1970s and early '80s sci-fi saga *Blake's 7*. We were meant to be a comedy double act in the series, Rats and Seedy, two low-life characters both somehow mixed up in the sci-fi story. He was Seedy and had a costume to match – flared trousers, open-necked shirt, medallion and toupee. We passed each other on the stairs of the studio.

'Ah, Mr Darrow, a pleasure to meet you, sir,' I ventured.

'You must be David.'

'Yes. I have to say, sir, the outfit is amazing.'

'Thank you. I chose it myself.'

'The toupee is very funny.'

'Why thank you. It was my idea.'

'And I love the comedy teeth.'

There was a pause.

'Comedy teeth?' he said.

'Yes . . .'

I looked closer. They were real. I watched every episode of *Blake's 7* but I must have completely forgotten about his real teeth, which although being large and protruding, were definitely not from a joke shop.

'I must go to make-up,' I said.

To my horror I saw that we were sharing a dressing room. The embarrassment was set to continue. When I couldn't put it off any longer I knocked and entered.

'Oh hello again, Mr Darrow, sir. I have to say you were absolutely stunning as Avon in *Blake's 7*. It's one of my favourite programmes of all time . . .'

'You were joking about the teeth?'

'Yes,' I lied.

Paul spoke about himself as if he was one of the biggest stars in the world.

'Do you go to sci-fi conventions at all, Mr Darrow?' I asked over lunch.

'Yes, I love them. But I did one in America —'

'*Blake's 7* is big there?'

'Huge. And as I arrived there were thousands of people all calling my name: "Paul!" "Mr Darrow!" "Avon!" I went out to greet them, and the security man pulled me over.'

'Security?'

'Yes, I had security. And he said to me, "You must never ever do that again." And I said, "Why, I was just greeting my many fans." He said, "Remember what happened to John Lennon."'

'Sound advice,' I said, screaming inside, *AS IF ANYONE IS GOING TO ASSASSINATE PAUL BLOODY DARROW FROM* BLAKE'S 7*!*

When we were filming the second series of *Little Britain* we asked if we could vomit on him in a Maggie and Judy (named after Dames Smith and Dench) sketch.

'I'm only doing this because it's you, you understand?' he said. I'm sure he was also pleased with the fee and the being-on-TV-again, though.

Matt had seen Paul in a daytime advert for mobility scooters. Casting directors think you're past it when the only work you get is advertising hearing aids, walk-in baths and the like. I had told Matt that Paul was quite a character, so he couldn't resist asking him about the advert between takes.

'Mr Darrow, I saw you in an ad on TV for mobility scooters,' said Matt.

Without a pause Paul replied, 'Favour for a friend.'

'Favour for a friend' became our new catchphrase, and we even wrote a series of short sketches for the next series of *Little Britain* about an out-of-work actor seen doing a number of increasingly humiliating jobs. When spotted by someone he knew while cleaning toilets he would merely say, 'Favour for a friend.' Sadly the sketches never made it to TV. Matt and I could never decide whether the idea was only funny to us because we had actually met Paul Darrow.

But for all the laughs he had given me and Matt, I loved every moment I spent with Paul, and when *The Strangerers* finished, I missed him . . .

Friday 27/8/1999

Last day on *The Strangerers*. My feelings for Darrow have come full circle, and despite him always doing his Humphrey Bogart impression which is only fifty years too late, and going on and on about how he once played Macbeth, I was very sad to say goodbye to him. At the end of the day I could tell Paul had grown fond of me too. In our shared dressing room he said, 'I used the small towel. I left the big towel for you.'

Perhaps one day I will be advertising mobility scooters.

Other minor roles followed. In *Alexei Sayle's Merry-Go-Round* I had one line as a newsagent. Even though I acted with Alexei Sayle, he didn't speak to me, not even to ask me my name. (When I became a star on *Little Britain* I made sure I would at least always say hello to all the supporting actors and ask them their names. Not just out of common courtesy, but also to put them at their ease.)

In *Spaced* I played the performance artist Vulva. The role was a homage to the great Leigh Bowery, whom Matt was also soon to play in the Boy George musical *Taboo*. It was the best part anyone had ever written for me, and Simon Pegg, Jessica Stevenson and Edgar Wright welcomed my input. I added a tiny moment at the end of Vulva's performance where he bows and then says, 'It's not finished . . . It's finished.'

Paul Kaye played Vulva's co-star Hoover. Amazingly, despite swinging a vacuum cleaner around his head in the performance scene at the end, he never hit me with it. Paul and I were close friends at the time, and worked together on many occasions. First on *The Sunday Show*, then on a spoof rock band documentary with Annie Griffin for Channel 4 called *Wrath* about a fictional band called Spunk, and on his Dennis Pennis video *Rest in Pennis*. I hero-worshipped Paul. He was talented and glamorous, and women found him irrestistible – one day he turned up to meet me with Hollywood star Chloë Sevigny on his arm, at that time the hottest girl in the world. Paul was not a trained actor; he really wanted to be in a punk band. He had seemingly fallen into comedy by accident, and had an amazing rock 'n' roll approach to performing.

In *Wrath* Paul played someone full of anger. His character Seamus, the lead singer of Spunk, took his frustrations out on me, Gavin, the guitarist. Paul didn't like to rehearse much and liked performing scripted lines even less. So most of what he did was improvised. In character he threw a great many objects at me, one beer bottle narrowly missing my head.

Even though I never missed an episode of *Shooting Stars* and even sat through the whole of the unwatchable *Sunnyside Farm*, Matt never watched my episode of *Spaced*. Nor anything else I did at that time.

'Did you see it?'

'See what?'

'The episode of *Spaced* I was in.'

'No, I was on the phone.'

'Oh. Could you not have videoed it?'

'I was recording something on the other side.'

'Aren't you interested in what else I'm doing? I mean we are a double act, aren't we?'

This made me sad.

Annie Griffin remembered me from a summer course she had run at Bristol University, where she taught me to do something I never thought I could do: a cartwheel. I have never attempted one since, but my huge lumbering frame spinning wildly through the air must have stuck in her mind. After *Wrath* she cast me in her comedy drama series *Coming Soon*, which concerned the events leading up to an alternative theatre troupe's first night. Annie, an American performance artist who later in life developed a desire to become much more mainstream (she went on to write and direct *Book Group*), assembled a retrospectively astonishing cast: Julia Davis, Ben Miller, Omid Djalili, Paul Kaye and Billy Boyd (who went on to play Pippin the hobbit in the *Lord of the Rings* trilogy).

The production was shot in Annie's adopted hometown Glasgow. On Friday 12 February 1999 I missed my plane as I was in the airport bookshop buying J. D. Salinger's *Catcher in the Rye* (I had no plans to assassinate anyone, not even Paul Darrow). It was the last flight that night, so the plan was for me to go to Euston and get the overnight train at midnight. That gave me four hours to kill . . .

Leaving Heathrow, I found myself on the travelator next to a beautiful blonde British Airways stewardess called Ina. She was Norwegian.

Russell Brand would later say to me when we were

both taking regular flights to LA for work, 'You're wasting your time with BA. The stewardesses are much fitter on Virgin. And they're all up for it.'

Well if that was the rule, this lady was the exception. Blonde, shapely and her eyes twinkled with sexual desire. Incredibly for me.

'I live nearby,' she said. 'Would you like to come back for some coffee?'

'I only drink tea,' I said, not used to the euphemism.

After we had had sex a few times back at her flat, I lay there smugly and said, 'I've never picked anyone up at an airport before.'

'I picked you up!' she said.

She had indeed picked me up. Despite now being in my late twenties, it was my very first one-night stand, though I couldn't actually stay the night as I still had to be in Glasgow first thing the next morning to film. She called a minicab for me, but even though Ina's flat was near Heathrow, the driver had no idea how to get to London, let alone Euston. So I missed my sleeper train, and the whole filming schedule had to be changed. The consequences of my adventure were:

- Annie Griffin never employed me again (I would have loved to have been in her follow-up *Book Group*).
- I read *Catcher in the Rye*. Which is astonishing. Though quite short.
- Most importantly I proved Russell Brand's theory wrong before he had even thought of it.

At this time I had little money to speak of and was praying for a job which meant I could at least buy a small flat. Unfortunately, adverts almost always eluded me. The best thing about adverts for struggling actors is that they pay well, which means your card doesn't get declined in the supermarket when you're buying food. As mine often did. My face, according to readers posting comments on the *Daily Mail* website, is 'creepy', 'frightening' and like 'a bag of spanners'. So perhaps I never looked friendly enough to sell anyone anything. Advert castings tended to be humiliating.

Tuesday 7/12/1999
I had an advert casting in the afternoon. The name of the director, John Lloyd, excited me – he is the legendary producer of *Blackadder*, among others. However, it couldn't be more demeaning: wearing only my pants, I had to beg like a dog for a Quality Street. I might as well have been begging for the job.

I did once get cast in an advert though – for the Home and Leisure channel. There was an amazing set of a garden, so what would have been outside was actually inside. I had no lines, but was playing a husband who had to come in through a garden gate carrying a gnome for my wife. On the first take I smiled as I opened the gate.

'Cut!' shouted the director.

On the second take I smiled some more.

'Cut!' shouted the director again.

For take three I was a little nervous. *What did the director want that I wasn't giving?*

'Can you come through the gate,' he said, 'with a look on your face that says, "Hello, I've got a gnome for you"?'

'Of course!' Quickly I flicked through Stanislavski's books about acting in my head. I had studied them all at university, but unfortunately neither *An Actor Prepares* nor *An Actor's Work* nor *My Life in Art* had any mention of what expression you should adopt when carrying a gnome for your wife through a garden gate.

So I pulled an even bigger smile and tried to twinkle my little piggy eyes.

'Cut! We've got it!' shouted the director. 'That was exactly it!'

'Thank you,' I said. 'I studied drama at Bristol University for three years and we did a whole module on acting with gnomes.'

'Really?' he said, not getting the irony.

'Yes,' I said, after an uncomfortable pause.

To its great credit Channel 4 was always trying to break new talent, and a sketch show was commissioned called *Barking* with unknown performers doing separate scenes – people like myself, Catherine Tate and Peter Kay. Matt co-wrote some sketches with me, but was already too well known at the time to appear in a show of unknowns.

Monday 19/1/1998
A solitary *Barking* writing day. Matt phoned and gave me some great thoughts for which I felt very grateful. He has a sense of absurdity that can really enliven some of my more straightforward ideas.

I performed a few characters, such as a posh wedding planner who would like to serve Ginster's pasties, the royal watcher turned stalker from our live shows (a spoof of real royal expert James Whitaker), a police sketch artist who wants to pin every crime on Ruth Madoc, and an out-of-work actor who writes threatening letters to try and get work. They were all reasonably amusing, but slight. There was certainly nothing of the quality of the characters that would later capture people's imaginations in *Little Britain*.

Barking was instantly dismissed by the critics, and no one I have ever met watched it. I mentioned it to Catherine Tate recently, and she had never seen it either.

Sunday 21/6/1998
The *Sunday Times* today – *Barking* – C4 11.30 p.m.

'Dire new sketch show. If anybody ever tells you that television comedy writing is desperately competitive and only the brightest and best come through a rigorous selection process, show them a tape of this.'

However, it was Victor Lewis-Smith's review that hurt the most. The headline was BLAME IT ON THE HUMOUR ERROR, and underneath was a large photograph of me as spoof royal watcher Peter Andre, with 'Barking Up the Wrong Tree' underneath.

Thursday 25/6/1998
Paul Putner phoned and spoke to Matt. He wanted to warn me I had been badly reviewed for *Barking* in

the *Evening Standard.* I rushed my pudding and went out to discover my fate at the newsagent. [Lewis-Smith] hated every minute of it it. He hated my sketch.

Victor Lewis-Smith is a great writer and I loved reading his criticism. Though not of me. That night I prayed that one day I would do something he would like.

Even though no one yet had digital television, the BBC was preparing to launch a digital comedy and music channel. Its first name was UK PLAY, which then for no apparent reason changed to, wait for it . . . PLAY UK. Finally it became BBC3. A whole host of comedians were asked to provide links to go between the music videos. As Matt and I were never ones to wing it – I in particular like to plan meticulously – we took some time to think about what we were doing and write the links as a script. Our idea was simple: as we were linking music videos we would portray famous pop stars. Matt was Gary Barlow and I had my shoes on my knees as Mark Owen from Take That. We did Brian May and Anita Dobson as a two-headed monster as they had the same black curly hair. We even did a very imaginative act called Keith Harris and Bjork in which I was the ventriloquist and Matt the dummy, his head pushed through a curtain over a tiny doll's body.

So impressed was someone (it can't have been the viewers because there weren't any), the BBC asked us to make a full series of these spoofs. Matt was initially quite reluctant. It was quite a step down from being on a hit

BBC 2 series (*Shooting Stars*) to a channel no one had heard of. However, I was keen as it was an opportunity to earn money and stave off what I was now beginning to think was inevitable – getting a proper job.

I had seen this happen to a number of my friends. Like them I was approaching thirty, and I had always felt this was something of a cut-off point. If you hadn't made it by that age, you probably never would. By then you had been trying to break through for nearly a decade after leaving drama school or university, and if you weren't working on good projects you were looking increasingly like you never would.

After a few days talking at each other's flats (Matt now had a huge and expensive apartment in West Hampstead bought from the proceeds of his Creme Egg adverts and *Shooting Stars* tour, whereas I was still renting a tiny one-room dwelling), we came up with a concept which we called 'Rock Profile'. We would dress up as pop stars, and Jamie Theakston, who at that time was the face of pop music on the BBC, presenting *Top of the Pops* and *The O-Zone*, would interview us. We knew Jamie a little through our mutual friend Steve Furst, and sometimes we would perform at Steve's cabaret club, the Regency Rooms.

Having Jamie Theakston was vital to the show's success – he would give it authenticity. Jamie had some experience of acting (let's not forget he was in the National Youth Theatre's production of *Marat/Sade* playing a mentalist) and didn't mind being sent up. With him on board, Matt and I set about deciding which pop stars we could portray. Matt can do almost any voice on the planet, and even when he can't do an exact impression he can approximate somebody's way of speaking and make it funny. However, I really can't do anyone other than Frankie Howerd, so we had to decide how to approach this. We arrived at the concept of 'non-impressions'. Matt and I would dress up as particular people but not especially bother to do their voice. There had been hundreds of high-voiced spoofs of Michael Jackson; when I played him I just used my own. In that episode Matt played Elizabeth Taylor with a cockney accent. We hoped the approach would make us stand out and counter any criticism that we weren't impressionists.

The first series of *Rock Profile* ran for thirteen episodes, and probably about half of those are good. The Take That spoof of an embittered Gary Barlow and his live-in servant Howard Donald during the wilderness years was by far the best, as it had some emotional truth. Some were surreal, such as Matt doing Prince as a Scottish tramp with me as his social worker. Others were simply unwatchable. Matt and I as a middle-aged husband and wife who were Prodigy fans just didn't work at all. It was all done incredibly cheaply. We filmed two episodes a day, and catering was some stale sandwiches from the local garage.

The presence of Jamie and the quality of some of the episodes led to a second series. However, there was a problem: Matt had accepted the role of Thersites in a touring production of Shakespeare's *Troilus and Cressida* and wouldn't be around to write it with me. So we planned out the episodes together, and I wrote the scripts on my own. This time we were much more confident about what we were doing, and the ABBA, Bee Gees, George Michael and Geri Haliwell, Tom Jones and Shirley Bassey, and best of all Sir Elton John and David Furnish episodes became cult viewing.

I was inspired by the brilliant documentary David made about Elton called *Tantrums and Tiaras*. In that Elton is given a dog as a present, and in the spoof I wrote Elton (played by Matt) is given a puppy and says, 'I love it I love it I love it. I am going to call her Doggy. Right, now put it in the bin.'

Similarly there had been a documentary about Shirley Bassey called *Divas Are Forever*, in which she had said of Tina Turner, 'Tina's wonderful but not for Bond. She doesn't have the range!' 'She doesn't have the range!' became a catchphrase in our spoof. Another time you see Shirley on the Eurostar shouting, 'Champagne!' For me as a writer, the documentary was a gift, and in her episode of *Rock Profile* she repeatedly calls for 'Champagne! Champagne for everyone!' So brilliantly funny was Matt as Shirley Bassey, we decided to base a character on his take on her. She emerged in the second series of *Little Britain* as Bubbles De Vere. The catchphrase 'Champagne!' remained the same.

A best-of was edited for BBC2, and all the indications were that we might be asked to make a full series of *Rock Profile* for terrestrial television.

But the channel said no. We were back to square one.

24

'Pick up the phone, let's fight'

So Matt and I started work on yet another project, a sitcom about life in a T.G.I. Friday-style restaurant called Crazy Jonathan's. It seemed an ideal setting for a comedy series, and we had assembled a dream cast for an on-stage run-through: Reece Shearsmith, Nick Frost, Jessica Stevenson, Morwena Banks, Roger Sloman (from *Nuts in May*) and Jack Wild, the Artful Dodger in *Oliver!*

'It won't get commissioned,' said my girlfriend at the time after she watched the performance. She was right. She knew a fair bit about comedy herself. Her name was Caroline Aherne.

At that time Caroline was the undisputed queen of British comedy, one of the biggest stars in television, with a second hit even better than her first. She had followed up the brilliantly funny *Mrs Merton Show* with the brilliantly funny and moving *Royle Family*. I had met Caroline years ago at one of Matt's gigs, where she had been on the bill as Mrs Merton, then more agony auntie than chat-show host. At the time she was married to Peter Hook, the legendary bassist from Joy Division and New Order. Now Caroline was divorced, and her deeply unhappy private life, struggles with alcoholism and depression and a suicide attempt meant that she was often front-page news in the tabloids.

I liked her from the first moment we met. Caroline was eight years older than me, and she was funny, northern and pretty in my favourite sort of way – blonde hair and big tits. Of course I was aware of her troubled life, and like most men who were attracted to Caroline thought I could save her.

'I met her in a bar and knew she was trouble' sounds like a sentence from a Raymond Chandler novel, and the second time I met Caroline was indeed in a bar, the Groucho Club. In the 1990s the Groucho was the place to be. Its unofficial rulers were the triumvirate of Damien Hirst, Alex James (the floppy-haired bassist from Blur) and Keith Allen. The Groucho's reputation as a place where famous people could party in private made the thought of going there thrilling. As it was a private members' club, you couldn't get in without a member present. Bob Mortimer was and went there a lot, and sometimes Matt would go to meet him and I would tag along.

The night my love affair started with Caroline the first episode of *Sir Bernard's Stately Homes* was being broadcast. We were celebrating with a drink at the club – little did we know what Victor Lewis-Smith would write in the *Evening Standard* the next day – and she was drunk. We kissed on the snooker table, and our affair began . . .

Wednesday 12/5/1999
So we decided to watch the first episode of *SBSH* in a room at the Groucho. Me, Matt, Edgar, Paul and

Myf (Foxxey missing in action) sat in the bar waiting. My stomach churning with anxiety. To make matters worse, comedy greats Caroline Aherne and Craig Cash were in, and determined to watch it with us. After some panic finding the right channel, he heard the BBC2 announcer say: 'This is BBC2, home of innovation and the odd, but then would you expect anything else from Matt Lucas?' I thought, *Odd? It's just supposed to be funny.* Anyway, no one laughed very much, not least me. Craig and Caroline laughed at exactly the same moments. When the ten minutes had elapsed, Caroline sat on the snooker table and started dispensing very long-winded career advice, with Craig intermittently heckling her with comments like 'What are you try-ing to say, love?' She became quite bossy and ordered me to lie beside her on the snooker table, and then, champagne glass in hand, the flirting started. On both sides.

The two of us went back to her house, and there she dispensed more advice. 'Whatever you do, don't lose your anonymity. It's the most terrible thing to lose.' Caroline talked and talked and it was either heartfelt or funny or both. I talked too, and tried to be heartfelt and funny but can't be sure if I was either, because the thought *I'm about to kiss Caroline Aherne* was racing through my mind. Elvis came and went on the stereo as did Sinatra ('Fly Me to the Moon' again and again and again), before she put on Charlotte Church, and that first kiss finally arrived.

Caroline kissed me really quickly and then retreated, laughing. 'Not everything has to be funny,' I said and then we started getting passionate on her sofa. The house in Notting Hill was posh and aside from the BAFTA, strangely anonymous. Our hands were all over each other, then I said: 'Why don't we go upstairs?' to which came the baffling reply 'What for?' We did anyway, with the promise of 'no sex', which we stuck to. We got under the covers, and as is so often the case with someone who I feel really connected to, the cuddles were the best bit. We did spoons and I suppose I slept a bit, next to this comedy genius.

Thursday 13/5/1999

The alarm went off at 8 a.m. 'Come on, Caroline,' I said. 'Go out there and bring joy to millions.' She laughed as she had last night, which of course delighted me. I don't ever remember meeting anyone who talks so much and we swapped numbers.

A few nights later we went out for dinner and soon we were together. This was before the plague of paparazzi hit London and newspapers had you under surveillance by listening to your private messages, so we managed to keep our relationship secret. I was pleased as I was relatively unknown at the time, and did not want to become known for dating someone famous. People might have assumed any future success was because of her. My diary entries then give a flavour of what it was like sharing my life with this troubled genius.

Sunday 13/6/1999
'Am I your girlfriend?'
'Yes.'
'Well you haven't asked me out yet.'
'Do you want to go out with me then?'
'Yeah.'

I bought her a hat; she immediately lost it. She got drunk at dinner and started having a go at me. She wrote me a letter into the wee hours full of contradictions as I lay in bed. But all this couldn't stop me adoring her.

Tuesday 29/6/1999
I was in bed by 10.30 p.m. in anticipation of my early start tomorrow at Elstree Studies. In the darkness I heard the phone ring. It was just before midnight. A strange woman with the voice of Caroline Aherne started saying completely out-of-character things to me. 'You've got no love in your heart – you're incapable of it. Don't phone me again . . .' After about fifteen minutes I put the phone down. It rang another five times, but I had to try and sleep. 'Come on, David. Pick up the phone, let's fight.'

What you have to understand is that Caroline sober, the real Caroline, is the sweetest, kindest, gentlest, most loving person you could ever meet. Innocent as an angel. However, when she drank the alcohol poisoned her mind. It was only when she was drunk that she said hurtful things to me. The morning after, I would take flowers round to her flat, and she would be full of remorse, crying about how everything had gone so wrong again.

Wednesday 30/6/1999

At lunchtime I phoned Caroline at work. 'I'm so sorry. What did I say last night?' she said. After work I cabbed my way to Pembridge Mews, fantasizing about how I would take her in my arms and tell her I loved her when she opened the door and everything would be all right. But when she did open the door she wasn't quite ready for that. So I listened and comforted her and didn't judge her but was firm enough to tell her she did have a problem. 'I can't guarantee it won't happen again,' she said. But she was sorry and sad and that's what I needed to see so I kissed her arm and then her neck and then her lips. 'I love you,' I said. 'You're everything I ever wanted.' I continued repeating myself.

Then we retreated to the cosy domesticity of her bed and I watched the end of *Diamonds Are Forever* and she ate a pizza and then we slept.

One night we encountered someone whose problems far outweighed Caroline's. Michael Barrymore.

Tuesday 13/7/1999

Dinner at head of Granada Andy Harries's house was a strange ordeal. I arrived before Caroline and sat with Amanda Donohoe, praying she couldn't tell by looking at my face that as a teenager I'd had fantasized about her over and over again (in *Lair of the White Worm*, an abysmal Ken Russell film made watchable only by her beautiful naked body). When Caroline did arrive it was with Michael Barrymore. Barrymore was not invited to the dinner, but he's doing a series with Andy at the moment. Caroline had a drink with him after filming (her *Royle Family 2*, him *Bob Martin*); he seemed high on something and decided to invite himself. At first I was delighted and told him so as I had seen him on stage in 1988 with Robin at Bournemouth. However, after he had played far too roughly with Andy's ten-year-old twin sons on the trampoline ('Look, Daddy, I've got marks on my arms'), Barrymore danced around the room with Caroline to a Sinatra CD, desperately trying to be the centre of attention and shouting repeatedly, 'Do you take it up the chutney larder?' By the time he had shouted 'Do you take it up the chutney larder?' for the hundredth time, everyone was willing him to leave. What was most surprising was how unfunny he was. Amanda Donohoe grew so sick of him asking her about the moistness of her quim she had to move to the other end of the table. 'Has he rooted around your handbag yet?' I asked Caroline as he whisked her around the room again like an old lady he might pick on in his stage act. 'Yes,' she answered.

After Barrymore left I said, 'He tones it down for TV.' It made everybody laugh, and like all good jokes was true. Caroline kept on repeating the line in the cab on the way home.

'You are a very funny boy, Dasid.'*

Caroline was forever breaking up with me, and then instantly we would get back together . . .

Tuesday 27/7/1999

I went to Putney today for my dental brace fitting for *The Strangerers*. The dentist told me my jaw was out of alignment and that this was responsible for neck pain, stomach problems, leg numbness, headaches and chronic tiredness, which seemed a little far-fetched.

At 9 p.m. I went to room 432 of the Landmark Hotel, where Caroline is living right now. She was strangely wearing glasses when she opened the door, and didn't kiss me. Caroline had decided she didn't want me. Immediately I knew something was very wrong. She complained about my lack of sensitivity and my always wanting to go to bed rather than stay up all night drinking. After a while I said, 'But what if I got this dental brace fitted?' which made her laugh and say, 'That's the funniest thing you've ever

---

* One night Caroline and I babysat Craig and Steph Cash's beautiful little sons Billy and Harry. Harry was very young and couldn't pronounce 'David'. Caroline never called me David again. To this day, she still calls me Dasid.

45. (*left*) With Mark Gatiss and Paul Putner in a *Doctor Who* spoof. Mark had to be the doctor.

46. (*above*) With *Blake's 7*'s Paul Darrow just after I insulted his teeth.

47. (*below*) I just can't believe I am working with the great Richard Wilson. The great Jack Shepherd is lurking.

48. With God – Tom Baker, of course – on the set of *Randall & Hopkirk (Deceased)*.

49. Expressing my deep love and admiration for Vic Reeves.

50. On the set of *Attachments* with my TV dad Andrew Sachs, just before I asked him another question about *Fawlty Towers*.

51. (*above*) As Ruth Madoc in *Blankety Blank*.
Painfully thin and painfully unfunny.

52. (*below*) Matt as Andy Warhol…

53. … and how it turned out. As Lou and Andy. 'Yeah, I know'.

54. Emily Howerd debuts in *Little Britain* with a bit too much make-up on.

55. Everything about this photograph is wrong.

56. (*left*) Matt and I just before we put our costumes on to film.

57. (*above*) The very PC Anne.

58. (*below*) With Sally Rogers, filming *Little Britain*.

59. Ray McCooney. Not everyone thought he was funny.

60. Backstage at *Little Britain* with the long-suffering Tony Head.

61. A world record attempt on *Little Britain*. Paul Putner and Steve Furst squeeze into the Mini.

63. In some very tight shorts, with James Corden, shooting *Cruise of the Gods*.

62. Marjorie Dawes under inspection.

64. I couldn't believe I was working with two greats – Coogan and Brydon. And pulling a face to prove it.

said. You're a genius! Craig is still laughing about your "He tones it down for TV" comment about Michael Barrymore.' I told her I loved her and she told me she loved me, and then we kissed and for a moment everything seemed all right.

Sunday 8/8/1999

We lazed around in the hotel room for more of the day, waiting for Caroline's mum to arrive from Manchester. When we went to Paris together, Caroline told her that I was gay and that we were just good friends and she has continued with this lie ever since. Reminding Caroline of the scenario she had created, she said 'It's like a sitcom, isn't it?' 'Yes,' I replied, 'but not even a good one. Definitely ITV.' When we met her mother at Euston I knew this was some kind of test. 'Do you like David, Momo?' Caroline asked her before we had even left the station. She had come to help Caroline move out of Pembridge Mews, and I surprised myself by revelling in my role as man about the house, unscrewing shelves, sealing boxes and the like. I had to stop myself being too affectionate to Caroline in the presence of Momo, and came close to stroking her hair as I walked past on a couple of occasions. Of course I couldn't resist making lots of silly jokes, which Momo loved, but like her daughter she is such a warm, loving, caring woman, pretty much anything I cared to do or say would have delighted her. Caroline told me she had sent her mother to see Richard Wilson in Samuel Beckett's play *Waiting for Godot*.

'Did you enjoy it, Momo?' Caroline asked afterwards.

'Well, it was these two men waiting for Godot. He never came, but I still enjoyed it.'

Thinking about that always makes me laugh.

Caroline couldn't resist pausing over every single one of her belongings. In a plastic bag she found Mrs Merton's old costume. 'I bought these shoes from Oxfam for five quid,' she said. 'I thought, *This better bloody work or I've lost a fiver.*' This perfect comic mythology left me silent with awe, not least because she tossed the comment over her shoulder with not the least bit of sentimentality.

Saturday 23/10/1999

Today my beautiful friend the artist Sam Taylor-Wood and her art dealer husband Jay Jopling invited me to their daughter Angelica's christening. Entering the chapel at Westminster Palace, I was very nervous. I was alone and hardly knew anybody. The people I did know I didn't know well – Janet Street-Porter, Gary Hume, even Sam and Jay really. After the service there was a lunch at St John's restaurant in EC1. Who was I to sit next to? I sat down facing some people I didn't know – who turned out to be the artists Jake and Dinos Chapman – then I heard a familiar voice ask, 'Do you mind if I sit here?' The face was familiar too. More attractive than I'd anticipated. It was Geri Halliwell. 'I'd be delighted if you sat there,' I said. We had an interesting time talking about lots of silly stuff like star signs and food and kissing and clothes and her hair extensions, and although she's not an intellectual, she was sweet and kind and listened. Against my better judgement I was really rather attracted to Geri. Her lovely flat tummy was showing. And she had a completely unrehearsed vulnerability – 'I had never had a birthday party until last year.' Though she did say something that rang alarm bells as to her sanity.

'You know your brain is in the small of your back? That's where you actually do a lot of your thinking from.'

Maybe I can use that line in the next series of *Rock Profile*.

In the evening I went to see Caroline. It started well enough. She was a teensy bit jealous that I had met Geri but we went to see a film and then went out for dinner. I could have set my watch to what happened next. The warm loving comments at the start of the meal – 'I love being with you . . . There's no one who I'd rather listen to, I love your ideas on things' – turned cold. Little things I might have said or done were brought up in an attempt to create an argument (of course her champagne glass had been refilled many times by now). I said, 'Right, I can't listen to this any more. I'm leaving. I'll walk you home though.' She carried on being impossible on the street telling me to go as she stumbled into the road. I became quite angry and guided her by the arm back onto the pavement but she started shouting as the

Saturday night crowd in central London looked on. I was praying they did not recognize her. She calmed a little towards the last steps. She stood at her door. A tear rolled down her cheek, just visible in the dark. 'I'm sorry it didn't work out, Dasid,' she said. Whether she meant the evening or our relationship, I didn't know. I walked to Charing Cross Tube and on the way home tried to convince myself I couldn't save her from herself.

It was so sad. I loved her so much. Caroline and I had so many deliriously happy times, and often our minds would be completely in synch. With all my heart I believed if only I loved her enough she would be free of all the pain. I was wrong. After a year or more of trying, I realized no one could take it away from her. Caroline's father had been a violent alcoholic, and the scars ran deep within her. One night when she split up with me for the hundredth time I didn't go back. The situation was making me unbearably sad. It broke my heart that we couldn't be together. We would have laughed every day for the rest of our lives.

Sometimes she would call me in the morning. . . 'Dasid, put on *Trisha* now!"

Caroline would have spotted something amusing about one of the participants and had to share it with me. Sometimes it was the subtlest thing – a word, a gesture – but her mind had homed in on its absurdity. Caroline has the greatest comic mind I have ever encountered. Most comedians create a distance between themselves and the characters they create. Caroline never did. She loved people. Her work has always been deeply compassionate.

'I'd be the best girl you ever had,' Caroline said to me one night after we had split up, imploring me to return. And in her heart she meant it.

Without the drink it might well have been true.

25

A Poetic Soul

On the last day of filming the second series of *Rock Profile* me and Matt's new agent Melanie Coupland at Talkback (replacing Samira at ICM after the Hat Trick debacle) called me. 'You've got the job in *Burn Rate*.'

This was a BBC2 drama series that changed its title to *Wired* and finally to *Attachments*. It came with an excellent pedigree: the executive producer was the legendary Tony Garnett (*Cathy Come Home*, *Kes*, *Beautiful Thing*). His most recent hit on television had been *This Life*, the series about young professionals in the 1990s which had launched the careers of Jack Davenport and Andrew Lincoln. *This Life* had been a huge critical hit and is still talked about as a seminal piece of television drama. *Attachments* was his follow-up, following the lives of a number of characters in an Internet start-up company. It was an ambitious project in which viewers would be steered to the website the characters were working on, seethru.co.uk. How could it possibly fail?

Being cast as one of the lead characters, website designer Jake, felt momentous at the time.

When I told my mother, 'Mum, I've been cast as one of the leads in a new BBC2 drama series . . .'

'That will be good experience,' she replied.

Experience? I thought. *No, this is actually it. This is not experience. This is the thing! I am getting paid and everything!*

It was a huge endorsement of my talents as a serious actor, and there had been endless auditions and workshops to land the role.

Andrew Sachs played my dad. This was a treat, as not only was he in one of my favourite comedy series of all time (he, of course, played Manuel in *Fawlty Towers*), he was more than happy to talk about it. Soon I was fielding questions from fellow comedians to him . . .

'Andrew, my friend Graham Linehan would like to know how much the scripts were rewritten in the rehearsal room.'

'Actually very little,' purred Andrew in his soft warm tones, so instantly familiar from a thousand voiceovers. 'John and Connie worked so long on the scripts that by the time us actors received them there was no need to change a word. There was three years, don't forget, between the first series and the second.'

'Thank you, I will tell him that.'

I even asked him about the film of *Are You Being Served?* to which his reply was, 'Same performance. Different moustache!'

We filmed the first series of *Attachments* over the summer of 2000, and by the end the young and mostly sexy cast were doing shoots for newspapers and magazines. The *Radio Times* lined us up against a wall in an effort to make us instantly iconic. Some of the girls in the cast went out on shopping sprees and came back with designer handbags that must have cost thousands of pounds. Why not? We were stars already, weren't we?

No.

Attachments flopped. Badly. It was both too late and too early in its depiction of an Internet start-up company. More importantly too much of the drama was derived from one of us looking at the screen and saying 'The server's crashed!' which to the viewer at home doesn't seem all that dramatic. Certainly no one had died. Fortunately I did not buy a designer handbag. The show made me the tiniest bit famous . . .

Sunday 20/05/2001

I was in the showbiz page of the *People* today; Sean O'Brian's 'Hot People' column.

'The other night I had that TV comedian DAVID BADDIEL and *Attachments* star DAVID WALLI-AMS in my car . . .'

A nation asks who?

It continues . . . 'Just a small cab ride from a party to their north London homes. Diamond geezers, the pair.'

The first and I hope last time I've been referred to as a 'diamond geezer'.

Around this time I fell madly in love.

Nothing else mattered. I was completely overwhelmed by this girl. My heart danced every time I saw her. Her eyes killed me. Just the thought of her was enough to make me want to sing. I longed for the world to stop turning so I could be with her in a moment in time for ever.

She had a boyfriend.

I waited a year.

She split up from her boyfriend.

We were finally together.

This girl had a genuinely poetic soul. Like a heroine from an eighteenth-century romantic novel. When we watched the planes crash into the Twin Towers in New York over and over again on the news on 11 September 2001, she said to me, 'It's a day which makes you scared to fall in love.'

Friday 8/9/2000

She arrived at my flat at 1 p.m. and didn't leave until 8 p.m. It was raining heavily outside so we only went out for a brief walk. The rest of the time we spent lying on my sofa or bed with our arms wrapped around each other. I kissed the small of her back, I kissed her stomach. 'I feel so safe,' I said. And I did, what could possibly go wrong with her arms around me? Then the kissing started, long lingering kisses. When I showed her to my door I kissed her again. I closed my eyes. It was so beautiful. I literally went weak at the knees.

'You're so gorgeous, I adore you,' I said to her many times.

'I love you, you're lovely,' she said to me.

I walked her to the station. I wanted to spend every moment I could with her. Our legs slinked together as we made our way up the road. I carried her bag. My other arm was around her. We're good together.

Sunday 8/10/2000
'You smile and I am rubbing my eyes at a dream come true,' sings Neil Tennant on the Pet Shop Boys song 'It Always Comes as a Surprise'. This morning I woke up in bed with my beautiful angel. We made love, went out to get the papers, showered together, had smoked salmon and poached eggs, made love again. 'Being with you makes even the simplest things magical,' I said. And it's true.

Thursday 02/08/2001, Friday 03/08/2001, Saturday 04/08/2001
From Thursday evening to Saturday evening she never left my side. She came over for dinner at 8 p.m. on Thursday night and we were together for the next two days. Here are some snapshots of our time together:

- her reading poetry alone to me on my sofa wearing only her knickers
- us kissing passionately under a tree on Hampstead Heath where we were sheltering from the rain
- us eating a picnic on the lawn of Kenwood House

- me prancing around in my new velvet jacket for
  her amusement

It's like I've been given this amazing reprieve.
Another chance of happiness.

I loved her so much that when the relationship ended
I was completely destroyed. So destroyed that there was
very nearly no *Little Britain* . . .

26
Two Words

The first television series of *Little Britain* launched in the autumn of 2003, but the origins of the series go many years back. It may have had the longest period of development of any comedy show.

Even though our pilot of *Sir Bernard Chumley's Soirée* failed to become a series on Radio 4, there was always the opportunity for us to go back to the station with another idea. Radio 4 was an important gateway to BBC television, as many series – from *Hancock's Half Hour* to *Goodness Gracious Me* – had started there. However, Matt and I were reluctant to return as he felt insulted that Radio 4 had taken a year to say no to the *Soirée* pilot.

Years passed and a meeting was called with Matt and me to discuss making another pilot. Frustratingly Matt told the head of Radio 4, 'I'm not doing a show with a laughter track. They're old-fashioned, and no good comedy programmes have them any more. Look at *The Day Today* or *Brass Eye*.'

While it was true the laughter track had become seriously naff in the late 1990s, we were not, nor ever would be, Chris Morris. Moreover, sketch comedy is particularly hard to do without laughter. To me a series of sketches is not unlike a comedian telling a series of jokes, and not hearing laughter can be disconcerting.

Matt wouldn't budge; everyone left the meeting frustrated, but eventually Radio 4 relented, and against my better judgement we made a pilot in a studio with no audience present. The only good thing was that Matt and I were finally writing sketches. Having started our career together performing a cabaret show, and having found cult success on digital television doing spoofs, we had written very few sketches. Sketches were what other people did. It was hard for us to imagine that we could compete with the great sketch shows of the day, most notably *The Fast Show* and *The League of Gentlemen*. The *League*'s sketches in particular were so perfectly written, some even worthy of Alan Bennett ('The Cave Guide'), all Matt and I felt we could do was stand back and gaze in awe.

Perhaps the only link with *Little Britain* in this our second radio pilot was the character of Dennis Waterman, another of our non-impressions. Aside from that, there were historical sketches and spoofs. In need of a linking device, we enlisted the Brigadier Nicholas Courtney to read some lines as if Matt and I had taken him prisoner. I was even embarrassed recording them, they fell so flat.

The problem was Matt and I didn't know who we were as us.

Ronnie Corbett later told me, 'Ronnie B and I didn't have any shtick. We weren't like Eric and Ernie, who could bounce off each other so naturally as themselves. That's why we did the news stories at the start and end of the show.' It was the only way we felt we could be us.

Whether through awkwardness or shyness or whatever, Matt and I didn't have any shtick either. It wasn't a lack of chemistry – we had amazing chemistry when we were characters – we just felt ill at ease trying to be Morecambe and Wise, but then Morecambe and Wise never did characters. Later in our careers we were offered many hosting jobs together, award ceremonies such as the Brits and the BAFTAs. However, we knew we would be no good at it, so we turned them all down.

So Matt and I handed in this ragbag of sketches with a linking device that didn't work, which we had recorded one rainy afternoon in a studio with no audience to laugh and bounce off. Radio 4 responded with just two words: 'Lacks conviction.'

Matt was incensed. 'I am never ever doing anything for Radio 4 ever again.'

However, I knew Radio 4 were right, even if the brevity of their response felt insulting. What we had produced could in no way take its place alongside the great sketch shows of the day. So we were adrift yet again.

Shooting Stars had run for three series between 1995 and 1997 but had now finished, as far as Matt knew at the time, for ever. He was becoming increasingly anxious about how his career, his earnings and his fame were all rapidly declining. I had experienced little success in any of these fields, but I was starting to wonder whether we were stronger together or apart. As I am sure he was too.

Then one day something magical happened. I put together two words that would change our lives for ever: little and Britain.

We still had one ally left in the BBC, Myfanwy Moore. She implored us to have one last try at writing a script for a sketch show pilot for television. By now we had been writing sketches for quite a while and had a number we believed in. They were disparate though. One involved revisiting Neville Chamberlain's speech on the eve of the Second World War in which the piece of paper turned out to be blank and he had lied about the appeasement deal with Hitler. Another concerned the witch from *Hansel and Gretel* doing a site visit while her house made of sweets was still under construction and talking to the builders. Once again, though, we needed a concept. *The League of Gentlemen* was all set in one town; *The Fast Show* did what it said on the tin, the sketches came thick and fast; *Goodness Gracious Me* was a brilliant take on British Asian culture.

So we sat in Matt's office for a couple of days trying to think of something that would bind our sketches together. The trick was to avoid inventing things that had already been invented while at the same time steering clear of ideas along the lines of 'It's all set in a giant space station' – i.e. crap. Eventually an idea emerged.

'How about a spoof documentary series where we look at life in modern Britain?' I suggested.

'No,' said Matt.

'Why?'

'Well our Neville Chamberlain sketch is set in the past – that wouldn't fit in.'

'Yes, but it's only one sketch.'

'It's a great sketch. We can't lose it.'

'OK, well try and think of something else then.'

'I am trying,' he snapped.

We sat in silence for quite a while. I have always found silence distinctly uncomfortable and after a while I broke it.

'I really think the documentary idea could be a good one, Matt.'

Gradually I talked him round. Yes, we would have to lose a sketch, but it was only one, and if we were to do a successful sketch show series we would need at least a hundred. Then we found ourselves looking for a title, and of course many bad ones tumbled out until I said . . .

'What was *Eldorado* originally going to be called – *Little England*? We could call it something like that. *Little Britain*?' I thought for a moment. 'No, I don't like that.'

'No,' said Matt. 'It's good. *Little Britain*.'

We both said it out loud a few times to get used to it.

'*Little Britain* . . .'

'*Little Britain* . . .'

'*Little Britain* . . .'

'It hasn't been used before for anything, has it?' I asked. 'It sounds familiar.'

'I don't think so,' said Matt. 'The phrase is usually Little England or Little Englanders.'

'And it's a documentary-style series about life in Britain. We can shoot it all with a hand-held camera. It can be about all the people who live there. We could even have a narrator, like on a real documentary.'

'OK, *Little Britain* it is.'

I have always been in awe of people who write TV comedy on their own, like David Renwick (*One Foot in The Grave*), John Sullivan (*Only Fools and Horses*) and Roy Clarke (*Open All Hours*). You have to have such finely tuned instincts about what is funny. When someone else is there, their response to your ideas is crucial. I had dismissed *Little Britain* as a title as soon as I had thought of it. Matt was right though: it was good. Teamwork.

Matt and I hurriedly wrote a pilot script. The concept helped focus our minds on what we should write. Every sketch had to take place in modern Britain, so there could be no spoofs or historical sketches. Everyone did spoofs anyway, and historical sketches could be too obscure and uninvolving for many. Now we had the chance to forge ahead with some kind of social satire, which had much more chance of resonating with a large TV audience.

Together we wrote the first Daffyd sketch for this script. Amazingly, neither Myfanwy nor Matt liked it.

'I don't think it's very good,' was his judgement on one of the characters that would make him a superstar.

However, it stayed in, and we presented the finished script to Jane Root, who was then the controller of BBC2. The rest is history.

Except it wasn't. She turned it down.

So we had to grovel our way back to Radio 4. Now at last we had a strong concept. We rewrote the script for radio, adding characters as we went.

'How about Tom Baker as the narrator?' I suggested. I knew he would be terrific but I also wanted to meet him again. A few years previously I had queued up with a large group of Whovians – or gay men as they are more commonly known – at a bookshop on Oxford Street for him to sign his autobiography.

'Could you sign it, Sir Tom Baker, please? As I think you should be made a sir,' I creeped. He rolled his eyes, no doubt thinking *Another mentalist* before wordlessly signing my book.

'Or Michael Sheard?' suggested Matt.

'Who?'

'You know, Mr Bronson in *Grange Hill.*'

'Oh yes, of course. He'd be good. Or Harold Pinter?'

'Harold Pinter?'

'Yes, he acts occasionally and he has a very mellifluous voice,' I replied. Once again, this was really someone I wanted to meet, so in awe was I of his work. 'OK, so let's make a list. Tom Baker first choice?'

'OK.'

'Then Harold Pinter?'

What makes me laugh so much now is that we thought that the world's greatest living playwright would have gone anywhere near a Radio 4 comedy sketch show and read out lines like, 'But just who are Britain? Over the next twelve weeks we aim to find out by following the lives of ordinary British folk. What do they? Who is them? And why?' Or, 'One thing that drags Britain down is fat people. They take up space. They're rude. And in summer they smell.' Or, 'Britain's national food dish is burger 'n' chips, which has been enjoyed since medieval times. Along with nuggets, fillet 'o' fish and toffeenutbobbin.'

I couldn't imagine Harold Pinter reading those lines myself, even if he had yet to receive the Nobel Prize for Literature.

'OK,' said Matt. 'And then Michael Sheard.'

In retrospect I would have loved to have added Peter Wyngarde to the list. He has the most superb voice. Wyngarde made his name in *Department S* and *Jason King* on British television in the late 1960s and early '70s. He was then arrested for 'gross indecency' in a public lavatory at Gloucester bus station in 1975. He didn't really resurface until 1980, when he played General Klytus in *Flash Gordon*, though his face was hidden behind a mask. I would have liked to have brought him back to the public's attention. He had paid the price for being gay at a time when it was not accepted. He needed the break a lot more than Tom Baker.

Of course Tom Baker said yes, and we met him with our producer Ashley Blaker (an old school friend of Matt who was starting out on radio) at BBC Broadcasting House at Portland Place in London to record his links. Tom was early, as he often was, and I missed an amazing monologue from Tom that Matt and Ashley excitedly relayed to me as soon as he had gone.

'He said,' said Matt breathlessly, '"I don't watch TV any more. Whenever I watch TV, I look at all the faces of the people and I think, *He's dead. She's dead. I fucked her. He fucked me. He's dead!"*'

Tom's not gay but he would say outrageous things like that just to make us laugh. He was prone to making extraordinary pronouncements like . . .

'My dick has died on me.'

'I cannot abide the smell of neglected quim.'

'They wear their trousers back to front in Denmark. Have you never read *Hamlet*?'

'Life was so much simpler in the days before penicillin.'

'Rowan Atkinson only likes polishing his cars. That's what gets his dick hard.'

'I want to play Lady Bracknell from *The Importance of Being Earnest* in blackface with a gun.'

Listening to Tom talk was infinitely more entertaining than hearing him read the lines we had written, though suddenly he would become restless telling stories and hurry through the work so that he could disappear off into the streets of London. Tom told us that he had been offered a part in Yasmin Reza's play *Art*, which would change its cast every three months over a decade-long run. He said, 'I asked to meet them before taking the job. They said there was no need; the role was mine. I insisted. I went to meet them. And then they withdrew their offer.'

Having spent time with him I was not surprised. Tom Baker is bonkers. We used his bonkersness to our advantage though.

The writing for *Little Britain* on radio was sometimes difficult. A sketch show eats ideas so you need hundreds.

Monday 26/03/2001
'Shall we work on some radio ideas?' I asked Matt. It was 3 p.m. and we'd spent the morning finishing off our 'Rock the Blind' spoof.*

* A forty-five-minute special episode of *Rock Profile*.

'Yes,' he said. Then he went to the loo. Then he spent an age creating a file on his computer like a schoolboy who hadn't done his homework. He was putting off the moment of truth for as long as he could. He hadn't thought of anything. I'd spent the last four months writing down ideas when they came to me . . . in the pool, in the street, out with friends. I had around fifty. All good starting points for us to work from.

'Did you think of these over the weekend?' he asked, having listened to my long list.

'No, when I think of something funny I write it down.'

I always liked to write any ideas I had down in a little black notebook that I carried around everywhere with me. You never knew when you might hear something funny, or have an idea that you might be able to use one day.

Thursday 29 /03/2001
Overheard in the YMCA this morning:

Ten-year-old girl: You're flabby.
Nine-year-old girl: No, you're flabby.
Eleven-year-old girl: You're both flabby.

The truth is they were all flabby.

Idea for a sketch. Some lads are exchanging Xmas presents in the pub.

Lad 1: I got you that *X-Files* video you wanted.

Lad 2: OK, thanks. I've got something for you. Close your eyes ... (*He produces a box from his pocket. In it is an emerald necklace which he puts around his friend's neck.*) Emeralds. To go with your eyes ...

Every six months or so Matt and I would have a big falling-out, but that was generally a good thing. It would clear the air.

Wednesday 17/1/2001

So because I was in a mood with Matt I said little when we recorded Tom's voice for *Little Britain*. When we'd finished I plucked up the courage to speak and it all came pouring out – how he'd been lazy in the writing, how his bad behaviour with others has held his and maybe even our career back, how unwelcome he makes me feel when he opens the door in the morning. How he hates work. Everything I'd wanted to say for ages but hadn't. He listened, accepted most things and came back at me with others. Which I accepted. I am not easy either. What was important was that we were talking like this. It ended with a hug on Tottenham Court Road. I was so pleased and happy afterwards.

Sometimes a strike would get in the way.

Monday 5/2/2001

Today there was a Tube strike.

Today we were due to rehearse *Little Britain* at 10.30 a.m.

I walked from my flat in North London and arrived at 10.20.

Paul Putner cycled, Samantha Power walked and Ashley Blaker got up early and caught a bus.

Matt arrived at about 11.45. He phoned me at 10 a.m. from his flat in West Hampstead wanting to call the whole thing off.

'I'm at Camden,' I said.

'How did you get there?'

'I walked.'

'You walked?'

'Yes, if you started walking now you'd be there by 11 a.m.'

'Walk? To the West End?'

'Yes.'

'Well . . .?'

Ashley received bulletins every fifteen minutes or so. By the time he finally arrived Matt had developed a hitherto unseen limp.

However, at our best as a writing team we made each other laugh. When one of us was laughing we knew the sketch was OK. If both of us were laughing we knew we had something good. And of course most often we wrote something together that neither of us would have been able to come up with alone.

The *Little Britain* radio pilot recording took place at the Drill Hall, just off Tottenham Court Road in central London. We of course asked all our friends. We had invited all our friends to the performance of *Crazy Jonathan's* and they had laughed only for the first few minutes. This time they laughed all the way through and immediately we knew we were on to something. But, despite everything falling into place so beautifully – Tom's links, the classical music, the sketches – Radio 4 still made us wait an agonizing three months before they said yes.

I was getting frustrated. I was completely broke; my debit card was being declined in the supermarket every week or so, and I was too proud to ask my parents for help. I didn't want them to know quite how little money I was making, and I knew they thought, particularly my father, that I should give up on this dream and get a proper job. Much of our work was unpaid – our Edinburgh performances for example just about covered their costs. Developing ideas and scripts was mostly undertaken on spec, and unlike Matt I had no income from adverts or *Shooting Stars*, with its lucrative book, tour and videos.

However, with the radio pilot of *Little Britain* I knew Matt and I had produced something of undeniable quality, something I could be proud of. I knew it was the best piece of work we had ever done. So I was exasperated by the long wait.

Finally we received the call. Radio 4 would like to pick up a series of four episodes. The fee would be £500 each for writing and performing in each one. We spent the next six months working on them, so I lived on seventy-six pounds a week. I would have been better off claiming unemployment and housing benefit, but I knew we were getting closer and closer to our dream . . .

27

The Comedy Pope

The best thing about making a comedy show on the radio (apart from not having to learn your lines) is that you don't need any sets, costumes or make-up. So you can rewrite the script at very short notice, invent a new character or sketch on the day. That's much harder if not impossible on television.

We recorded the episodes once a week, which meant we could gauge how the characters were received by the audience. If they liked them, we could feature them more.

Vicky Pollard is a case in point. All our *Little Britain* characters started with one sketch. We wrote a two-minute piece about the most inarticulate person in the world being put on trial. Matt's performance was extraordinary, and no one had heard anything quite like it before. Buoyed by the audience's laughter, we wrote more and more. Other characters never made it past their one sketch, but it didn't matter. Soon we had a cast of characters to equal our contemporaries. Not just Vicky, but Daffyd, Emily, Sebastian, Kenny Craig, Jason (who fancied his friend's grandmother), Mr Mann and Roy, and Little Dennis Waterman made their debut in front of an audience on the radio show. Marjorie Dawes had appeared

CAMP DAVID

as George Dawes' mother on a couple of episodes of *Shooting Stars*, but this was a different incarnation of her – as a 'Fatfighters' group leader.

Some of our best sketches were written at this time. Because radio humour can never be visual, you have to work doubly hard on the words. The 'Pirate Memory Game' sketch, the first appearance of Mr Mann and the long-suffering shopkeeper Roy, may just be my favourite piece we ever wrote.

In the days when I was pretty much anonymous I could while away time idling down the street without any feeling of self-consciousness. After a drink at the Hollytree pub in Hampstead with Graham Linehan I looked in the window of the toy shop opposite and saw in the display Yo Ho Ho: A Pirate Memory Game. The specificity of it amused me, and I thought how funny it could be if someone came into that shop, asked for something as specific as a 'pirate memory game' and then rejected it as 'not quite what I had in mind'. I told Matt the next day at work. Many people cannot believe that writing comedy sketches can be regarded as work.

'I guess you come up with it all down the pub. Have a few beers then just get talking?' and 'Do you write the stuff in advance, or just make it up on the day?' are just a couple of the questions I get asked. Now writing may not be going-down-a-mine hard work, but it is still work, and can be exhausting, mentally. Matt and I wrote the 'Pirate Memory Game' quickly, like all our best sketches. The ones you labour over and rewrite ten times generally turn out the worst. The sketch was old-fashioned, but in my

288

opinion old-fashioned in a good way. For me the 'Pirate Memory Game' was important, as it proved we could write a 'classic'-style sketch, with a proper beginning, middle and end. It would not have been out of place in an episode of *The Two Ronnies*.

Little Britain was to be broadcast at 6.30 p.m. on Radio 4, and so it couldn't be too rude either. It could explore some adult themes, but there could be no swearing or explicit sexual references. Again that made us work harder as writers, as both swearing and sexual references are easy buttons for comedians to press to get a laugh.

We assembled a little repertory company of actors around us: Paul Putner of course, Samantha Power (who we had met on *Spoofovision*) and Jean Ainslie. Jean was eighty when we worked with her. She was a rare talent, an old lady who never acted being an old lady; she just was one. We had seen her be naturalistic in *Brass Eye* and knew she would be perfect as the grandma Jason fancied in those uncomfortable sketches. Very sadly Jean died between the recordings of the first and second radio series, so we never had the chance to bring her with us to the television series.

The reviews for the first radio series of *Little Britain* were all positive, only my dad was unable to give me a full endorsement. When I asked him if he had heard it, he replied, 'I was driving back from seeing your mum on Brownie camp with someone and I didn't think I could just put the radio on and listen to it with him.' This struck me as very strange. If I'm a father one day and my son makes his own radio show, I hope I make everyone in the world listen to it.

Despite the good reviews, television was still not tak-ing much notice of the series. Graham Linehan was and still is a close friend. He's a legendary and much loved figure in the world of comedy, his work at the time includ-ing *Father Ted*, *Big Train* and *Black Books*. I told him that even with a successful radio series we were struggling to make it on to TV.

'I want to help you and Matt,' he told me one night at the pub. '*Little Britain* is a good show – it's a great show. I'll direct the pilot for you.'

'Oh Graham, thanks . . .'

'I won't do the series. I can't. I've got too many other projects to do. But if my name can help you get *Little Britain* on to television, then I'd be happy to help.'

His endorsement was like being anointed by the Com-edy Pope. Suddenly BBC television executives sat up and took notice: 'If Graham Linehan thinks it's good, then it must be . . .'

The new channel BBC3 was preparing to launch in a year. Having already made two series of *Rock Profile* (and the strangely unfunny special *Rock the Blind*) for a digital channel, we were reluctant to give the series to them. We needed to be on terrestrial television with our contempo-raries. Matt and I wanted a large audience to see us, and to be able to tour after the series had come out. It was pretty much impossible to sell a tour unless you were on one of the major TV channels. Our success at Edinburgh convinced us we could deliver a good live show as per-formers, and now we had the material too.

However, Jane Root, who ran BBC2 at the time, never

warmed to us, so we went to see Stuart Murphy, the controller of BBC3.

BBC3 had trendy offices, and on the wall a poster which read:

> **The BBC3 viewer is –**
> Jacqui
> 23
> Likes pubs and clubs
> Single but dating regularly
> Drinks Bacardi Breezers
> Works in PR
> Earns £25,000+ a year
> Spends her money on CDs and clothes
> Holidays in Greece

As Matt, Graham and I sat outside Stuart's office, I stared at it and said, 'Is that their only viewer?'

Of course 'Jacqui' was meant to be representative of who their viewers might be; whether our show would appeal to 'Jacqui' was beyond me. The average age for listeners on Radio 4 was fifty-five.

A secretary took us into Stuart's office.

'Have you heard the radio series?' prompted Graham.

'I haven't had a chance to listen to it yet,' Stuart said, 'but I've got the tapes right here on my desk.' My heart sank. 'But I'm a big fan of *Rock Profile* and of course *Shooting Stars.*'

'Thanks,' said Matt.

I nodded a thank you, as I had only been in *Shooting*

Stars for ten seconds so didn't feel I was in any position to take any credit for it.

Stuart's ideas were not to any of our tastes.

'We can put dance music on all the sketches and release a CD of it afterwards,' he said.

'That's not important,' I said.

'It is important, David. The marketing of the show is very important.'

Tense.

'What's important to me is that it's funny,' said Graham. 'And I think it's very funny.'

'We want to be as big as the Two Ronnies,' said Matt.

This is what clinched it for Stuart.

'I love the Two Ronnies,' he said. 'I will give you the money to go and make a pilot, and then I can put it out on the launch night of BBC3 next year.'

Walking out of the office, I said to Graham, 'What about the thing about having dance music on the sketches? That would kill them stone dead.'

'Oh that doesn't matter. We'll just take his money and make the show we want to make,' he said, obviously a great deal more experienced at dealing with television executives than me. 'He won't remember what he said in the meeting. They never do.'

Graham is not only a master of comedy, he's also a student, forever reading books about the art of screenwriting, and expounding upon it. He bought me a book by William Goldman (screenwriter of *Butch Cassidy and the Sundance Kid, All the President's Men, Marathon Man, The Stepford Wives, Heat, The Princess Bride*) called *Adventures in the*

Screen Trade for my birthday one year. Its first sentence is 'Nobody knows anything.' Goldman was writing about Hollywood and how no one truly knows how to have a hit movie. The same of course can be said of a hit TV series.

However, Graham knew more than we did. He certainly knew something about comedy. Delivering three consecutive television hits – and co-creating Ted and Ralph for *The Fast Show*, that sublime comic reworking of *Lady Chatterley's Lover* along the way – was no fluke.

'This is TV, not radio!' he would tell us over and over again, when we dusted off another successful radio sketch and presented it to him. 'Just because it worked on the radio doesn't mean it will on TV.'

'I'm going to fight these changes every step of the way,' said Matt to Graham after one particularly strong set of notes. I was so embarrassed as Graham was my friend, and I had brought him to the project, which he was doing as a huge favour.

'I'm only trying to make it better!' said Graham. 'If you don't want me to I've got plenty more things I could be getting on with.'

Fortunately I managed to talk Graham round, and work continued. He made Matt and I work really hard, creating strong visual humour for the pilot episode:

- Sebastian jumping on top of the PM when he says there's a sniper outside.
- Ian and Ian, the world record breakers, with their one box of dominoes.

- Jason's point of view when he sees his friend's nan for the first time, complete with soft focus and romantic music.

And he generously suggested some of the visual jokes that accompanied Tom Baker's narration.

Graham encouraged us to be ambitious with casting too. Instead of trying to get 'a Tony Head type' for the role of the PM, we just called Tony Head.

Wednesday 29/05/2002

Anthony Head came into rehearsals for the first time today and was brilliant. His performance was so still and truthful. It's amazing how working against a quality actor can lift your own performance.

The location sketches went well, though I was surprised Matt didn't feel it necessary to be there when he wasn't in a sketch. He was never a one for getting up early, however much was at stake. The night in the studio went brilliantly, and I remembered the Richard Wilson trick of talking to the audience before and making them laugh between the takes to keep them entertained.

I still felt very much in Matt's shadow and knew I had to earn my right to be perceived as a partner rather than a 'sidekick'. The audience's reaction was tumultuous. Of course there were lots of friends there. If you listen closely to the audience laughter you can hear Edgar Wright's distinctive guffaw. However, most weren't friends, and they still laughed. It was a glorious night. The show was received as if it was an old favourite, rather than something new.

Matt and I both knew that this pilot was something really special and deserved to be seen by more people than the tiny audience that was going be available to BBC3, so we had to go back to Jane Root at BBC2. It was 20 August 2002. I remember it well because it was my thirty-first birthday. It seemed I was at least a year late on my deadline for success.

'What sketches do you think don't work?' the wiry blonde bespectacled channel controller asked. This was a horrible question to have to answer – a bit like when the great Sir David Frost famously made Tony Blair squirm by asking him, 'What do you think is your worst quality as prime minister?' No one wants to emphasize their failures; they want to concentrate on their successes.

'Well,' I said, trying to be assertive even though I knew that my future was in her hands, 'there are many sketches we think are good.'

'Yes, but I asked you what ones do you think don't work?' she said as I squirmed.

'Well, which ones don't you like?' Matt asked.

'The Scottish hotel one is awful,' said Jane Root. She even screwed up her face at the thought of it.

I shifted on my seat some more; this involved Ray McCooney, a character I played.

'Well we can have another look at that . . .' I said.

'You have to cut it,' she said.

Jon Plowman, then head of comedy at the BBC, leaped

in to save us from more embarrassment: 'Look, Jane, I really believe in this show. I've got a good feeling about this one. It's going to be good. It can be big.'

Jane looked at us all, then muttered something and walked off.

'What did she say?' asked Matt. In the large open-plan office neither of us had heard her.

'She said go away and make it,' said Jon.

'Did she?' I asked.

'Yes.'

'So we've got the series?' I asked.

'Yes,' said Jon.

'Was that it?' asked Matt. We were expecting a little more fanfare than a mumbled aside.

'Yes,' said Jon

'Then let's get out of here before she changes her mind,' I said.

28

In Bed with Rob Brydon

The night *Little Britain* was commissioned for BBC2 I celebrated my birthday in a bar on Shaftsbury Avenue. My girlfriend hobbled in on crutches. She had kicked the wall while we were having an argument over the phone a couple of days before and broken her toe. This was a relationship with constant drama.

Sunday 18/8/200

When I spoke to her this morning she was on her way to the casualty department of her local hospital. During last night's argument she had kicked the wall and had broken a bone in her foot. So I made a cheese, ham and pickle sandwich for her and made my way down to the hospital to care for her. She thought I was coming down to tell her I didn't love her any more, but of course I was there to tell her I loved her more than ever. Nothing can stop this tidal wave of love I have for her.

Every couple of days our relationship would go into meltdown. She would break up with me twice a week, sometimes leaving my flat shouting and screaming at me.

I loved her so much, I was lost. I couldn't get enough of her. Her mind and her body electrified me. Despite her broken toe, this was one of the happy times, though it was not to last.

Before the writing for the TV series of *Little Britain* started, I had to shoot a comedy drama called *Cruise of the Gods*. For a programme that few have seen, it has been written about a great deal. Russell Brand, James Corden and Rob Brydon all devoted chapters to it in their autobiographies. So here is mine.

Steve Coogan and Rob Brydon were the stars. I was a huge fan of Steve Coogan's work. I had been to recordings at the BBC as a fan of *Knowing Me, Knowing You* and *I'm Alan Partridge*, and enjoyed watching him work from afar. To me Steve Coogan is the Peter Sellers of our generation. Like Matt, Steve combines technical brilliance with a real sense of anarchy. Unlike Matt, he liked to drive sports cars, take drugs and shag birds. That gave him an old-fashioned aura of stardom in the mostly unglamorous world of comedy. However, Steve was a mass of contradictions.

Wednesday 12/12/2001

'Do you wanna come back to my hotel suite?' said Steve Coogan.

It was 1.30 a.m. in the Century bar in Soho. The Baby Cow Christmas party was coming to an end. I looked to Graham and Edgar's faces and like mine theirs were filled with excited anticipation. However, the vision I conjured up of cocaine and lap dancers was soon replaced by the dull reality of

Steve Coogan reciting Monty Python records. It was a bit like being trapped by Nigel from accounts.

Rob Brydon I had met briefly in the cafe at the Curzon Soho Cinema with Julia Davis. At the time he was writing *Human Remains* with her. He was very unfriendly that day. I had never seen him do anything on television before, and when I asked him, 'Do you do comedy too?'

'YES!' was his rather hostile reply.

Rob stood there in moody silence as I caught up with Julia, who I had acted with in *Coming Soon*. In fact he made me feel so unwelcome that I had to leave after a few brief exchanges. He seemed jealous of my friendship with her. Little did I know then that Rob would become one of my absolute best friends. Soon after *Marion & Geoff* made him a star, I met him again by chance in a bar on Shaftesbury Avenue in London. Rob was a little drunk and this time happy and relaxed. We were not competing for the attention of Julia Davis, and I joined him for a drink.

'I liked your Tom Jones on *Rock Profile*,' Rob said. This was merely a pretext for him to do his Tom Jones, which was of course infinitely superior.

'You've got to do the cough. Huh! You see the cough. Tom always coughs. HUH!' he continued.

Rob swiftly moved on to his peerless Ronnie Corbett impression. That night neither of us could have known we would soon be sharing a bed on a cruise liner.

The character I played in *Cruise of the Gods* could have been written for me. Jeff 'Lurky' Monks was the head of the fan club of a second-rate sci-fi programme that Steve and Rob's characters had starred in decades before. Mostly I had to lurk behind them in a creepy manner. Amazingly it was Steve himself who had suggested me for the role. Tim Firth (*Calendar Girls*) wrote the script, and Steve and Peter Baynham (one of the *Partridge* writers) did a polish.

'I said to Pete, "How about David Walliams as the super-fan?"' he later told me. 'And Pete said, "Great, he'd be perfect."'

I couldn't believe either of them knew who I was, but even if *Rock Profile* had not been seen by a mass audience, people in the industry had watched it, and I was very occasionally recognized.

Sunday 7/10/2001

6.55 p.m. and back on the train to Manchester to film the BBC1 comedy drama *Ted and Alice*. A big group of drunk hairdressers who'd been taking part in a Toni and Guy competition shrieked their way back north. One of them recognized me.

'You're Elton John's boyfriend!' he squealed.

'Not the real one,' I answered.

He asked for my autograph, and of course I obliged. However, this turned out to be something of a curse because for the rest of the journey all the other hairdressers shouted across the aisle at me.

'Who are you?!'

'Daniel what?'

And best of all, 'Have you ever been in *Emmerdale*?'

And a man who worked in a phone shop gave me pref-
erential treatment . . .

Friday 28/09/2001
Scene: Carphone Warehouse

Me: My screen keeps crashing.
Assistant: I'm afraid that's gonna take at least fourteen days
to repair.
Manager: I can get an engineer downstairs to repair it for
you. Come back in an hour.
Me: Thank you.

I came back and received my phone repaired with
no charge.

Me: I must say this is a great service.
Manager: To be honest I've seen you on *Rock Profile* and I
think it's brilliant.
Me: Thank you.

I left the shop pondering first how even a tiny
morsel of celebrity is well worth having and second
why can't they repair everyone's phone in an hour?

Having auditioned and won the role in *Cruise of the
Gods*, I saw in the *Guardian* a photograph of people queuing up outside the Royal Albert Hall for the last night of
the Proms. One man was quite fat, and wore glasses, a
polo shirt tucked into tight shorts and sandals with socks.
I knew that was what Jeff should look like. The tight

shorts were the key. To have someone lurking behind you in too-tight shorts would be deeply unsettling.

Wednesday 18/09/2002
Entering Soho House for the read-through of *Cruise of the Gods* was pretty daunting. I made some conversation with James Corden and Niall Buggy but was glad when we sat down to read. 'Do we read it out loud?' I quipped before we started. Rob and Steve laughed loudly, and it was their approval I valued most highly as we read. The script read well – I had lots of funny things to say and do.

Thursday 19/09/2002
In the morning I rehearsed *Cruise of the Gods*. I left on a real high, still unable to comprehend

1. That I'm in a show with Steve Coogan.
2. That I'd been making Rob Brydon laugh.
3. That we were filming this in Greece.
4. That I am not struggling at all with the material.

In short I was flying.

Yes, a baby-faced James Corden was in the cast too, as my assistant. Once we'd had the conversation about the Channel 4 boy band spoof that Matt and I had created but been dismissed from which James ended up starring in – not that he was in any way responsible for anything but it was the elephant in the room – we became close friends too. I was totally bowled over by his acting ability.

His character Russell was a more serious role than the others. James played the quiet fan who turned out to be the son of Andy van Allen (Rob Brydon). James had already worked with two giant talents of British cinema, Shane Meadows and Mike Leigh, when I first collaborated with him, and his assurance as an actor showed. As a person he was a lot less assured. On the coach to the cruise ship on which we were filming he passed around photographs of his girlfriend.

'Shelley is really pretty, isn't she? Isn't she?'

I thought it was strange that he needed us to tell him. I thought his size must have made him insecure, and he dearly wanted us all to know that although he was seriously overweight (he was really heavy then) he still had an attractive girlfriend.

A still-using Russell Brand joined the cast in a small role as one of the fans. This is what he wrote about me in *My Booky Wook* . . . 'I didn't like David at first . . . He had a certain charm, but there was inevitably something of a clash between his effete head-boy and my subversive truant.'

I hated him. He talked and talked and never listened. Utter bollocks. In place of true wisdom he relied on the words of others.

'Have you never read Descartes?' he would say.

'No,' I replied.

'Well, Descartes said . . .' Etc., etc., etc.

I doubted he had really read Descartes. It felt like he was spouting the York Notes version of the French philosopher.

There were real people having a holiday on the cruise ship – elderly couples who had no doubt saved up for years to make as many trips to the hot buffet as possible. Eating themselves to death as they celebrated their golden wedding anniversaries. At dinner the arrival of dessert was applauded. The lights were dimmed for 'The March of the Baked Alaskas', and the whole dining room burst into applause. None of these people wanted a film crew getting in the way of their holiday. And they certainly didn't want to see a drugged-up loon like Russell Brand at dinner in trousers hanging so low that you could see his bum cleavage.

One night though I glimpsed his genius. My God could he spin a yarn. When we stopped in Istanbul Russell left the boat alone at the dead of night to look for a prostitute. In a city where you could hear the calls to prayer from the mosques five times a day. Of course it ended in disaster. Russell paid a thousand euros to be threatened by some Arab heavies and then have a deeply frustrating encounter with a tearful girl who spoke no English. However, he told the story as if it was the greatest adventure of his life.

'Then the poor dejected wench, her eyes stung red by her own river of tears, refused to divest herself of her vestments . . .'

Rob, James and I crowded around and listened to this story, and I thought how like Tom Sawyer he was. In Mark Twain's *The Adventures of Tom Sawyer* Tom is made to whitewash a fence but convinces the other boys that it's fun, and they trade marbles, apples and all kind of treasures for the

privilege of doing his work. Russell had that power. However, this escapade, combined with taking drugs onto the
boat – and of course the bum cleavage – meant he was
sent back to London and his part was taken by an extra.
Soon after Russell became sober, we developed a very
close and lasting friendship. I love him.

'I was born when she kissed me. I died when she left me. I
lived a few weeks while she loved me . . .' says Humphrey
Bogart in Nicholas Ray's masterpiece *In a Lonely Place*.

My girlfriend split up with me over the phone a few
days into the trip. Although we didn't live together, she
had keys to my flat and had come in and read my diary
from cover to cover. I had kept one since 1997. In the
years before I had met her I had done some things I was
ashamed of. The night with the BA air hostess was the
first of numerous meaningless encounters. I thought sex
could take away my sadness. However, it just made it
worse. And I sank lower and lower into despair. I had
become a sex addict.

I started seeing a psychotherapist and kept the diary
really as a record of this struggle with my shame. Despite
our problems, I loved this girl so much, beyond anything
I had ever experienced before. Jack Nicholson says to
Helen Hunt in *As Good As it Gets*, 'You make me want to
be a better man.' That's what I felt about her. With her by
my side I thought I could put so much of the unhappiness of the past behind me. She was young, beautiful,
intelligent and, compared to me, innocent. Deep in my
heart I felt her love for me was some sort of redemption.

In my head she took away all my ugliness, shame and despair.

I asked the psychotherapist – the brilliant Bruce Lloyd, who Caroline had recommended – in his office overlooking the Oval cricket ground, 'Should I tell her about my past?'

'No, no, no. That *is* the past. It's dead. You have to move on from that. Maybe one day, if you were getting married. But even then you wouldn't have to. We all have our own shame; that's yours. You need to move on and be happy . . .'

I had taken his advice, but now this girl had found out my secrets for herself. No doubt she had been looking for answers to why I was often so sad. What she read deeply upset her. My past hurt her so much that she could never love me. All the ugliness and shame and despair returned a hundredfold.

The next day the liner docked at the Greek island of Mykonos. I walked to the top of a cliff and looked down at the rocks below. I thought how easy it would be to hurl my body down and be rid of this torment that had blighted so much of my life. This girl had confirmed what I had always thought about myself: that I was a bad person. It seemed liked the inevitable end to my story. I sat on top of the cliff and called my friend Edgar Wright. I didn't tell him I was planning to kill myself, but I talked to him about what had had happened with my now ex-girlfriend. Like most of my friends he hadn't approved of the relation- ship. There had been more unhappiness than happiness in my time with her, and most weeks I was miserable about things having gone wrong between us. Edgar's anger at her gave me some small sense of perspective, and I walked down the cliff back to the ship.

Rob Brydon turned out to be something of a rock. When the liner hit a rock leaving the Greek island of Patmos and we were moved to another ship, the members of the cast were asked to share cabins. Rob and I chose to share with each other. The twin beds were right next to each other.

The maid asked, 'Shall I move the beds apart?'

'It's OK,' I joked.

'Yes, please,' said Rob. The maid moved the beds about an inch apart. The cabin wasn't big enough to move them much further. The best thing was that I wasn't alone; I was with my new best friend. He helped me get through the night. I felt safe with him there.

Friday 18/10/2002

Today we boarded the *Olympic Explorer*, the sister ship of the *Voyager*. Because of a shortage of room, Rob and I are now sharing a cabin.

I instantly loved sharing with Rob. And so relieved he was there. I couldn't face being alone at the moment, with everything that's happened. It took me back to being about ten and having a friend to stay over. And in that tradition we put the light out and talked into the early hours with the constant preface 'Are you still awake?'

Rob had recently gone through an agonizing divorce

and was struggling with the pain of no longer living under the same roof as his three young children. We were completely and utterly honest with each other. I told him everything about my past, and we tried to help each other as much as we could. However, we laughed together too. I couldn't sleep, so when he got up in the night to pee, as older men have to, I would wait until I could hear the water being passed into the bowl and moan, 'Oooh, my Rob.'

That never failed to give us both hysterics.

As the last drops tinkled out I would sigh, 'Oooooooohhhhhh.'

Like some of the best jokes, you're not sure why they are funny, but you laugh anyway. Other times we behaved like an old married couple and I would bring him a gin and tonic while he was in the bath. Yes, I have seen Rob Bryden's penis.

When you hate yourself as I did, playing someone else can be an escape. So I put all my energies into my work and delivered a strong performance. Certainly one that impressed the master, Steve Coogan, whose company was producing the programme.

Wednesday 23/10/2002

'Steve's been saying nice things about you,' said Caroline Hickman, Steve's fianceé.

'Oh yes?'

'Yes, I heard him talking to Henry Normal. He said he'd been writing up your part because you were so good.'

As if that wasn't good enough, Steve approached me in the make-up room.

'I just watched the scene you did with James where you were running down the corridor,' he said. 'Very funny, very detailed.'

I shrugged it off, but inside I was dancing.

Later I was shooting a scene with Rob and Steve, and thought, *Can work get any better than this?*

After dinner the talk turned to the new *Partridge* series. Steve has acted out so much of it on this trip I now think I have seen most of it.

'You should have been in *Partridge*,' he said to me.

'I love acting. I love being someone else,' I told Niall Buggy, a member of the cast. Niall was much older, more experienced and ultimately a hugely superior actor to me. What's more, he had worked with many theatrical legends.

'The best actors reveal something of themselves when they act,' he said.

I hadn't thought of that. Playing comedy characters is so often about externalizing something, demonstrating the absurdities of other people. However, I never forgot what Niall said, even though I wasn't ready to reveal anything intimate about myself on stage or film any time soon.

Being away filming was like being in a bubble. I was never alone, and there were constantly new experiences to savour: sailing into Venice as dawn rose, visiting the Acropolis in Athens, travelling to the top of the island of Santorini on donkeys . . .

So when I finally returned home the reality of what had happened finally hit me.

29
4.48 a.m.

It was impossible to sleep. Anxiety stopped me from falling asleep; depression woke me up. The recurring nightmare of being smothered in my own bed visited me over and over again. Every night I could feel myself being pushed into the pillow, my breathing stopping. Every night I told myself it was a dream, but this was a nightmare in which I was lying in bed awake. It terrified me.

In my diary at the time I wrote, 'I dreamt that I was lying awake in my bed and someone was pushing me hard into the pillow. It really felt like someone was there. I can understand why people believe they've seen a ghost; I've felt one. Then I saw a big python squeezing the life out of me and that's when I woke up. My nightmares always follow the same pattern: lying there frozen with terror and powerless because I don't know that I'm asleep.'

At 4 a.m. I would wake in a cold sweat. Sarah Kane's last completed play before she committed suicide was *4.48 Psychosis*, the time she frequently woke up in her depressed state. Many people who suffer from depression confirm early morning is the worst time. At 4 a.m. you are totally alone. There is no one to call. Your friends or family tell you, 'Call me any time,' but at 4 a.m. you don't feel you can. It's dark outside; there isn't even the sound of the birds to keep you company. So I would lie there until the curtain edges grew light and the room took shape. It was not just the terrible elemental sadness I felt, but fear. Fear of death, fear of life, fear of love, fear of everything. This went on for six months. My diary entries at the time make for bleak reading.

Sunday 17/11/2002
The day started with me walking down to Primrose Hill planning my own death. *If only I could get my hands on a gun*, I thought. Not enough pills in my house, I don't have a car so I can't do the exhaust/hosepipe thing – thinking about that, I don't have a hosepipe, and my oven is electric.

Monday 18/11/2002
Today the stone in my heart turned into a rock.

I was back at Shepperton filming scenes for *Cruise of the Gods* we had lost through the boat running aground. News reached me that my ex-girlfriend had a new boyfriend. The tears started. I went outside. Suddenly the crying was uncontrollable. I stood out in the car park, bent double with grief. I crawled back to my dressing room and lay on the floor, sobbing. I thought this was it. I would never stop crying. I would never be able to get up. What I had been thinking had been confirmed. I had ruined my life. Because of what had happened to me and what I'd done, the girl I loved had rejected me. I could never love again. I was unlovable. How could I ever love anyone again, when I had to carry around this poison inside me? How could I give that to anyone else and break their heart just like I had broken hers?

I had never experienced this level of pain or emotion before. It was terrifying. I was shaking. It was like I was having a nervous breakdown or going mad or both.

Tuesday 19/11/2002

This was a day I'd never thought I'd see. Tuesday the 19th of November came as a complete surprise. Last night I genuinely could not envisage surviving until the morning. But here it was, cold and dark but a new day nonetheless. A new life started today. It was back to Shepperton, and the vague embarrassment of acknowledging the faces of all those people who had seen or heard me cry or at least heard about it smile at me in that supportive way. I swear my eyes were still bloodshot from crying. My face couldn't hide what had happened. In my dressing room James Corden had left a present of a Peter Kay live DVD. He had heard me crying yesterday and wrote a note saying he hoped this might cheer me up. What a wonderful friend he is.

Thursday 28/11/2002

My life is a living death. Yes, I wrote *Little Britain* with Matt, yes, I went to the gym and yes, I went to Hampstead in the evening to see Graham Linehan, but I wasn't there. All I could think about was how I wanted to die. If she can't love me then I don't want to live. What has surprised me is this impulse to destroy myself hasn't mellowed at all as the days have passed. It's really scary. I can't trust myself to be on my own. Back in my flat, I lay in bed and watched the hours go by on my clock, thinking how many sleeping pills I have in my house.

Saturday 21/12/2002

I couldn't get out of bed. Then when I did I sat with porridge and cried and cried unable to cope with the pain. I silently screamed then looked out the window to David's Baddiel's house and thought tonight I will go into his living room and hang myself from his roof supports. I had to be serious this time. Really to do it. Edgar was having a party later. I could say goodbye to everyone there.

'I won't see you in a while,' I could say. All I needed was some rope.

Wednesday 25/12/2002

It's Christmas Day. I am lying in bed in my sister's old room at my parents' house and I am weeping. I had been close to tears all day. In the cab on the way over this morning I wanted to turn back, thinking I couldn't face my family while I am in this state. When my mum sat next to me on the sofa to show me some photographs she had given Nanny of the family I could feel the tears welling up. I'm crying now. As quietly as I can. Because I can't begin to tell my parents what's wrong. Because everything is wrong.

Monday 30/12/2002

4.30 a.m. was when I woke up this morning. Forty minutes later than yesterday. That still left me hours and hours to stare into the abyss until daylight came. Matt came round at 10 a.m. and we got straight to work. Thank God for work. It is a momentary escape from this nightmare.

I became obsessed with the Nick Cave album *The Boatman's Call* and listened to it every night. It was so full of sadness and longing, and every song seemed to help define what I was feeling, especially the opening track on the album, 'Into My Arms'. I chose it for one of my Desert Island Discs years later. Never has a song been so full of longing . . .

> Into my arms, O Lord
> Into my arms, O Lord
> Into my arms, O Lord
> Into my arms
> And I don't believe in the existence of angels
> But looking at you I wonder if that's true

Night after night with no sleep. I was so tired during the days they were like a walking death. Round and round in my head spun the same thought: *I can't change the past. The past means she can never love me. I can't change the past. The past means she can never love me. I can't change the past . . .*

After a while those close to me realized something.

I was going mad.

Suicide was all I thought about. I needed an end to the pain.

Somehow I got through some additional work Matt and I had taken on to pay the bills before *Little Britain* was filmed. I sleepwalked my way through some unfunny performances on the yoof TV series *Born Sloppy*, quite possibly the worst Channel 4 programme ever produced. Once again we reprised *Rock Profile* with some new characters, though somehow it seemed like the law of diminishing returns was operating. Matt's brilliance as a performer dragged us through it, but I was barely able to crack a smile let alone raise one.

Wednesday 1/1/2003

I slept a few hours and then stayed in bed hiding from the world. When I did get up I started crying uncontrollably and had to lie on my sofa.

'I can't handle this I can't handle this I can't handle this,' I kept saying to myself.

I looked at the sleeping pills again, thought about writing, 'When the person you love rejects you for what you are, how can you go on?' on a piece of paper and leaving it in a prominent position but didn't. Then I ran a bath, took out the longest sharpest knife from the kitchen drawer, and lowered myself into the water. I ran the knife along my wrists and throat, just drawing blood. The determination wasn't there. But the pain is too much to live with. Wanting to die has always been in me. At the moment it's winning. No one need take the blame if it beats me tonight or tomorrow or the next day.

Monday 10/2/2003

It's 4.46 a.m. on Tuesday morning and I could not be more awake. I have given up trying to sleep and am sitting on my sofa in my pyjamas cold from sweat.

Wednesday 19/2/2003

The end of the story is this, me hanging from the rafters.

The torment was unbearable today. I wasn't working. I lay on my bed and cried and cried and started to think about my dead body hanging there and thought this is why I don't like being emotional. I kept on thinking is it today that I die? Why not now?

Friday 28/2/2003

Torment. Despair. Pain. In alone, writing *Little Britain*. I cried in the morning. Then again at lunchtime. My body buckled in my kitchen. It was frightening. I thought will I ever come out of this? Is this the moment I don't come back from? When the grief overcomes me and I finally surrender to it and find refuge in madness.

During a yoga class later I started composing suicide notes in my head and imagined myself dead hanging from the door with my belt around my neck.

My friend Mark Morriss came over in the evening. He played me his new Bluetones album, which on first listen sounded very strong, and told me about how his stepdad used to be violent towards him and his mum.

'Sometimes I think the pain of life is unbearable,'
I said.

One night, after seeing *Catch Me If You Can* with Edgar
Wright near his home in Islington, I let my feet stray near
the edge of the Tube platform. As the train thundered
out of the tunnel I thought about how easy it would be to
step in front of it. I imagined my body bouncing off the
front of the train, then torn into a bloody mess on the
tracks. It was horrifying. I stepped back just as the warm
wind of the train whooshed past me.

Saturday 1/3/2003

11.30 p.m. Just tried to hang myself. From the door
of my living room with my belt. Hung there for
about a minute in the dark. Wrote a suicide note first:
'To everyone who loves me, I can't bear the pain
any more. I can't get through another day or another
night. I am so sorry. David.'
I stared at the dark stained wood of the door as
the belt tightened around my neck and my head
started to buzz with pain. But I knew I didn't really
want to die, I just didn't want to live. I took my weight
again with my feet and sat down on the floor. Earlier
I had come close to stepping in front of a train. I am
in total despair.

That night I realized I needed some serious help. Going
to see a psychotherapist once or twice a week was not
enough. Bruce Lloyd suggested going to the Priory.

Monday 3/3/2003

'The torment is making you mad,' said Bruce after I told him what had happened. 'That combined with the fatigue is preventing you from getting better. You need more help than I can give. You need to go to a hospital.'

The Priory is a psychiatric hospital in Roehampton just outside London which became as famous as some of the people it treated for depression or addiction. If I stayed there for a while I would be safe from trying to kill myself, as if you are on suicide watch you are checked all through the night. There I would also be given medication to alleviate my depression and perhaps more importantly to help me sleep. Sleep. Something I had not experienced properly for nearly a year. Caroline Aherne once said to me, 'I think depression is mainly caused by a lack of sleep. If you can't sleep at night you're going to be in a very down mood all day, and if you're in a very down mood all day you can't sleep at night . . .'

Most of the symptoms of depression support this. Tiredness, being unable to concentrate, losing your appetite. So both the depression and the insomnia have to be treated. I had hoped I could think my way out of depression with Bruce's help. I was wrong. As I couldn't sleep, I couldn't think straight. I was obsessing about the past and deeply anxious about the future. As a result I was unable to live in the present, and all those simple things that bring me pleasure, such as a nice meal, seeing friends or writing comedy, became joyless.

However, you can't just turn up at the Priory even if you are suicidal – you have to be referred by a doctor or psychotherapist and they need to have a bed for you.

Another nightmarish week passed.

Tuesday 11/3/2003

4 a.m. and the fear is on me. If hell is in your mind then I have been to hell.

At any moment I knew I might get the call from Bruce telling me they had a place for me. The call finally came on Friday. Matt and I were at the BBC filming a sketch for Comic Relief, a spoof of *Blankety Blank* that Peter Serafinowicz had written showcasing his astonishing impersonation of Terry Wogan. Matt and I were cast opposite each other as *Hi-de-Hi!* cast members Su Pollard and Ruth Madoc respectively. The cast was uniformly brilliant. Simon Pegg was an anarchic Hitler-obsessed Freddie Starr, Nick Frost an incomprehensible Willie Rushton, but I was dismally unfunny. And painfully thin too. I was down to twelve and a half stone, which for someone six foot three inches tall is underweight.

After filming the sketch, Matt and I went to Myfanwy Moore's office at the BBC for a meeting about the forthcoming filming of *Little Britain*, which was now only weeks away. There I finally received the call, and stepped outside the room to take it.

'David?'

'Hi, Bruce.'

'I've got you a place.'

'Oh thank you so much.'

'And most importantly you'll be under the care of Dr Mark Collins. He's the best man there.'

'Thank you.'

'Pack your bag and get there as soon as you can. Dr Collins will come round and see you tonight. Good luck, David. Call me if you need anything.'

'Thank you. I will.'

So I had an announcement to make. Despite Matt and I being in the last stages of writing a series that could change our lives for ever, I needed time off. Maybe weeks. Maybe months.

I ended the call and stepped back into the office. Trembling, I turned to face Matt and Myf.

'As I'm sure you both know, I'm not well, and haven't been well for quite a while. I need to go away and try and get better. The psychotherapist I've been seeing has secured me a place at the Priory and am going there tonight . . .'

Matt mumbled something about his own problems, but Myf was more sympathetic. 'Oh, you poor thing. Yes, Lovely,' she said. Myf often called you Lovely, which made you feel a little bit lovely. 'Of course. You should go. Let us know if you need anything and let me know when you feel ready to return to work.'

So I boarded a train packed with commuters at Waterloo, got off at Barnes and walked to the Priory . . .

30

'Don't fall in love here'

In 2003 the Priory's fame had not reached epic proportions. It was just somewhere people went when they were
fed up with life but didn't want to die. I knew I was edg-
ing closer and closer to killing myself, but ultimately I
knew that would not be the end of my story. An actress
friend from *Attachments*, Sally Rogers, said to me, 'You're
a nice middle class boy who wants to get his homework
in on time. You know you mustn't kill yourself.'

I wouldn't have gone to the Priory if I wasn't bothered
about my homework, this being the scripts to the first
series of *Little Britain*.

'Hello, I'm Dr Collins, but you can call me Mark,' said
a portly man with a kind voice. To my relief he wasn't
dressed in a long white gown. I was sitting on my bed in
a room at the hospital, an old country house with acres
of grounds set behind high walls. It wasn't nice though;
it's a psychiatric hospital. 'Bruce has told me a little bit
about what has brought you here. But I thought you
might like to tell me in your own words . . .'

I did, and when I finished he said, 'Don't fall in love
here.'

'What do you mean?'

'Well lots of vulnerable people come here and they start relationships. It's not a good idea. You would be replacing one dependency with another.'

He prescribed me some antidepressants and I was given some pills to help me sleep. When I put my head on the pillow in the gloomy pictureless room, my mind still raced, fighting the pills as much as it could. Every hour or so the night nurse came in to check I hadn't tried to hang myself with my shoelaces.

I had arrived on a Friday night, and there wasn't much happening over the weekend – many of the patients went home on Saturday – so the following morning I trundled around the largely empty building alone. Rob Brydon lived nearby in Richmond and invited me out for lunch and to play football with his three lovely children in the park. In the dining room that night there were just two others: a young woman with only one arm and a man who looked so ill with depression that his skin was grey. Being among other depressed people gave me perspective. I immediately felt better off than either of them. When it filled back up on Sunday night, I realized I was worse off than some. There were people who had had nervous breakdowns at work and were still there two months later, funded by their company's health insurance. Which is why the Priory is regarded by many as some kind of holiday camp. Who wouldn't want a few months away from the stresses of their life?

I didn't tell my mum and dad I was there. Not only did I not want my mum to worry – she was always such a worrier – at the time I couldn't find the words to tell them why I felt this way. My sister Julie spotted that I didn't come on and take a bow with the rest of the cast that night live on television after the *Blankety Blank* sketch played out on Comic Relief. She came to visit me, which was very kind, and relayed to our parents where I was but that I was all right.

The days at the Priory were scheduled not unlike school, with classes designed to put you in touch with your feelings, such as art and dance therapy. Comedians tend to be natural cynics, so I was not able throw myself into these activities with the same abandon as others. There were group therapy sessions where I witnessed the scale of other people's madness. A dozen of us had to sit on chairs in a circle, and at the start of the session the therapist prompted us all to say our name and how we were feeling today.

'Hello, my name is David, and I'm feeling down today.'

'Hi, I'm Chris, and I'm feeling a bit more positive than yesterday.'

Round the circle we went, until it was the turn of a small wiry-looking lady in her fifties.

'Someone came up to me and touched me in the dinner queue today and I have said a million times before I cannot abide being touched so I thought I would complain to the staff nurse so I went all the way up the stairs but she was not at her station so I went back down again . . .'

On and on she went. It was as if she was never going to stop.

'. . . but who did I see only Geoffrey well Geoffrey is a

nuisance at the best of times then lo and behold as he is talking to me his elbow brushes past me well that was the final straw –'

The therapist tried to butt in: 'Thank you.'

'– and then I discover that the tomato soup is cream of tomato not just plain tomato and of course they didn't say that not that I am allergic to dairy but it does not agree with me one bit just ask my sister –'

'THANK YOU!'

'– she herself is a slave to her bowels but then I enquired about badminton lessons . . .'

I glanced around the room looking for someone to share a smile with. This lady was quite mad. It was tragic but also funny. Critics of comedy always want to erroneously divide up the tragic and the comic into two distinct lists. That way they can have a roll of subjects they deem unsuitable for comedy, be it Derek and Clive shouting, 'I've got fucking cancer!' or Chris Morris making a *Brass Eye* special about the media's reaction to paedophilia. But life can be tragic and funny at the same time.

I didn't fall in love at the Priory even though there were one or two beautiful and emotionally damaged girls there who I became strongly attracted to; I took Dr Collins' advice and stayed away from them.

One night at dinner I asked the man whose skin was grey to join a group of us on a table. He was wearing his pyjamas and dressing gown. I couldn't bear to see him sitting alone in the big room.

'Thank you so much,' he replied with tears in his eyes. 'That is so so kind of you.'

The man was so moved by this simple act that I wanted to cry too. Depression seemed to have utterly destroyed him. Most of the time we never saw him. Most likely he didn't have the energy to go to the classes. Instead he would lie on his bed day in, day out. His room was next to mine, and I would pass it and see his grey feet at the end of the bed if the door was open. Just thinking about him now makes me want to cry.

The most useful sessions at the Priory were with Dr Collins. I saw him daily. A fresh pair of ears and eyes was very helpful, and every day he would tinker with my medication, which I collected from the on-site pharmacy instantly. That way he could ensure that the sleeping pills could help me sleep without making me into a zombie for the rest of the day. And the antidepressants started working. It wasn't that they made me feel happy; the feeling was more akin to being able to shrug off the bad thoughts. Soon my brain wasn't repeating and repeating and repeating the same thought with quite so much frequency.

I can't change the past. The past means she can never love me. I can't change the past. The past means she can never love me. I can't change the past . . .

Without health insurance I couldn't afford to stay long, and when a week was up I left with a paper bag full of antidepressants and sleeping pills and a follow-up appointment to see Dr Collins. My knight in shining armour Rob Brydon picked me up from the hospital, much like his minicab driver character Keith Barrett in *Marion & Geoff*. His fiancée (now wife) Claire Holland cooked us all a lovely meal (she even does a starter), and

I took my pills and went to sleep in one of the children's bedrooms under a Spiderman duvet. Rob really is the best friend I could ever have hoped for. Naturally caring, brilliantly funny, and having suffered unhappiness himself, he could really help me through an incredibly difficult time. I will always love him. Even if he has more hair now than he did then.

My parents found the whole thing baffling. A psychiatric hospital? Dad assumed that after my stay in the Priory I was now free of depression.

'So you're feeling fine now?' he said.

It was easier to say yes so I did.

Now I had to go back to work. Matt and *Little Britain* were waiting.

31

'Yeah, I know'

Some days I just couldn't wake up. The sleeping pills needed to be so strong I slept through my alarm. A few times Matt woke me up knocking on the door of my flat. For someone who had valued punctuality from a very young age I was deeply disappointed in myself for not being ready for work in the morning. At home my father had two clocks in the kitchen, one of which was visible from the hall. That was set seven minutes fast, so he could shout at us children for making him late for his train to work, even though we hadn't. Even after my father died in 2007 my mother still might turn up forty minutes early for something. Timekeeping was drilled into us all so much.

My mind was dulled by all the sleeping pills, and the shrug-it-off feeling that the antidepressants induced affected everything, not just the negative thoughts. Therefore it was hard for me to feel that enthusiastic about the writing. Fortunately we had already done a great deal of good work, and soon we would be filming.

The League of Gentlemen's Mark Gatiss was our script editor. Matt and I admired his work greatly, and we trusted his instincts implicitly. Mark often had great ideas too. For example he suggested killing Mollie Sugden at the end of the sketches about a woman who claimed to be her brides-maid. Another one he virtually wrote for us off the top of his head was the one-off in which a lady goes into a charity shop and asks if anyone had died in the clothes she's buy-ing, then chooses a pair of pyjamas a man had definitely died in. It wouldn't have been out of place in the League's TV series. One morning we read through a sketch Matt and I had great faith in that in the end only made it as a deleted scene on our DVD. This involved a cure for can-cer being found at the offices of Cancer Research and everyone who worked there being disappointed. Just after we read it Mark received a call from his sister.

'My mother has just been diagnosed with cancer,' he told us.

'Oh my God, I am so sorry,' I said.

Matt and I instantly felt distinctly uncomfortable that we had been trying to make people laugh about the dis-ease that was soon to take his mother's life.

'The sketch must stay,' said Mark. The mark of a true comedian. He believed that you should be able to joke about anything. I so respected him for that.

Mark encouraged us to be as edgy as possible. At the time we had no idea that *Little Britain* would one day be on BBC1 and watched by ten million people. The first series was made for BBC3, with a repeat on BBC2. How-ever, as Matt and I moved into darker territory, egged on by Mark, there was a voice of caution. Myfanwy Moore.

In the early days of BBC3 Ralf Little (Anthony from *The Royle Family*) was so popular he had his own chat show. Matt and I were asked to do some *Rock Profile* sketches based on the MTV series *Cribs*, in which stars showed you around their homes. The best of these sketches was one in which Lou Reed's lodger was Andy Warhol. I performed Lou Reed with the lisp I had used for the cockney film star in *Spoofovision*, really only because they had the same look. It was an in-joke that only Matt and I understood, but we enjoyed it so we left it in. Matt's years of working with Reeves and Mortimer had made him trust his subconscious imagination, so with his encouragement I wasn't too frightened of committing to something unexplained or unexplainable. I generally preferred to be more logical, but I couldn't do an impression of Lou Reed even if anyone wanted to hear one, so I was pleased to go along with the idea.

Matt had the most magnificent take on Andy Warhol. He was a scouser, appeared to be not all there and said little more than 'Yeah, I know.' We wrote some dialogue that amused us both greatly:

'What do you want for your tea?' I asked as Lou.

'Chips,' Matt replied as Andy.

'Well you're having chips for your lunch.'

'Yeah, I know.'

'You can't have chips for your lunch and your tea.'

'Yeah, I know.'

'So what do you want for your tea?'

'Chips.'

So it went on. The relationship between the characters was one we instantly felt we wanted to pursue. Obviously we didn't want to pursue a spoof, albeit a bizarre one, in *Little Britain*. Neither Lou Reed nor Andy Warhol (who died in 1987) fitted into a series depicting life in contemporary Britain. But we kept the first names and the relationship of carer with someone who needed care. In the script read-through sessions we started improvising the characters and realized there were many situations where we could use them. But even though we had a strong idea of how they should look and sound we still didn't really know who they were. Brothers? Father and son? Nurse and patient?

'Matt's character should be in a wheelchair!' I announced.

It was such a shocking idea, almost everyone laughed. But I could see out of the corner of my eye that Myfanwy Moore was not amused.

'We can't have an able-bodied actor play someone in a wheelchair,' she said. As an employee of the BBC Myf knew there were taste and decency guidelines that had to be adhered to.

'What about Daniel Day-Lewis in *My Left Foot*?' I asked unhelpfully.

'That's totally different,' she replied.

There was silence for a while, as the idea of having Andy in a wheelchair that Lou had to push drifted off into the universe, never to be seen again.

'What if he doesn't need the wheelchair?' said Myf. 'He isn't really disabled.'

At first nobody was convinced. Groucho Marx once told a reporter, 'All comedy comes from pain. To illustrate, consider this . . . You can take a young man and dress him up as an old woman. Put him in a wheelchair.

Push him down a hill where he runs into a brick wall. That's funny. But you take a *real* old lady, put her in a wheelchair, push her down the same hill into the same brick wall . . . and *that's* comedy.'

As comedians we wanted to be as hard-edged as possible.

'It's a bit of a cop-out,' said Mark.

'It could be funny though,' said Myf. 'Matt could get out of the wheelchair behind your back.'

'In a kind of "He's behind you" at the panto kind of way?' I asked.

'Yes,' said Myf.

So we started thinking up scenarios in which we could do this joke. The more we thought about it, the funnier it became. The most elaborate idea was where Matt ran up to the top of a diving board tower and jumped off. In an effort not to offend BBC licence payers, Myf had given us the germ of our most famous sketch ever.*

Steve Bendelack was the director of all *The League of Gentlemen* TV series and had directed me in the forgotten Dawn French and Stephen Tompkinson BBC1 comedy drama *Ted and Alice*. Some directors are craftsmen, others are artists. Steve is an artist. He encouraged Matt and me to think visually about the series. We had developed a sense of costume and make-up. Our favourite game was sitting on the top deck of a bus travelling through London and pointing out people who we deemed to have 'the

---

* It was voted the best comedy sketch of all time by viewers of Channel 4 in 2005.

look'. This meant they looked more like a comedy character than a real person. However, neither of us had any sense of an overall aesthetic for our work.

Steve Bendelack – Bendybum, as Caroline Aherne called him – had given *The League of Gentlemen* such a unique look and feel, it was arguably the most distinctive sketch show series since *Monty Python's Flying Circus* thirty years before. Steve wanted to make *Little Britain* different from *The League of Gentlemen* and so did we. We really needed it to be as different as possible as our concept was similar to theirs. It was wise for us to avoid comparison with an established and brilliant series.

Martin Parr is a visionary British photographer who had recently had a retrospective exhibition at the Barbican. In his photographs Martin Parr celebrates the mundane. He makes his subjects, such as a group of poor holidaymakers on a litter-strewn beach, look somehow iconic. Through his lens the ordinary becomes extraordinary. We wanted our characters, however ugly or grotesque, to be iconic too. Neil Tennant once told me that the mark of a great pop band was 'if you could draw cartoons of all the members and recognize them. The Beatles, the Spice Girls, Blur. Look at Julian Opie's cover for Blur's greatest hits.'

That set me thinking that our characters should be as instantly recognizable as cartoon characters. Think of the colour-themed costumes – Vicky Pollard was never out of pink whether it was a tracksuit top or a bikini. The make-up reflected this too: each character's look had to be markedly different from the rest. However, much of

Little Britain was set in the real world, so the characters needed to sit within a recognizable reality. Martin Parr held his camera back most of the time, documenting people who were larger than life.

'That's what I'll do,' said Steve over dinner just before we started shooting. 'Hold the camera back. Observe.'

There was still the difficult question of the title sequence. These can be really difficult to get right. How do you define a new show in the first thirty seconds and grab the audience's attention? For the pilot we used some stock footage, having neither the time nor the money to shoot something original.

Many Martin Parr photographs depict people standing awkwardly outside their home or car, and his work dominated conversation that evening.

'We could have still portraits,' said Steve.

'People and places,' I said.

'What?' said Matt.

'That's what *Little Britain* is about – people and places.'

'So have Marjorie outside the community centre?' he asked.

'Yes, and Sebastian outside Number 10 Downing Street and —'

'And I can shoot it all on 35-mil film!' said Steve. 'I can shoot it fast and then slow it down afterwards . . .'

Suddenly it felt like we really had a show. We had defined *Little Britain*. Now all we had to do was film it.

Just before we started I went out on a date. Louisa McCarthy, a great friend from National Youth Theatre days, set me up with one of her friends who I had fancied for years. However, I just wasn't ready to go near another woman for the foreseeable future. I couldn't even try and kiss her, I was so terrified of rejection. A kiss was impossible. And love was unthinkable.

All I had was work. That's all I had to live for. So I threw myself into it. Having a comedy series on BBC2 was my dream. Most of the series that I had loved – *Not the Nine O'Clock News*, *The Young Ones*, *The Day Today*, *The Smell of Reeves & Mortimer*, *I'm Alan Partridge* – had been on the channel. It was where comedy fans traditionally went to see the programmes they would love but not everyone would like. Up to this point pretty much everything I had done on television had felt disposable. The odd episode of *Rock Profile* was good, but a spoof of anything is limited. Now we had a chance to create a proper legacy for ourselves.

The first *Little Britain* sketch for the series we shot was the one in which Emily has to go to hospital to have an X-ray. I was pleased this one had me in the funny role. I was often (and probably still am) perceived as Matt's sidekick. He had proved himself to be supremely funny in *Shooting Stars*, and most people didn't see me as his equal. I don't either, and never will. That doesn't bother me. To me Matt is one of the all-time greats, and will one day take his place alongside the likes of Ronnie Barker, John Cleese and Rowan Atkinson. But since I had been struck down by depression I was not feeling funny. On the *South Bank Show* Barry Humphries said, 'You have to feel funny to be funny,' and I was feeling desperately sad.

However, on that first morning the crew very duti-
fully laughed. The quasi-French pronunciation of 'testicle'
seemed to resonate with people, and we were off. The shoot
was done on a very tight budget, so much so that neither
Matt nor I had anywhere to change. It's quite normal on a
TV programme for the actors to have small (or if they are
stars, large) trailers to get dressed or wait or learn their lines
in, but we needed every penny to be seen on screen.

Soon into the shoot though something absolutely
disastrous happened. We very nearly became the series
famous for killing two old ladies . . .

Tuesday 6/5/2003
Evie Garrett, the lady who plays Nan, launched herself so hard at the lady playing her sister, when she
kissed her they fell over and had to be taken to hospital. And all because I'd written a lesbian love scene
for them. I felt so responsible.

The relationship between Matt and myself was mostly
harmonious, but at times became strained.

Tuesday 13/5/2003
Today I got angry. I hate being angry. Me and Matt
were being filmed for the behind-the-scenes documentary and he did what I always knew he would do,
claimed to have come up with ideas he hadn't.

'I don't know if you remember, David,' he said,
'this person at the National Youth Theatre called
Shadwell . . .'

He was the basis for Daffyd. Of course I remembered. I came up with the idea. Matt didn't even believe in it at first. I was upset and took him into a corridor.

'I honestly don't remember who came up with it,' he protested.

'If I said I'd invented Vicky Pollard or Marjorie Dawes you'd be rightfully pissed off.'

We agreed to use 'we' from now on.

Again it was ultimately a constructive falling-out, but by pure chance the next day I received some terrible news from my *Attachments* co-star Sally Rogers.

Wednesday 14/5/2003
'I've got something to tell you,' said Sally on the phone. 'Shadwell killed himself a couple of weeks ago.'

'What?'

'Of course his real name was Paul. Apparently he did it in the manner of Virginia Woolf – walked into a river with stones in his pockets. I thought you should know.'

I couldn't believe what I was hearing. It made me desperately sad that another person I knew had lost their battle with depression.

Lisa Cavelli-Greene, our make-up designer on *Little Britain*, had spent years at Thames Television, and had worked with many of the great British comedians of the twentieth century, most notably Morecambe and Wise and Benny Hill. Sometimes she would give one of us a wig to wear that had a little name-tag inside reading 'E. Morecambe' or 'B. Hill'. It was strange wearing a legendary comedian's wig and made me try as hard as I could to be funny so as to honour their hairpiece! It was magical thinking there is a mystery to being funny. The greatest comedians of all time can turn in an unfunny performance. Someone can be hilarious for years and then one day simply not be funny ever again. You can have a standing ovation one night and be booed off the next.

As soon as the location filming was over we went into rehearsals for our studio recordings. This was some of the best material: the Sebastian scenes for example were filmed in front of a studio audience. Tony Head came back from the pilot to reprise his role as the prime minister. He was such a joy to work with. He played everything so straight, and kept so still as I flounced around him as Sebastian.

Sebastian was probably the character I felt I inhabited the most successfully. It was not hard for me to portray someone who was consumed with unrequited love. Playing him, I realized the best comedy characters had an emotional truth. Lou Todd, the long-suffering carer, had it too. Others I realized existed much more on the surface, such as the Scottish hotelier Ray McCooney or rubbish transvestite Emily Howard. When we toured from 2005 to 2007, completing over 250 performances to a million people, I tired of playing these characters much sooner.

The last night of recording in front of the audience was in fact the Sebastian scenes.

Wednesday 16/7/2003

We went out on a high with the 10 Downing
Street sketches. At last I felt totally at home in front
of the audience in complete control of what I
was doing. Mum, Dad and Julie were in, and I was so
pleased they were for me so on form.

I hated it when we wrapped though. I am so scared
of being without work to distract me from my thoughts.
Filming this series has proved to be such an anchor.

The very last sketch of the first series we recorded was
the one featuring the Italian prime minister and his translator. It was one of my favourite sketches and ended with
neither of us on screen. When Sebastian flounces off in a
huff the translator turns to the British PM and says, 'The
Prime Minister says if you love him, go after him . . .'

It brought the house down. My parents were in that
night, and Steve Bendelack asked my dad, 'Did you enjoy it?'

'Well you can't laugh at everything,' was his reply. Once
again, my father couldn't say anything nice.

Already moving in show-business circles, Matt had
met Patsy Kensit, and she came to one of the *Little Britain*
recordings. The first thing that hit me about her was not
so much her beauty, but her smell. She smelt lovely. Of
course she had been the fantasy of me and many other
boys my age in the 1980s, when she found fame in *Absolute Beginners* and with the band Eighth Wonder, and Robin
and I had seen her mime on *Top of the Pops*. Now she was
in our green room at the BBC and she flirted with me.
Patsy Kensit flirted with me.

'David, that was amazing. You are both so funny. I loved it tonight. I really did,' she said, flicking her famous blonde bob away from her face. As she was now the ex-wife of three rock stars I was more perplexed than flattered and, still hurting from the events of the last year, I did not flirt back.

On Thursday 10 July I wrote in my diary, 'In exactly a week I will be finished shooting *LB* and I am very scared of all that free time that is stretching out before me like a desert.'

As it happened I kept myself busy, and, unwilling to have a day off, went straight into developing a series with Rob Brydon called *Home*. A sitcom about two brothers running an old people's home, we imagined Ronnie Corbett as the only male resident, a kind of octogenarian lothario. Sadly our busy work schedules mean we have still not made the show. Perhaps one day we will.

When I wasn't busy, thoughts of suicide still haunted me. I now had a cache of sleeping pills. Whether I had enough to kill myself I didn't know, but I spent a long time obsessing about it. As well as the depressive behaviour, I was often manic. The manic and the depressive went hand in hand for me. I disgraced myself and amused everybody at Simon Pegg's engagement party.

Friday 17/10/2003
In the evening I went out to Simon and Maureen's party. My friend Mark Morriss from the Bluetones was DJing and put on 'Relax' by Frankie Goes to Hollywood. I was dancing with Julia Davis and to

amuse her on the word come, I pretended to come over her. I did it again and realized everyone (including Julia) had stopped dancing and was crowded around clapping as if I were a champion dancer. I started improvising a routine, coming over different people around the room. I could hear the end coming and needed a finale. Fortunately Simon's friend Claire, who is in a wheelchair, was watching, and as the song reached a crescendo I pretended to come all over her as she played very gamely along. The crowd applauded. I was relieved it was over and realized I was totally out of control. Graham Linehan said afterwards, 'That's the funniest thing I've ever seen in my life.'

On 20 August 2003 I celebrated my thirty-second birthday. My neighbour and friend the comedian David Baddiel let me host it in his garden, as I lived in a tiny flat. The night before I wrote in my diary, 'Tomorrow night I am having a birthday party. I have been thinking about saying goodbye to everyone and going back to my flat to sleep for ever. The selfishness of it disturbs me. How much pain it would cause my mum and dad? Maybe an "accident" would be better.'

The night after the party I wrote, 'I didn't take an overdose. I won't kill myself today. Like an alcoholic who promises himself he won't drink today. One day at a time. I hate this feeling though. Hate it.'

A couple of years earlier I had done a day's filming on

a deservedly forgotten comedy series entitled *World of Pub*. The very friendly Phil Cornwell (from *Stella Street*) was in it, and we had talked about his alcoholism.

'How do you deal with thinking you will never ever have another drink?' I asked him. At the time I was searching for answers to Caroline Aherne's troubles.

'I don't,' he said. 'I just think I won't have a drink today. And when the next day comes I just have the same thought. One day at a time.'

I remembered this and it helped. My depression was like I was walking through a storm. Not today. I wouldn't kill myself today. As the days and weeks passed the rain got a little lighter.

Having earned the most money I ever had in my life – for writing and performing the eight episodes of *Little Britain* – I felt rich, so I flew to LA for Lee Lodge's wedding. Lee is a friend from university who now puts together visuals for rock concerts. Robbie Williams was one of the guests, as Lee's bride Josie Cliff was his PA. The ex-Take That member had seen the pilot of *Little Britain* and was quoting a lot of the catchphrases already. He said, 'Come out to my house tomorrow.'

I couldn't believe it. Robbie was one of the biggest stars in the world.

'What time?' I asked.

'Any time,' he said.

'Yes, but I don't want to come at the wrong time. How about 3 p.m.?'

'Perfect,' Robbie replied.

The next day I took a taxi all the way from the Standard Hotel to the gated community just off Mulholland Drive where he lived. At 3 p.m. exactly I rang the bell.

'Hello?' came a voice.

'Is Robbie there?'

'Who is this?'

'David Walliams.'

'Who?'

'David Walliams.'

'David Williams?'

'No, David Walliams.'

'What do you want?'

'Robbie invited me over to his house today at three o'clock, so here I am.'

'Call back later.'

'Well I'm here now.'

There was a pause before the voice said wearily, 'Wait there.'

A bald-headed man I later found out was his manager David Einthoven appeared.

'Oh it's you! Robbie is asleep. Can you come back later?'

'When?'

'Any time later. Just not now.'

'Oh.'

I was too embarrassed to tell him I had let the cab go, so I walked up the steep hill to the security gate, and the guard took pity on me and called me a taxi. Two hours and a hundred dollars later I was back at the hotel. I never did go back to his house that day.

Soon after, however, Lee invited me to Moscow, to see Robbie's live show. That night Robbie and I had a heart-to-heart conversation that I recorded in my diary.

Saturday 8/11/2003

Back at the hotel after the concert, I had a quiet drink with Robbie, and despite being in the presence of this superstar I managed to relax and talk to him normally.

'When's the last time you had a girlfriend?' I asked him.

'Natalie Appleton.'

'When was that?'

'For eight months, five years ago.'

'And you haven't had a girlfriend since?'

'No.'

'Were you in love with her?'

'No, I've never been in love. Have you?'

'Three times'

'Three? That's a lot. What's it like?'

'Well the first time I fell in love it was with this girl who I had been friends with for three years. So it felt totally natural. It didn't feel like I was "going out" with someone. It's like your best friend is your lover. Imagine if Jonathan Wilkes was your girlfriend!'

'Ha ha!'

'Just like that.'

'Are you on antidepressants, David?'

'Yes.'

'Which ones?'

'Cipralex.'

'I thought so. You used to have a kind of darkness around you . . .'

'An aura?'

'Yes, a dark aura around you. I think it's gone. How long have you been on them?'

'Six months. I've had a really sad year.'

'Why's that?'

'I was really in love with this girl and it all went wrong. She ended up reading my diary. She read about things that happened before I had even met her, and she broke up with me.'

'How did that make you feel?'

'Like I didn't want to live any more. I think I want a woman who when I look into her eyes I will see my own death.'

'That's what you're looking for?'

'Yes. Someone once said you find a knife to fit the wound.'

'That was then, when you were ill. You're better now. I can see it. You will find someone else . . .'

At it happened, I only had to wait one minute . . .

32

Tonight Is Forever

As word was out in Moscow that Robbie Williams was staying at the Hotel Kempinski, there were soon hordes of beautiful girls floating around the bar, trying to catch his eye. One had been in the hotel for a few days, and everyone had noticed how astonishingly sexy she was. Kind of textbook sexy, with blonde hair and a perfect figure. She was so sexy in fact that on seeing her for the first time all Rob's friend Max Beesley and I could do was laugh.

Inevitably this girl approached Robbie and me and asked, 'Can I join you?'

I looked to Rob and he nodded.

'Of course,' I said.

She sat next to me. After a while Rob left to play Scrabble in his hotel room with his dad.

'I'm sorry you're stuck with me,' I said to this girl, who I learned was a singer from Stockholm called Natascha.

I was really quite embarrassed by her beauty and at first didn't know what to say, but after a while I relaxed, and thinking I was just really holding the fort for Rob, I became quite playful with her.

Rob came back briefly and picked up some other girl.

But Natascha didn't want to leave. And neither did I. It was now about 3 a.m. She brought the conversation around to sex and it finally dawned that she was flirting with me.

'Shall we go for a walk?' I said, my heart pounding, my head spinning.

'Yes. Where are we going?'

'Outside? I don't know.'

'I'll get my coat.'

She went upstairs and I thought she wouldn't come back, but she did and we ventured out into Red Square and the surrounding area.

'I wish I could sing and dance,' I said.

'Why?'

'Because I feel like I want to.'

I danced a little in a park, jumping on and off a bench.

'Do you ever feel there are moments you want to live in for ever?'

'Yes,' she said.

'Well, I want this night to never end. I want to spend the rest of my life walking around Moscow in the early hours of the morning with you.'

She laughed.

'Whatever happens between us, Natascha, and I know nothing probably will, no one can take this night away from us. It's ours and ours alone.'

'What are you thinking?'

'I'd like to kiss you.'

'My lips are too cold.'

We went back to the hotel. It was now 4.30 a.m. and I was pleased to see the bar was closed.

'Shall we go back to my room?' she asked.

'Yes,' I said, trembling with desire.

We sat on her bed.

'Are your lips warm enough yet?' I whispered.

'Yes.'

We kissed. I was kissing one of the most beautiful women I had ever seen in my life. I kissed her neck. I held her. She held me. Each touch felt like ecstasy.

'You are so beautiful,' I said.

'You are so sexy,' she said, which I thought was a good reply, because I know for sure I am not beautiful.

'I want to see you naked,' I said.

'I'm shy.'

'Please. You said you wouldn't be in London until spring. Please give me something to think about until then.'

'OK, you can see my top half.'

She took her bra off under her vest, then turned her back to me and pulled her vest up slowly to reveal the most perfect back. Beautiful enough to make the French Foreign Legion weep. Then she slowly turned and fixed me with her gaze, her hands over her breasts. It was heart-poundingly erotic.

She gradually removed her hands to reveal the most beautiful breasts I had ever seen. She looked into my eyes. I looked into hers.

'I can't believe it. You are so beautiful,' I said.

I kissed her neck from behind and embraced her. It felt so sexy, it could have been the first time anyone had touched me.

'I feel like I want to give up everything and move to Sweden. You can't move to London, can you?'

'No,' she replied.

'Here's my phone number and email address. You will email me, won't you?'

'Oh yes, I have to see you again,' she said. And I left.

I saw Natascha a couple more times, once in Sweden, another time in London, but it was not to be. It mattered not. Natascha gave me something that magical night in Moscow. Hope. Hope that one day I could love again.

When I returned to London, *Little Britain* was finishing its run on BBC3 and about to begin on BBC2. On Monday 1 December 2003 the first episode aired on terrestrial television and was an instant hit. Despite it being a repeat from BBC3, 3.2 million people tuned in. That Thursday Matt and I recorded our very first interview with Jonathan Ross. I sat embarrassed in his on-screen green room as properly famous people surrounded us. Boris Becker, Ozzy Osborne and the Strokes were the other guests. As our names were called I took a deep breath and stepped out onto the set so familiar to me from watching the programme for many years.

The audience received Matt and me rapturously, and I realized I now could be considered to be slightly famous.

Jonathan Ross is obsessed with homosexuality (I would call him bi-curious) and he asked, 'We all know you're gay, Matt, but what about you, David? There are rumours that you have dabbled.'

My brain whirred to find an appropriate response.

'You know what's it's like, Jonathan. You suck a few cocks, you get a reputation.'

That brought the house down but was edited out of the episode when it aired the next night, which was probably for the best.

The reviews were overwhelmingly good for *Little Britain*. In the *Evening Standard* on 17 September 2003 Victor Lewis-Smith had finally given us a glowing one, which pleased me no end . . .

A club recently opened in New York, based around an ingenious concept that originated in Aberdeen. The idea is called WC-TV, and some time ago I visited the Scottish club that pioneered the service by fitting waterproof television screens to the base of each urinal in the gentlemen's lavatory.

'When you want to strain the potatoes,' explained the proprietor in his colourful patois, 'just tell me the name of the TV presenter you can't stand, go to the lavatory, and we'll put a tape of them on for you.'

So it was, that after a hard day's journalism (aka the art of turning your enemies into money), I was able to spend the evening contentedly urinating over images of the selfsame celebrities whom I had earlier been metaphorically spraying in print. I understand that the new American club is taking the concept of WC-TV one stage further, but I'm not sure that's wise.

I mean, there's the cleaning up to consider, and anyway, isn't there already enough crap on TV?

There was a time when I would have called for a tape of David Walliams and Matt Lucas on a urinal screen, and happily given them the high-pressure hose treatment.

Indeed, if I might be allowed to quote myself (sorry, but I'm getting to that age), I once described the former as 'dismally untalented . . . living proof that you are only young once, but can remain immature indefinitely', and condemned the latter for doing 'a desperately unfunny Tony Hancock routine, although at least Hancock had the decency to commit suicide afterwards'.

But either I was wrong (there's a strong possibly, and certainly wouldn't be the first time) or the pair have got a lot better over the past couple of years, because their *Rock Profile* series revealed a comedic deftness of touch that had hitherto seemed absent from their work. And with the arrival of *Little Britain* (which began last night on BBC3) there's ample evidence that the erstwhile untalented Walliams and unfunny Lucas are now two of the hottest comedy properties on television. Now will somebody remove this sword from me?

In the Nineties, documentary makers like Paul Wason used to boast that they were 'taking the temperature of Britain', and that's what these two writer-performers are doing now in a series of rapid character sketches, only with more acute powers of observation and a rectal thermometer. Take Vicky Pollard, whose incoherent scatological outbursts brilliantly captured the hormone-crazed confusion of the adolescent mind, or the verruca-covered urchins who splashed around aimlessly in the municipal swimming pool, a place that no self-respecting person would be seen dead in (unlike, say, Michael Barrymore's private pool).

More disturbing still was the world's least convincing transvestite, Emily Howard, whose motto is 'I'm a lady, I like to do ladies' things', and whose appearance is fifty per cent Emily Bronte, fifty per cent Reggie Kray. She reminded me of the wig-and-suspenders-wearing transvestite flasher I read about in my local rag only this week, who, when apprehended on a golf course by police and asked 'Have you ever sought medical attention?' got his/her own back by replying, 'Well . . . I did have a bit of sinus trouble recently.'

With Steve Bendelack as director, and Mark Gatiss as script editor, a certain *League of Gentlemen* influence was inevitably apparent (although I'm certainly not complaining, because what better influence could there be for a comedy?)

Cake-crazy Marjorie Dawes is certainly a near relative of the pen-obsessed Pauline, but that didn't make her insane slimming advice ('Cut your favourite food in half, and it's just half the calories! And because it's half the calories, you can have twice as much!') any less plausibly ridiculous, or less funny.

Darker moments included the appearance of teenage gerontophiliac Gary, and two gay Government advisers who both wanted to do to the Prime Minister what he's recently been doing to the country, but most surreal of all was the sight of two Black and White Minstrels listening anxiously to a radio, on which the Home Secretary was promising to 'send them all back to Minstrel-land'. Incidentally, I'm currently trying to obtain a copy of the Black and White Minstrel radio show, which they used to record in full make-up and costume, an act that was almost as pointless as the magician I heard on LBC in the Seventies, saying: 'Yes, caller, I can confirm that this is your card.'

As with Avid Merrion's *Bo' Selecta!* (a programme that must have been inspired by this duo's characterisations), this series succeeds because its stars are accomplished straight actors, as well as gifted writers.

The result is a comedic masterpiece that's innovative, funny, and very, very British, full of characters who (once the series gets a terrestrial showing) are destined to become as well-known as the dramatis personae of *The Fast Show*.

The kakopyginous [sic] Marjorie will certainly become celebrated for her unhinged approach to weight loss, with methods almost as odd as my own idea for winning the 'Slimmer of the Year' title in one of the hundreds of diet magazines that currently infest the shelves at WH Smith. I won't actually lose any weight for the award, of course. I'll just buy a pair of trousers with 158-inch waist, put them on, point at the huge amount of slack, smile for the photos, and collect the dosh.

YES!

The Wednesday after the *Jonathan Ross Show* was recorded I won the Best Newcomer award at the British Comedy Awards. Despite having been active in the world of comedy for the best part of a decade. I kept quiet about that. When my name was called the room erupted in cheers. This was before our monumental success jaded the response of some of our peers. I had planned to say nothing as I accepted the award, as I really had no idea what to say anyway, so I kissed Jonathan on the lips and ran off in an outrageously camp way. It was original and funny, and for the first time in my life I felt as if I was at the centre of something, rather than on the fringes. Still I couldn't quite let myself go. Instead of going to the party, I came home and read a book I had started called *The Gulag: A History of the Soviet Camps*. Clearly I still didn't quite know how to enjoy myself.

The next morning I was walking through Covent Garden, doing some Christmas shopping. A teenage girl recognized me and pulled on her father's sleeve. The man approached me. 'You're off that *Little Britain*, aren't you?'

'Yes, I am.'

'Can my daughter here have a photo with you?'

'Of course,' I said. And the teenager came and stood next to me as her dad fiddled with his mobile phone, and eventually took the picture.

'Thanks,' he said. 'She likes all the famous people.'

I looked at them both. 'I'll tell them. They'll be thrilled!'

Every Christmas Day my family visits my dad's brother's family. Uncle Leslie and Auntie Vivien's daughters Laura, Natalie and Sarah are the cousins my sister and I performed with in little made-up plays as children. I never spent that much time with them as a child, and less in adult life. Sometimes the once-a-year Christmas visit was all I would see of them.

This particular year everything changed. Cameras came out for the first time. I don't remember them ever taking a photograph of me before. Now a record was needed of my visit. Autographs were requested for friends. Some of the children even watched me drive off.

It was strange.

I was famous.

I hadn't changed but the world had changed.

And my life would never quite be the same again.

*

'Patsy fancies you,' said Matt. I didn't take much persuading to meet up with her. When I did, that sweet smell of hers was the first thing I noticed. Matt, Patsy and I went to see Paul Kaye in an awful play called *Dinner* together. At the end of the evening Patsy and I swapped numbers. Immediately the texts started going back and forth.

Then Patsy invited me round to her house in Notting Hill. Then we were kissing. Then I was being photographed leaving her house in the morning. Then I was in the newspapers for something not to do with my work. Then I became so well known that when I walked down the street every second person recognized me. Women threw themselves at me. And sometimes I caught them. Then I became rich. Then I swam from one country to another.

Over the next decade my life became curiouser and curiouser. Like Alice in Lewis Carroll's novel, I entered Wonderland. A place of dreams and nightmares.

To be continued . . .

Acknowledgements

First I would like to thank myself for writing the book. That was the hard bit.

Reluctantly I would also like to acknowledge the help of the following people:

The managing director of Michael Joseph, Louise Moore.

My literary agent Paul Stevens at Independent.

The editor Katy Follain.

Katy's colleague Rowland White.

Anna Mrowiec the editorial assistant.

Beatrix McIntyre the editorial manager.

Catriona Hillerton and Lisa Simmonds, who work in production.

John Hamilton and Lee Motley, who are responsible for the design.

Hugh Davis the copyeditor. If you find any spelling mistakes, take them up personally with him please.

Katya Shipster the deputy publicity director.

God there are a lot of people to thank, this is getting quite boring now.

Ruth Spencer the marketing manager.

What do they all really do?

Viviane Basset the marketing director.

I have never even met half these people.

ACKNOWLEDGEMENTS

Alex Elam the head of rights.
Not a clue what he or she does.
Anna Derkacz the sales manager.
Thank you all so very much. I love you all dearly.

DW

Permissions

page 55 'Tom, Dick and Harry' sketch by Richard Curtis

page 60 *The Complete Poems* by Philip Larkin. Copyright © Estate of Philip Larkin. Reprinted by permission of Faber and Faber Ltd.

page 65 *Against Interpretation and Other Essays* by Susan Sontag (first published 1961, Penguin Classics 2009). Copyright © Susan Sontag 1961, 1962, 1963, 1964, 1965, 1966

page 104 'Later Tonight' lyrics by Neil Tennant & Christopher Lowe. Copyright © Sony/ATV Music Publishing. All rights reserved. Used by permission

page 109 'The Collection' taken from *Plays* 2 by Harold Pinter. Copyright © Estate of Harold Pinter and reprinted by permission of Faber and Faber Ltd.

page 109 'The Collection' by Harold Pinter. Copyright © 1963, 1964 by H. Pinter Ltd. Used by permission of Grove/Atlantic, Inc.

page 188 Review, Ben Thompson, *The Independent*, 18 August 1996

page 228 Review, Victor Lewis-Smith, *Evening Standard*, 13 May 1999